# VICTORY THROUGH SURRENDER

*Confessions of a Prisoner of Grace*

A 365-Day
How-To Guide

VOLUME TWO

# Tim Tremaine

Tim Tremaine

© Copyright 2021 by The Tremaine Company, LLC

All rights reserved. No part of this collection may be reproduced or transmitted in any form or by any means, electronic or mechanical, including photocopying and recording, or by any information storage and retrieval system, except in the case of brief quotations for use in articles and reviews, without written permission from the author.

The views expressed in this book are the author's and do not necessarily reflect those of the publisher.

7710-T Cherry Park Dr, Ste 224
Houston, TX 77095
713-766-4271

Cover design: Harvest Creek Ministry by Design, www.harvestcreek.net

VICTORY THROUGH SURRENDER

Dedicated to my family:

Dottie,
Taylor and Laura,
Chase and Paige,

for
Selah

## Other books by Tim Tremaine

*Officer Up! Creating a Climate for Appropriate Officer Behavior*
*Victory Through Surrender: Confessions of a Prisoner of Grace, Volume One*

# TABLE OF CONTENTS

| | |
|---|---|
| Introduction | 7 |
| Month Seven | 13 |
| Week Twenty Seven | 14 |
| Week Twenty Eight | 21 |
| Week Twenty Nine | 27 |
| Week Thirty | 34 |
| Week Thirty One | 40 |
| Month Eight | 41 |
| Week Thirty Two | 47 |
| Week Thirty Three | 54 |
| Week Thirty Four | 61 |
| Week Thirty Five | 68 |
| Month Nine | 71 |
| Week Thirty Six | 76 |
| Week Thirty Seven | 82 |
| Week Thirty Eight | 88 |
| Week Thirty Nine | 95 |
| Month Ten | 101 |
| Week Forty | 102 |
| Week Forty One | 109 |
| Week Forty Two | 115 |
| Week Forty Three | 122 |
| Week Forty Four | 129 |
| Month Eleven | 131 |
| Week Forty Five | 137 |
| Week Forty Six | 144 |
| Week Forty Seven | 151 |
| Week Forty Eight | 158 |
| Month Twelve | 163 |
| Week Forty Nine | 166 |

| | |
|---|---|
| Week Fifty | 173 |
| Week Fifty One | 178 |
| Week Fifty Two | 185 |
| Epilogue | 194 |
| Index of Authors | 196 |
| Index of Weekly Themes or Featured Authors | 198 |
| Bibliography | 199 |

# INTRODUCTION

If you have completed Volume One, congratulations! I am gratified that you found value in that material and want to continue here growing in your Christian walk as a surrendered disciple of Christ. If you have come across this volume first, do not worry. Each volume can stand on its own. You will have enough information to begin here and go on to Volume One later. The primary difference is that the first week of Volume One covers issues related to a person's salvation experience and personal relationship to Christ. These books are written for believers as an aid to discipleship. If you do not have a personal born-again experience, I encourage you to begin with Volume One and get that issue settled in your heart now. You cannot learn how to live the life surrendered to Jesus Christ as Lord until you have first surrendered your life to Jesus Christ as Savior through confession, repentance, and faith.

When Volume One was published, I tried to find it on Amazon and discovered other books with the same title. I bought them and read them as well. I was already familiar with the 1966 book by E. Stanley Jones. I used it in Volume One. A second is from 2013 by Air Force veteran and minister Dr. Raymond P. Findlater. He uses accumulated messages, devotionals, and social media posts to emphasize the necessity of surrender related to the Great Commission. Findlater asserts that "being a field worker in the service of the Lord requires total dedication and selflessness. Our salvation is not just a badge of honor to be worn conveniently. Jesus has called us to take up his cross and follow him, to give up our own will for our heavenly Father's. We are sent out as lambs among wolves, stripped of our own usual means of survival, to be totally reliant on God (Luke 10:3–4). The believer thus becomes the representative of Christ in the highways and byways of life; preaching and teaching the gospel, healing the sick and casting out devils in the name of Jesus. Whether on a secular job or in full time ministry the commission is the same; to give hope to the hopeless, sight to the blind, light where there is darkness, and peace where there is turmoil" (p. 12).

One book had "Victory Through Surrender" in the subtitle. It was a workbook called *The Incredible Power of Kingdom Authority* by the late Dr. Adrian Rogers. In week two, Rogers records part of a conversation he had with a Romanian pastor friend about the difference between commitment and surrender. The friend said he noticed that the word "surrender" had been replaced with "commitment" in most American settings in recent years. Rogers asked why that was significant. The friend replied, "When you make a commitment, you are still in control. Surrender is different. If someone holds a gun and asks you to lift your hands in the air as a token of surrender, you don't tell that individual what you are committed to. You simply surrender and do as you are told. Americans love commitment because they are still in control. The key word is surrender. We are to be the slaves of the Lord Jesus Christ." Rogers concluded that "There are many things we may be committed to in a godly and wholesome way, but nothing can take the place of absolute surrender" (p. 28-29).

The oldest book is a small but powerful work from 1892 by Benjamin Fay Mills. I begin Week 27 with an excerpt from this book. Mills contends that "We need to continually keep in mind the fact that the principles that govern the entrance into the Christian life are the same principles that govern every advanced step, and the development of the life of God in man" (p. 44). I completely agree. We are saved by faith, and we work out that salvation daily by faith. Regarding the need for absolute surrender to God, Mills concludes that "The secret of the Lord which is with them that fear him… (is) that God is satisfied not with our simply being dependent upon him, but with our being independent of everything else" (p. 68). "The infinite life of God, in purity, and wisdom, and peace, and strength, and power, is waiting for the one who is willing to receive it" (p. 81).

All this to say that the message of absolute surrender is far from unique to me. In fact, that is one of the purposes of these two volumes; to demonstrate that the message of surrender and dependence upon God alone is a constant theme of teachers and preachers throughout the centuries. Hopefully, you have been exposed to many new voices and resources in Volume One. If not, you can begin that journey now. I hope that at least some of these voices will reverberate in your spirit and bring encouragement, instruction, and insight into how you can live the life totally surrendered to our Savior and Lord Jesus Christ.

As in the first volume, I offer my own surrender prayer to you as a model or pattern for you to use daily in your walk of faith. The important thing is to pray the prayer every morning, as soon as you can, out loud, and believe that God hears it and accepts it, and works it out in you. I detail these points in Volume One, so I will simply reproduce the prayer for you here to use and modify as the Holy Spirit leads.

"My God, I am willing to be made willing (Psalm 51:12). Lord, I yield myself in absolute surrender to you, my God. I accept your terms of absolute surrender. By your grace, I desire to do your will in everything, every moment of every day. I give myself absolutely to you, to your will, to do only what you want. I give myself absolutely to you, God, to let you work in me to will and to do your good pleasure.

"I count, reckon, and consider myself dead to sin and alive to God in Christ Jesus my Lord. Help me not to let sin reign in my body so that I obey its evil desires or offer the parts of my body to sin as instruments of wickedness. I offer myself to you and the parts of my body to you as instruments of righteousness (Romans 6:11-14); so that in everything, you may be glorified through Christ Jesus my Lord (1 Peter 4:11).

"You are my God, apart from you I am nothing (Gal 6:3), I know nothing (1 Cor 8:2), I have nothing (1 Cor 4:7), and I can do nothing (John 15:5). I want to speak what you are speaking and do what you are doing (John 5:19). I am willing to lose what I have, or what I think I have, to gain what you are willing to give. I am putting my trust in You. Show me the way I should go, for to you, I lift up my soul. Teach me to do your will, for you are my God. May your good Spirit lead me on level ground (Psalms 143:8, 10)."

You may not think that you can, or feel like you can, surrender everything to Jesus. But if you are willing, God will do it! List the things you are willing now to surrender to Jesus. Begin with the obvious things and listen to the Holy Spirit for what he wants you to add to the list as you go along. You will probably begin with things, then move to activities, relationships, and finally, attitudes. The deeper you go, the deeper he will take you. Learning to live the surrendered life is not a one-time experience. You will not get where he wants you to be in 30 days or six months, or even one year. This will be an ongoing lifestyle until he comes, or you leave to meet him. It's not easy, but it is simple. Just pray for it and, by faith, receive it. God will do it!

## HOW TO USE THIS BOOK

Were you to pick up this book and flip through the pages, you might think this is a devotional based on the layout. But that is not quite accurate. I refer to it as a "confessional journal anthology." It involves something you speak, something you write, and something you read. The purpose is not just to teach lessons, although I have included a few and I trust you will learn something along the way. The purpose is to model for you how to live the Christian life in complete surrender to God and trust in God through daily confessing the truths of His Word. The **Confessions** sections, not unlike the confessions of faith throughout history, are based on Scripture as well as the Spirit-led words of other faithful men and women through the centuries.

These confessions are prayers, in the sense that you are talking to God, but not in the sense that they are requests, petitions, or intercessions. They are more like proclamations, declarations, or affirmations of truth. They will sound and feel like praise but are really your faith responses to truth. I have my own God-given filter that takes in truth and finds a way to speak it out that is meaningful to me. Maybe I can communicate in a way that is meaningful to you. I'm not trying to re-interpret Scripture or make a new translation, although it might sound like it. I simply want to model for you how you can take the truths in Scripture, accept them, incorporate them into your life, verbalize them as faith confessions, and let God transform you through them.

The approach is more like; "Since these things are true, therefore I will respond like this." I encourage you to read the Scripture passage first, then read the confession. I am simply sharing the style the Lord has given me and the styles I have found with other people. There is space at the end of each week to journal what you learn or write your own confessions and prayers.

God is always the primary audience, but not the only audience. You will be speaking to yourself as well. There is something powerful and wonderful about hearing the truths of God in your own ears spoken by your own voice. These confessions are not simply to be read. They are to be read *out loud*. You can recite them privately or as part of a group or congregation. But the point is, speak them *out loud*. Get them out of your brain and into the air. The powers of the air, the enemy with which we war every day, will also be an audience to your confessions. The strongholds you battle are like the walls of Jericho. But the walls did not fall from silent prayer and worship, they fell at the shouts of obedience! So, give voice to your devotion.

Spirit-filled words based on God's truth are powerful and effective when spoken into our atmosphere, sounded forth into the heavenlies, and endorsed by the awesome "Yes!" of the Lord Jesus Christ. The concept of words, the spoken word, or The Word is very important in the economy of God. Throughout the history of man, God has spoken to His people and given them words to speak. Phil Driscoll, the great trumpeter and general in the worship army of God, says that "words are process starters." He refers to 1 Corinthians 14 where it talks about words having significance. Speaking the truth to God, to yourself, and to others is an important and powerful part of the process of sanctification.

These confessions are not just made at the beginning of the Christian walk when a person is born again. Confessions of faith need to be made throughout our life as we grow in the Lord and learn how to trust Him and depend on Him and wait on Him every day. The walk of holiness, obedience, and surrender requires a continual confession of faith. Not that we have to be saved over and over, in terms of our regeneration, but in terms of working out our salvation on a daily, hourly, moment by moment basis. It's walking by the Spirit, step-by-step, less of me and more of Him, toward the goal of maturity and the fullness of Christ in our life.

Men and women of faith have been teaching these principles for centuries and I will highlight many of them in the **Insight and Encouragement** sections. When I read books, I often highlight, underline, or make notes, then I go back and type up those notes creating a synopsis of the book for my future reference. Throughout the book, I will share synopses, adaptations, and excerpts of other books that God has used over the years to help me along the way. Many are condensed or adapted for clarity and space purposes, but I strive to remain true to their message. I also include some insights that the Lord has given me. I hope they are helpful as well.

I have also included several poems and old hymns, written out in poem form, in the **Hymns and Poems** sections. Reading those great hymns of old as poems underscores that the saints of old had a pretty good handle on what it means to live the life "hidden with Christ in God." At times, the voice of the selection is changed from third to first person. Like the **Confessions** section, these also are meant to be spoken ***out loud***.

The believers referenced herein span the centuries and represent a wide range of theological perspectives and backgrounds. Just because I have used someone as a resource for this book does not mean that I agree with everything they ever said or wrote. It simply means that, in this instant, I and others have found some truth in what they wrote regarding the subject at hand, living the surrendered life. You may not like everything I have shared and that is ok. These are simply examples that spoke to me and helped me along the way. They are tools, part of the "how-to" of living the Christian life. I hope to demonstrate the consistency of the message and experience throughout the ages of the church era. Some will speak to you where others will not and that is ok too.

I encourage you to use my examples to "prime the pump" of your own faith confessions. Use mine until your thought categories are developed by the Holy Spirit to create your own. The purpose is to further your relationship with Him and teach you how to submit to that relationship in total surrender as a true disciple of Christ. If you question whether this is necessary, read and meditate on Luke 14 and I trust you will gain a fuller appreciation for the effort.

My hope is to encourage you by illustrating that this message, this process, this effort has been consistent throughout the centuries of the Church era. I have left most of the language as I found it in the source, so there will be some language you may not be familiar with. But I trust there will be many who speak to you in a way you can receive that will transform your life and walk with the Lord.

While researching the book, I came across a few books from the recent and distant past that follow a similar format. These resources (listed in the Bibliography) were a great source of encouragement and material for me. I am very grateful to those who "plowed the row" ahead of me: John Baillie, A. W. Tozer, Charles and John Wesley, Richard Foster and James B Smith, and John Shepperd.

Four times along the way, we take a break from the daily devotional format and spend a week delving into a particular subject. I hope you will be blessed by these expanded studies. They are meant to bring a deeper understanding and appreciation of Biblical topics that are crucial for living the surrendered life. Most weeks have a topic or a featured author so if you want to hear from a particular person or need to address a particular area you can jump around to those pages. Indexes are provided in the back. At the first of every month (or 30-day section), I include a short personal story about my background, successes, and failures living the Christian life. I hope these testimonies will be a blessing and encouragement to you.

Most of the selections are one-page long. Some are shorter, a few are longer. Once in a while, I insert a longer multiple day study. The order of the days is not important. I have tried to use each of the three sections almost every week for variety, but you are welcome to switch the order around as needed. If time is short one day, pick a day with a shorter section. Periodically, I will interject a note or comment on a page. These "Author Notes" are in brackets to identify them as mine.

**Pray** your surrender prayer at the beginning of each day. **Read** that day's devotion or confession as early in the day as you can. **Journal** whatever the Holy Spirit speaks to you as a record of what God speaks into your life. This is not information for you to learn, it is a lifestyle for you to live.

I suppose someone will ask, why do we need to spend an entire year studying one concept? The process is simple, but it is not easy. The purpose of this book is to help you work through some of the most difficult hurdles in living the surrendered life because it won't just be a one year study. You and I will be working on this for the rest of our lives. This is a process, a journey that will only end when you see Jesus face to face. It takes time, practice, and perseverance to succeed. There is no end to the insights God wants to reveal to us along the way. Experts say it takes anywhere from 18-254 days to establish a new habit. This is more than a habit – it's a way of life, a way of thinking, a way of processing and implementing Kingdom realities into earthly circumstances. Stick with it. You will not regret it.

I leave you with this verse: *He who has My commandments and keeps them, it is he who loves Me. And he who loves Me will be loved by My Father, and I will love him and manifest Myself to him* (John 14:21). Obey, and Jesus will show up!

Tim Tremaine

## MONTH SEVEN

One day at the beginning of my shift, I got a scolding from another supervisor much junior to me. I recently returned to his shift (my former shift) on a part-time basis but was acting like I was still the senior supervisor, walking right in and taking control. I was used to being proactive and making sure things were done right in a timely fashion. In doing so, he felt like I was steamrolling him, so to speak, and undermining his authority with the shift. Apparently, one or more of the troops had mentioned something to him about it. It was hard to listen to and harder for him to say. I don't think he knew what my reaction would be, but he found a way to say it in as non-confrontational a manner as he could.

As I listened to his concerns, I realized that God had shown me what I was about to do before I did it, but I missed it. As I was walking in the room, I got a quick mental image or impression, for lack of a better term, that what I was about to do would not sit well with them. But I did it anyway. The troops listened and complied, but my fellow supervisor told me after the fact that he had already covered those points. I had to agree with him and apologize. Although uncomfortable for me, we had a cordial conversation, and we established new boundaries.

God often puts up red flags or stop signs for us when we are about to go over the line or cross a boundary. I have trouble not running his stop signs. The funny thing about this situation was that, earlier in the day, I was reading an old journal from 1994 where I was talking about getting clearance from God before I did things. Same idea. I am a slow learner sometimes.

One of the biggest stop signs I ever ran happened in 2006. I had just retired from the police department and was trying to get back into full-time ministry. I knew a pastor looking for help as he was just called to a new church in the area. We began to talk about what that might look like and how we could make it work. I cannot speak for him, but I know now that I had no direction from the Lord and was moving totally in my strength, my wisdom, and my desires. The problem was, I had gotten a divorce a year earlier, which was a career killer in my circles. This pastor had gone through a divorce but was moving forward, and the church had been understanding and accepting. I thought this was God helping me find a way. It wasn't.

At the same time, I decided to apply for the department where I now work. As I approached the end of that process, this church opportunity came up, and I canceled the application process to pursue the church job. The night after we agreed on the church job, I suffered an anxiety attack so strong, I thought I was having a heart attack and went to the hospital. Testing showed there was nothing wrong with me physically. I realized much too late that was God putting up a stop sign – a really big one. I was so set on my own desires and my own plans that I plowed right through it. It led to three years of under-employment or unemployment. That job lasted only one year and was followed by four more short-lived jobs. It cost me three precious years of seniority in my present job and thousands of dollars of retirement savings just to stay afloat in the meantime. Being surrendered to God means you acknowledge his right to say yes or no to your plans and ideas. Pay attention to his stop signs and heed them. They are there to help you, not hurt you. God knows. Trust him.

**WEEK TWENTY SEVEN**  *INSIGHT and ENCOURAGEMENT*  **DAY 1**

Count It Done

Benjamin Fay Mills (1857-1916)

There never was, and there never will be any way to walk in the light of God other than by faith. In fact, the thing that God offers to us is his own faith, the principle by which he lives, and the knowledge that what he says shall be accomplished. The exact expression that the Master used and speaking to his disciples, as the word is recorded in the eleventh chapter of Mark (11:22), is not as the King James version puts it, "Have faith in God," but rather as the margin records it, "Have the faith of God." What Paul said to the Galatians (2:20) concerning the principle of the life that he lived with Christ was, that the life which he now lived in the flesh, he lived by "the faith of the Son of God." The gift which God makes to us in giving us faith, is that sublime confidence which enables us to count the things that are not as though they are and thus the faith is reckoned unto us for righteousness. When the Lord Jesus uttered a command, or worked a miracle, he had no question in his mind but that what he said would be perfectly accomplished; and just so far as we grow to be like him, and have no will but the will of God, abiding in Christ and having Christ abide in us, do we have the same sublimity of faith, and we shall ask what we will, and it shall be done unto us.

We need to make the words in the sixth chapter of Romans exceedingly practical, where Paul says, "Likewise reckon yourselves to be dead indeed unto sin, but alive unto God through Jesus Christ our Lord. Let not sin therefore reign in your mortal body, that you should obey it in the lusts thereof. Neither yield your members as instruments of unrighteousness unto sin, but yield yourselves unto God, as those that are alive from the dead, and your members as instruments of righteousness unto God. … Know ye not that to whom you yield yourself servants to obey, his servants you are to whom you obey; whether of sin unto death, or of obedience unto righteousness? … For as you have yielded your members servants to uncleanness and to iniquity unto iniquity, even so now yield your members servants to righteousness unto holiness. For when you were the servants of sin you were free from righteousness. … But now, being made free from sin, and become servants to God, you have your fruit unto holiness, and the end everlasting life. For the wages of sin is death, but the gift of God is eternal life through Jesus Christ our lord."

I would to God that we might see that when we present ourselves to God as if we were alive from the dead, that God does indeed make us alive from the dead, and that no practical faith was ever manifested toward him in vain. As a friend of mine said, in turning his back forever upon having any confidence in the flesh, and utterly surrendering himself to God, "I felt as though I walked out to the end of the ridge pole in the darkness, and jumped off, and Jesus caught me."

Excerpted from *Victory through Surrender; a Message Concerning Consecrated Living*. New York: Fleming H Revell Company, 1892. p. 47-50

VICTORY THROUGH SURRENDER

**WEEK TWENTY SEVEN**  *HYMNS and POEMS*  **DAY 2**

The Means of Grace (Part 1)

by Charles Wesley (1707-1788)

Long have I seem'd to serve Thee, Lord,
With unavailing pain;
Fasted, and pray'd and read Thy word,
And heard it preach'd, in vain.

Oft did I with th' assembly join,
And near Thine altar drew;
A form of godliness was mine,
The power I never knew.

To please Thee thus (at last I see)
In vain I hoped and strove:
For what are outward things to Thee,
Unless they spring from love?

I see the perfect law requires
Truth in the inward parts,
Our full consent, our whole desires,
Our undivided hearts.

But I of *means* have made my boast,
Of *means* an idol made;
The spirit in the letter lost,
The substance in the shade.

I rested in the outward law,
Nor knew its deep design;
The length and breadth I never saw,
The height of love Divine.

Where am I now, or what my hope?
What can my weakness do?
JESU, to Thee my soul looks up,
'Tis Thou must make it new.

Thine is the work, and Thine alone —
But shall I idly stand?
Shall I the written Rule disown,
And slight my God's command?

Wildly shall I from Thine turn back,
A better path to find;
Thy holy ordinance forsake,
And cast Thy words behind?

Forbid it, gracious Lord, that I
Should ever learn Thee so!
No – let *me* with Thy word comply,
If I thy love would know.

Suffice for me, that Thou, my Lord,
Hast bid me fast and pray:
Thy will be done, Thy name adored;
'Tis only mine t'obey.

Thou bidd'st me search the Sacred Leaves,
And taste the hallow'd Bread:
The kind commands my soul receives,
And longs on Thee to feed.

http://scriptoriumdaily.com/charles-wesley-on-means-of-grace/. Hymn No. 83, "The Means of Grace" (from Hymns and Sacred Poems, 1740).

**WEEK TWENTY SEVEN**  *HYMNS and POEMS*  **DAY 3**

The Means of Grace (Part 2)

by Charles Wesley (1707-1788)

I work, and own the labour vain;
And *thus* from works I cease:
I strive, and see my fruitless pain,
Till God create my peace.

Fruitless, till Thou Thyself impart,
Must all my efforts prove:
They cannot change a sinful heart,
They cannot purchase love.

I do the Thing Thy laws enjoin,
And *then* the strife gives o'er:
To Thee I *then* the whole resign:
I *trust* in means no more.

I trust in Him who stands between
The Father's wrath and me:
JESU! Thou great eternal Mean,
I look for all from Thee.

Thy mercy pleads, Thy truth requires,
Thy promise call Thee down!
Not for the sake of my desires–
But, O! regard Thine own!

I seek no motive out of Thee:
Thine own desires fulfill;
If now Thy bowels yearn on me,
On me perform Thy will.

Doom, if Thou canst, to endless pains,
And drive me from Thy face:
But if Thy stronger love constrains,
Let me be *saved by grace*.

Still for Thy loving kindness, Lord,
I in Thy temple wait;
I look to find Thee in Thy word,
Or at Thy table meet.

Here, *in Thine own appointed ways,*
I wait to learn Thy will:
Silent I stand before Thy face,
And hear Thee say, "Be still!"

"Be still –and know that I am God!"
'Tis all I live to know;
To feel the virtue of Thy blood,
And spread its praise below.

I wait my vigour to renew,
Thine image to retrieve,
The veil of outward things pass through,
And gasp in Thee to live.

http://scriptoriumdaily.com/charles-wesley-on-means-of-grace/. Hymn No. 83, "The Means of Grace" (from Hymns and Sacred Poems, 1740).

# WEEK TWENTY SEVEN — *INSIGHT and ENCOURAGEMENT* — DAY 4

Walk After the Spirit

by John Wesley (1703-1791)

Now "whosoever abideth in him, sinneth not"; "walketh not after the flesh." The flesh, in the usual language of St. Paul, signifies corrupt nature. In this sense he uses the word, writing to the Galatians, "The works of the flesh are manifest" (Gal. 5:19); and a little before, "Walk in the Spirit, and ye shall not fulfill the lust" (or desire) "of the flesh" (v. 16). To prove which, namely, that those who "walk by the Spirit," do not "fulfilll the lusts of the flesh," he immediately adds, "For the flesh lusteth against the Spirit, and the Spirit lusteth against the flesh (for these are contrary to each other); that ye may not do the things which ye would."

They who are of Christ, who abide in him, "have crucified the flesh with its affections and lusts." They abstain from all those works of the flesh; from "adultery and fornication"; from "uncleanness and lasciviousness"; from "idolatry, witchcraft, hatred, variance" from "emulations, wrath, strife, sedition, heresies, envyings, murders, drunkenness, revellings"; from every design, and word, to which the corruption of nature leads. Although they feel the root of bitterness in themselves, yet are they endued with power from on high to trample it continually under foot, so that it cannot "spring up to trouble them"; insomuch that every fresh assault which they undergo, only gives them fresh occasion of praise, of crying out, "Thanks be unto God, who giveth us the victory through Jesus Christ our Lord."

They now "walk after the Spirit," both in their hearts and lives. They are taught of him to love God and their neighbour, with a love which is as "a well of water, springing up into everlasting life." And by him they are led into every holy desire, into every divine and heavenly temper, till every thought which arises in their heart is holiness unto the Lord.

They who "walk after the Spirit," are also led by him into all holiness of conversation. Their "speech is always in grace, seasoned with salt"; with the love and fear of God. "No corrupt communication comes out of their mouth; but only that which is good," that which is "to the use of edifying," which is "meet to minister grace to the hearers." And herein likewise do they exercise themselves day and night, to do only the things which please God; in all their outward behaviour to follow him "who left us an example that we might tread in his steps"; in all their intercourse with their neighbour, to walk in justice, mercy, and truth; and "whatsoever they do," in every circumstance of life, to "do all to the glory of God."

These are they who indeed "walk after the Spirit." Being filled with faith and with the Holy Ghost, they possess in their hearts, and show forth in their lives, in the whole course of their words and actions, the genuine fruits of the Spirit of God, namely, "love, joy, peace, long-suffering, gentleness, goodness, fidelity, meekness, temperance," and whatsoever else is lovely or praiseworthy. "They adorn in all things the gospel of God our Saviour"; and give full proof to all mankind, that they are indeed actuated by the same Spirit "which raised up Jesus from the dead."

Tim Tremaine

*Sermons on Several Occasions, Vol. 1*. Digireads.com Publications, 2012. p. 121-122.

**WEEK TWENTY SEVEN**   *HYMNS and POEMS*   **DAY 5**

O Jesus, I Have Promised

by John Ernest Bode (1816-1874)

O Jesus, I have promised
To serve Thee to the end;
Be Thou forever near me,
My Master and my Friend;
I shall not fear the battle
If Thou art by my side,
Nor wander from the pathway
If Thou wilt be my Guide.

Oh, let me feel Thee near me;
The world is ever near;
I see the sights that dazzle,
The tempting sounds I hear;
My foes are ever near me,
Around me and within;
But, Jesus, draw Thou nearer,
And shield my soul from sin.

Oh, let me hear Thee speaking,
In accents clear and still,
Above the storms of passion,
The murmurs of self-will;

Oh, speak to reassure me,
To hasten, or control;
Oh, speak, and make me listen,
Thou Guardian of my soul.

O Jesus, Thou hast promised
To all who follow Thee
That where Thou art in glory
There shall Thy servant be;
And Jesus, I have promised
To serve Thee to the end;
Oh, give me grace to follow,
My Master and my Friend.

Oh, let me see Thy footmarks,
And in them plant mine own;
My hope to follow duly
Is in Thy strength alone.
Oh, guide me, call me, draw me,
Uphold me to the end;
And then to rest receive me,
My Savior and my Friend.

https://www.hymnal.net/en/hymn/h/465

**WEEK TWENTY SEVEN**   **Confession about the Nature of Obedient People**   **DAY 6**

Read Psalm 15

I understand that not just anyone can live in your presence and expect to be with you in eternity. Only those whose manner of life and daily walk is blameless are there. Only those who do right and good are there. Only those who speak honestly and earnestly and don't say mean, false things about other people are there. Only those who treat others with love and concern and compassion and don't say evil things about others are there. Only those who hate what God hates, who despise what evil people do but always honor those who live in obedience to the Lord are there. Only those who keep their promises even when it costs them something they highly value are there. Only those who are generous and kind and helpful and don't take advantage of another's difficult situation are there. Only those who absolutely refuse to be talked into hurting anyone, especially the innocent, are there. But I confess that in and of myself, I can't do any of these things. I confess that only through the grace and mercy of God am I able to live up to this standard. And it's not even me doing it but the life of the Lord Jesus Christ living in me that makes it all possible. When I do stumble, he is there to forgive and restore. By the grace and the life of Jesus, I am one of those, I am there.

**WEEK TWENTY SEVEN**          *INSIGHT and ENCOURAGEMENT*          **DAY 7**

The Coming of the Holy Spirit
by Andrew Murray (1828-1917)

Our Lord, on the last night that he was with His disciples, promised to send the Holy Spirit as a Comforter. Although His bodily presence was removed, they would realize His presence with them in a wonderful way. The Holy Spirit as God would so reveal Christ in their hearts that they would experience His presence with them continually. The Spirit would glorify Christ and would reveal Him in heavenly love and power.

How little Christians understand and believe and experience this truth. We fail in our duty as ministers if, in our preaching, we encourage Christians to love the Lord Jesus, without at the same time warning them that they cannot do this in their own strength. God, the Holy Spirit, will shed abroad His love in our hearts, and teach us to love Him fervently. Through the Holy Spirit we may experience the love and abiding presence of the Lord Jesus all the day.

But let us remember that the Spirit of God must have entire possession of us. He claims our whole heart and life. He will strengthen us in the inner man, so that we have fellowship with Christ, keep his commandments, and abide in his love.

When once we have grasped this truth, we will begin to feel our deep dependence on the Holy Spirit, and pray the Father to send Him in power into our hearts. The Spirit will teach us to love the word, to meditate on it and to keep it. He will reveal the love of Christ to us, that we may love Him. Then we shall see that life in the love of Christ is a blessed reality.

After our Lord had given the great command: "Go into all the world and preach the gospel to every creature," He again added another: "Tarry till ye be endued with power from on high." "Wait for the promise of the Father." "Ye shall be baptized with the Holy Ghost not many days hence."

All Christians agree that the great command to preach the Gospel to every creature was not only for the disciples, but is binding on us too. All, however, do not appear to consider that the very last command, not to preach until they had received the power from on high, is equally binding on us as it was on the disciples. The Church appears to have lost possession of that which ought to be to her a secret of secrets – the abiding consciousness, day by day, that it is only as she lives in the power of the Holy Spirit that she can preach the gospel in power. This is why there's so much preaching and working with so little result. It goes back to the universal complaint but there is insufficient prayer to empower the church.

*Growing in Christ.* Westchester, IL: Good News Publishers, 1979. p. 67-69.

**Record your insights, revelations, and meditations from this week. DATE:**

VICTORY THROUGH SURRENDER

**WEEK TWENTY EIGHT**  *HYMNS and POEMS*  **DAY 1**

Help, Lord, For Men of Virtue Fail

by Isaac Watts (1674-1748)

Help, Lord, for men of virtue fail,
Religion loses ground,
The sons of violence prevail,
And treacheries abound.

Their oaths and
promises they break,
Yet act the flatterer's part;
With fair, deceitful lips they speak,
And with a double heart.

If we reprove some hateful lie,
How is their fury stirred
"Are not our lips our own?" they cry;
"And who shall be our Lord?"

Scoffers appear on every side,
Where a vile race of men
Is raised to seats
of power and pride,
And bears the sword in vain.

Lord, when iniquities abound,
And blasphemy grows bold;
When faith is hardly to be found,
And love is waxing cold;

Is not thy chariot hastening on?
Hast thou not given this sign?
May we not trust and live upon
A promise so divine?

"Yes," saith the Lord,
"now will I rise,
And make oppressors flee;
I shall appear to their surprise,
And set my servants free."

Thy word, like silver
sev'n times tried,
Through ages shall endure;
The men that in thy truth confide
Shall find the promise sure.

https://hymnary.org/text/help_lord_for_men_of_virtue_fail

**WEEK TWENTY EIGHT**  *INSIGHT and ENCOURAGEMENT*  **DAY 2**

The Highest Perfection

by François Fénelon (1651-1715)

As soon as we discover a new insight into our faith, we are transported with joy like a miser who has found a treasure.  The true Christian, whatever the misfortunes which Providence heaps upon him, wants whatever comes and does not wish for anything which he or she does not have.  The more one loves God, the more one is content.  The highest perfection, instead of overloading us, makes our yoke lighter.

What folly to fear to be too entirely God's! It is to fear to be too happy. It is to fear to love God's will in all things. It is to fear to have too much courage in the crosses which are inevitable, too much comfort in God's love, and too much detachment from the passions which make us miserable.

So let us scorn earthly things, to be wholly God's. I am not saying that we should leave them absolutely, because when we are already living an honest and regulated life, we only need to change our hearts depth in loving, and we shall do nearly the same things which we were doing. For God does not reverse the conditions of his people, nor their responsibilities which he himself has given them but we, to serve God, do what we were doing to serve and please the world and to satisfy ourselves. There would be only this difference, but instead of being devoured by our pride, by our overbearing passions, and by the malicious criticism of the world, we shall act instead with liberty, courage, and hope in God. Confidence will animate us. The expectation of the eternal good things which are drawing near, while those here below are escaping us, will support us in the midst of our suffering. The love of God, which will make us conscious of God's love for us, will give us wings to fly on his way and to raise us above all our troubles. If we have a hard time believing this, experience will convince us. "Come, see and taste," said David, "how sweet is the Lord."

Jesus Christ said to all Christians without exception, "Let him who would be my disciple carry his cross, and follow me." The broad way leads to perdition. We must follow the narrow way which few enter. We must be born again, renounce ourselves, hate ourselves, become a child, be poor in spirit, weep to be comforted, and not be of the world which is cursed because of its scandals.

These truths frighten many people, and this is because they only know what religion exacts without knowing what it offers, and they ignore the Spirit of love which makes everything easy. They do not know that it leads to the highest perfection by a feeling of peace and love which sweetens all the struggle.

*Christian Perfection.* New York and London: Harper & Brothers, 1947. p. 37-38.

**WEEK TWENTY EIGHT**  *HYMNS and POEMS*  **DAY 3**

Moment By Moment

by Daniel W. Whittle (1840-1901)

Dying with Jesus, by death reckoned mine;
Living with Jesus, a new life divine;
Looking to Jesus till glory doth shine,
Moment by moment, O Lord, I am Thine.

*Refrain:*
*Moment by moment I'm kept in His love;*
*Moment by moment I've life from above;*
*Looking to Jesus till glory doth shine;*
*Moment by moment, O Lord, I am Thine.*

Never a battle with wrong for the right,
   Never a contest that He doth not fight;
   Lifting above us His banner so white,
Moment by moment, I'm kept in His sight.

Never a trial that He is not there,
Never a burden that He doth not bear,
Never a sorrow that He doth not share,
Moment by moment, I'm under His care.

Never a heartache, and never a groan,
   Never a teardrop and never a moan;
   Never a danger but there on the throne,
Moment by moment He thinks of His own.

Never a weakness that He doth not feel,
   Never a sickness that He cannot heal;
   Moment by moment, in woe or in weal,
Jesus my Savior, abides with me still.

Written in 1893, this was Andrew Murray's favorite hymn according to http://www.hymntime.com/. It was reprinted in his book "*Waiting On God.*"

**WEEK TWENTY EIGHT**  *INSIGHT and ENCOURAGEMENT*  **DAY 4**

Running the Race
by Gregory of Nyssa (331-396)

Since the letter which you recently sent requested us to furnish you with some council concerning the perfect life, I thought it only proper to answer your request. Although there may be nothing useful for you in my words, perhaps this example of a ready obedience will not be wholly unprofitable to you. For if we who have been appointed to the position as fathers over so many souls consider it proper here in our old age to accept a commission from youth, how much more suitable is it, inasmuch as we have told you, the young man, to obey voluntarily, that the right action of ready obedience be confirmed in you.

You requested, dear friend, that we trace in outline for you what the perfect life is. Your intention clearly was to translate the grace disclosed by my word into your own life. I am at an equal loss about both things: it is beyond my power to encompass perfection in my treatise or to show in my life the insights of the treatise. And perhaps I am not alone in this. Many great men, even those who excel in virtue, will admit that for them such an accomplishment as this is unattainable. As I would not seem, in the words of the Psalmist, *there to tremble for fear, where no fear was*, I shall put forth for you more clearly what I think.

The perfection of everything which can be measured by the senses is marked off by certain definite boundaries. Quantity, for example, admits of continuity and limitation. The person who looks at the number ten knows that its perfection consists in the fact that it has both a beginning and an end.

But in the case of virtue we have learned from the Apostle that its one limit of perfection is the fact that it has no limit. For that divine Apostle, great and lofty in understanding, ever running the course of virtue, never ceased *straining toward those things that are still to come*. Coming to a stop in the race was not safe for him. Why? Because no Good has a limit in its own nature but is limited by the presence of its opposite, a life is limited by death and light by darkness. Every good thing generally ends with all those things which are perceived to be contrary to the good.

If it is therefore undoubtedly impossible to attain perfection, since, as I have said, perfection is not marked off by limits: the one limit of virtue is the absence of a limit. How then would one arrive at the sought-for boundary when he can find no boundary? Although on the whole my argument has shown that what is sought for is unattainable, one should not disregard the commandment of the Lord which says, *Therefore be perfect, just as your heavenly father is perfect.* For in the case of those things which are good by nature, even if men of understanding were not able to attain everything, by attaining even a part they can yet gain a great deal.

Excerpted from Foster, Richard J. and Smith, James Bryan. *Devotional Classics*. New York: Harper One, 2005. p. 124-125.

**WEEK TWENTY EIGHT**         *HYMNS and POEMS*         **DAY 5**

Live Out Thy Life Within Me
by Frances Ridley Havergal (1836-1879)

Live out Thy life within me, O Jesus, King of kings!
Be Thou Thyself the answer to all my questionings;

Live out Thy life within me, in all things have Thy way!
I, the transparent medium, Thy glory to display.

The temple has been yielded, and purified of sin,
Let Thy Shekinah glory now shine forth from within,

And all the earth keep silence, the body henceforth be
Thy silent, gentle servant, moved only as by Thee.

Its members every moment held subject to Thy call,
Ready to have Thee use them, or not be used at all,

Held without restless longing, or strain, or stress, or fret,
Or chafings at Thy dealings, or thoughts of vain regret.

But restful, calm and pliant, from bend and bias free,
Awaiting Thy decision, when Thou hast need of me.

# VICTORY THROUGH SURRENDER

Live out Thy life within me, O Jesus, King of kings!
Be Thou the glorious answer to all my questionings.

From *A Selection of Psalms and Hymns* in 1864 according to http://www.hymntime.com/

**WEEK TWENTY EIGHT**     *INSIGHT and ENCOURAGEMENT*     **DAY 6**

Concerning the Nature and Extent of Christian Devotion
by William Law (1686-1761)

Devotion is neither private nor public prayer; but prayers, whether private or public, are particular parts or instances of devotion. Devotion signifies a life given, or devoted, to God. He, therefore, is the devout man, who lives no longer to his own will, or the way and spirit of the world, but to the sole will of God, who considers God in everything, who serves God in everything, who makes all the parts of his common life parts of piety, by doing everything in the Name of God, and under such rules as are conformable to His glory.

God alone is to be the rule and measure of our prayers; [but there is] as strong a reason to be as strictly pious in all the other parts of [our] life. For there is not the least shadow of a reason why we should make God the rule and measure of our prayers; but what equally proves it necessary for us to look wholly unto God, and make Him the rule and measure of all the other actions of our life. For any ways of life, any employment of our talents, whether of our parts, our time, or money, that is not for such ends as are suitable to His glory, are as great absurdities and failings, as prayers that are not according to the will of God. For there is no other reason why our prayers should be according to the will of God, but that our lives may be of the same nature, full of the same wisdom, holiness, and heavenly tempers, that we may live unto God in the same spirit that we pray unto Him. Were it not absolutely necessary to walk before Him in wisdom and holiness and all heavenly conversation, doing everything in His Name, and for His glory, there would be no excellency or wisdom in the most heavenly prayers. Nay, such prayers would be absurdities; they would be like prayers for wings, when it was no part of our duty to fly.

As sure as it is our duty to look wholly unto God in our prayers, so sure is it that it is our duty to live wholly unto God in our lives. But we can no more be said to live unto God, unless we live unto Him in all the ordinary actions of our life, unless He be the rule and measure of all our ways, than we can be said to pray unto God, unless our prayers look wholly unto Him. So that unreasonable and absurd ways of life are like unreasonable and absurd prayers, and are as truly an offence unto God. It is for want of knowing, or at least considering this, that we see such a mixture of ridicule in the lives of many people. You see them strict as to some times and places of devotion, but when the service of the Church is over, they are but like those that seldom or never come there. In their way of life, their manner of spending their time and money, in their cares and fears, in their pleasures and indulgences, in their labour and diversions, they are like the rest of the world. This makes the loose part of the world generally make a jest of those that are devout, because they see their devotion goes no farther than their prayers, and then, they live no more unto

God, till the time of prayer returns again; but live by the same humour and fancy, and in as full an enjoyment of all the follies of life as other people. This is the reason why they are the jest and scorn of careless and worldly people; not because they are really devoted to God, but because they appear to have no other devotion but that of occasional prayers.

Excerpted from *A Serious Call To A Devout and Holy Life* (1729). New York: Scriptura Press, 2015. p. 12-16.

**WEEK TWENTY EIGHT**　　　　　　　**Confession of Helplessness**　　　　　　　**DAY 7**

Read Habakkuk 1 and 3:17-19

Lord, how long must I cry out to you and call for help without getting an answer, with no reply at all? It seems like my voice cannot be heard. Even when people treat me harshly and commit evil acts against me, I cry for help, but help doesn't come. I constantly witness sinful behavior and sinful people cause trouble for me constantly. Theft and violence are all around me leading to constant fights and arguments. Man's law provides no relief because evil men are in positions of power and pervert justice for their own ends. I am absolutely helpless and confused. Why do you allow people to get away with this? Why do you not act to put an end to this? The wicked set their traps for whoever comes along and catch them in their webs of deceit. They celebrate themselves and worship their cruel devices. They lack nothing because they ruin other people's lives and rob them without pity. When will it stop? And yet, I still believe in you. I still trust that you are the answer. Even though I cannot comprehend what your purpose may be in all this, I will keep trusting. Even though I struggle to make it from one day to the next, I will continue to hope in my God. I do not yet see a solution, but I will continue to rejoice in the Lord. You will give me the strength to navigate the rocky steeps of this wilderness without falling I will continue to take joy in the God of my salvation.

**Record your insights, revelations, and meditations from this week. DATE:**

_____

_____

_____

_____

_____

**WEEK TWENTY NINE**  *INSIGHT and ENCOURAGEMENT*  **DAY 1**

Avoiding Spiritual Extremes
by John of the Cross (1542-1591)

With respect to the sin of spiritual gluttony, there is much to be said, for there is scarce one of these beginners who falls not into some of the many imperfections with respect to this sin, on account of the sweetness which they find at first in spiritual exercises. For many of these strive more after spiritual sweetness than after spiritual purity and discretion, which is what God regards and accepts throughout the spiritual journey. Therefore, besides the imperfections into which the seeking for sweetness of this kind makes them fall, the gluttony which they now have makes them continually go to extremes, so that they pass beyond the limits of moderation within which the virtues are acquired and wherein they have their being. For some of these persons, attracted by the pleasure which they find therein, kill themselves with penances, and others weaken themselves with fasts, by performing more than their frailty can bear, without the order or advice of any, but rather endeavouring to avoid those whom they should obey.

These persons are most imperfect and unreasonable; for they set bodily penance before subjection and obedience, which is penance according to reason and discretion, and therefore a sacrifice more acceptable and pleasing to God than any other. Inasmuch as all extremes are vicious, and as in behaving thus such persons are working their own will, they grow in vice rather than in virtue; for they are acquiring spiritual gluttony and pride in this way, through not walking in obedience. And many of these the devil assails, stirring up this gluttony in them through the pleasures and desires which he increases within them, to such an extent that they either change or vary or add to that which is commanded them, as any obedience in this respect is so bitter to them. To such an evil pass have some persons come that, simply because it is through obedience that they engage in these exercises, they lose the desire and devotion to perform them, their only desire and pleasure being to do what they themselves are inclined to do, so that it would probably be more profitable for them not to engage in these exercises at all.

You will find that many of these persons are very insistent with their spiritual masters to be granted that which they desire, extracting it from them almost by force; if they be refused it they become as peevish as children and go about in great displeasure, thinking that they are not serving God when they are not allowed to do that which they would. For they go about clinging to their own will and pleasure, which they treat as though it came from God; and immediately their directors take it from them, and try to subject them to the will of God, they become peevish, grow faint-hearted and fall away. These persons think that their own satisfaction and pleasure are the satisfaction and service of God.

When they have received no pleasure or sweetness in the senses, they think that they have accomplished nothing at all. This is to judge God very unworthily; they have not realized that the least of the benefits which come from this Most Holy Sacrament is that which concerns the senses; and that the invisible part of the grace that it bestows is much greater.

Excerpted from *Dark Night of the Soul*. Start Publishing eBook edition: 2012. p. 47-50.

**WEEK TWENTY NINE**  *HYMNS and POEMS*  **DAY 2**

A Soul in Its Earliest Love

by Charles Wesley (1707-1788)

O how happy are they
Who their Saviour obey,
And have laid up their treasure above;
Tongue can never express
The sweet comfort and peace
Of a soul in its earliest love.

That sweet comfort was mine,
When the favor divine
I received through the blood of the Lamb;
When my heart first believed,
What a joy I received
What a heaven in Jesus' Name!

'Twas a heaven below
My Redeemer to know,
And the angels could do nothing more

Than to fall at His feet,
And the story repeat,
And the Lover of sinners adore.

Jesus all the day long
Was my joy and my song:
O that all His salvation might see;
He hath loved me, I cried,
He hath suffered and died,
To redeem even rebels like me.

O the rapturous height
Of that holy delight
Which I felt in the life-giving blood;
Of my Saviour possessed,
I was perfectly blessed.
As if filled with the fulness of God.

Tozer, A. W. *The Christian Book of Mystical Verse: A Collection of Poems, Hymns, and Prayers for Devotional Reading*. Chicago: Moody Publishers, 2016. p. 80.

VICTORY THROUGH SURRENDER

**WEEK TWENTY NINE**  *HYMNS and POEMS*  **DAY 3**

What Shall I Give Thee, Master?
by Homer W. Grimes (published 1934)

What shall I give Thee, Master?
Thou who didst die for me.
Shall I give less of what I possess,
Or shall I give all to Thee?

What shall I give Thee, Master?
Thou hast giv'n all for me;
Not just a part or half of my heart,
I will give all to Thee.

What shall I give Thee, Master?
Thou hast redeemed my soul;
My gift is small but it is my all—
Surrendered to Thy control.

What shall I give Thee, Master?
Giver of gifts divine!
I will not hold time, talents or gold—
For everything shall be Thine.

*Refrain:*
*Jesus, my Lord and Savior;*
*Thou hast giv'n all for me;*
*Thou didst leave Thy home above*
*To die on Calvary.*

https://www.hymnal.net/en/hymn/h/446

**WEEK TWENTY NINE**  *INSIGHT and ENCOURAGEMENT*  **DAY 4**

Realize the Presence of God
by David McIntyre (1859-1938)

In the first place, it is necessary that we should realize the presence of God. He who fills earth and heaven "is," in a singular and impressive sense, in the secret place. As the electric energy which is diffused in the atmosphere is concentrated in the lightning flash, so the presence of God becomes vivid and powerful in the prayer-chamber. Bishop Jeremy Taylor enforces this rule with stately and affluent speech: "In the beginning of actions of religion, make an act of adoration; that is, solemnly worship God, and place thyself in God's presence, and behold Him with the eye of faith; and let thy desires actually fix on Him as the object of thy worship, and the reason of thy hope, and the fountain of thy blessings. For when thou hast placed thyself before Him, and kneelest in His presence, it is most likely all the following parts of thy devotion will be answerable to the wisdom of such an apprehension, and the glory of such a presence."

Our Father "is" in the secret place. Then we shall find Him in the inwardness of a "recollected" spirit, in the stillness of a heart united to fear His name. The dew falls most copiously when the night-winds are hushed. The great tides lift themselves "too full for sound or foam." The suppliant who prays with a true direction of spirit, "Our Father, who art in heaven," is oftentimes taken up into heaven before ever he is aware. "But, oh how rare it is!" cries Fénelon, "How rare it is to find a soul quiet enough to hear God speak!" So many of us have mistrained ears.

The realization of the Divine presence is the inflexible condition of a right engagement of spirit in the exercise of private prayer. John Spilsbury of Bromgrove, who was confined in Worcester jail for the testimony of Christ, bore this witness: "I shall not henceforward fear a prison as formerly, because I had so much of my Heavenly Father's company as made it a palace to me." Another, in similar case, testified: "I thought of Jesus until every stone in my cell shone like a ruby." And for us, too, in our measure, the dull room in which we talk with God, as a man may speak with his friend, will burn at times like a sapphire and a sardius stone, and be to us as the cleft rock in Sinai, through which the un-created glory poured, until the prophet's steadfast gaze was dimmed, and his countenance kindled as a flame.

Our realization of the presence of God may, however, be accompanied with little or no emotion. Our spirits may lie as if dead under the hand of God. Vision and rapture may alike be withdrawn. But we ought not therefore to grow sluggish in prayer. So far from interrupting the exercise at such times, we ought to redouble our energy. And it may be that the prayer which goes up through darkness to God will bring to us a blessing such as we have not received in our most favored hours. The prayer which rises from "the land of forgetfulness," "the place of darkness," "the belly of hell," may have an abundant and glorious return.

Adapted from *The Hidden Life of Prayer*. Originally 1891. p. 14-15.
https://www.scribd.com/document/176950429/The-Hidden-Life-of-Prayer

**WEEK TWENTY NINE**  *HYMNS and POEMS*  **DAY 5**

Lord Jesus Christ, With Us Abide
by Nikolaus Selnecker (1532-1592)

Lord Jesus Christ, with us abide,
For round us falls the eventide;
Nor let Thy Word, that heav'nly light,
For us be ever veiled in night.

In these last days of sore distress
Grant us, dear Lord, true steadfastness
That pure we keep, till life is spent,
Thy holy Word and sacrament.

Lord Jesus, help, Thy Church uphold,
For we are sluggish, thoughtless, cold.
Oh, prosper well Thy Word of grace
And spread its truth in every place!

Oh, keep us in Thy Word, we pray;
The guile and rage of Satan stay!
Oh, may Thy mercy never cease!
Give concord, patience, courage, peace.

O God, how sin's dread works abound!
Throughout the earth no rest is found,
And falsehood's spirit wide has spread,
And error boldly rears its head.

The haughty spirits, Lord, restrain
Who o'er Thy Church with might would reign
And always set forth something new,
Devised to change Thy doctrine true.

Oh, grant that in Thy holy Word
We here may live and die, dear Lord;
And when our journey endeth here,
Receive us into glory there.

And since the cause and glory, Lord,
Are Thine, not ours, to us afford
Thy help and strength and constancy,
With all our heart we trust in Thee.

A trusty weapon is Thy Word,
Thy Church's buckler, shield, and sword.
Oh, let us in its power confide
That we may seek no other guide!

Posthumously published in *Geistliche Psalmen*, in Nuremberg, Germany, 1611, according to http://www.hymntime.com/

**WEEK TWENTY NINE**  *INSIGHT and ENCOURAGEMENT*  **DAY 6**

Abiding in the Crucified One

by Andrew Murray (1828-1917)

Abiding in Jesus, the Crucified One, is the secret of the growth of that new life. I must learn to look upon the Cross as not only an atonement to God, but also a victory over the devil – not only a deliverance from the guilt, but also from the power of sin. I must gaze on Him on the Cross as wholly mine, offering Himself to receive me into the closest union and fellowship, and to make me partaker of the full power of His death to sin, and the new life of victory to which it is but the gateway. I must yield myself to Him in an undivided surrender, with much prayer and strong desire, imploring to be admitted into the ever closer fellowship and conformity of His death, of the Spirit in which He died that death.

On the Cross the Son of God enters into the fullest union with man – enters into the fullest experience of what it says to have become a son of man, a member of a race under the curse. It is in death that the Prince of life conquers the power of death; it is in death alone that He can make me a partaker of that victory. The life He imparts is a life from the dead; each new experience of the power of that life depends upon the fellowship of the death. The death and the life are inseparable. All the grace which Jesus the Saving One gives is given only in the path of fellowship with Jesus the Crucified One. Christ came and took my place; I must put myself in his place, and abide there. And there is but one place which is both his and mine - that place is the cross. His in virtue of his free choice; mine by reason of the curse of sin. He came there to seek me; there alone I can find Him. When He found me there, it was the place of cursing; this He experienced, for "cursed is every one that hangeth on a tree." He made it a place of blessing; this I experienced, for Christ has delivered us from the curse, being made a curse for us. It is as I abide daily, deeply in Jesus the Crucified One, that I shall taste the sweetness of His love, the power of His life, the completeness of His salvation.

I fear there are many Christians who are content to look upon the cross, with Christ on it dying for their sins, who have little heart for fellowship with the Crucified One. They hardly know that He invites them to it. Or they are content to consider the ordinary afflictions of life as their share of Christ's Cross. They have no conception of what it is to be crucified with Christ, that bearing the cross means likeness to Christ in the principles which animated Him in His path of obedience. The entire surrender of all self-will, the complete denial to the flesh of its every desire and pleasure, the perfect separation from the world in all its ways of thinking and acting, the losing and hating of one's life, the giving up of self and its interests for the sake of others – this is the disposition which marks him who has taken up Christ's Cross, who seeks to say, "I am crucified with Christ; I abide in Christ, the Crucified One."

Excerpted from *Abide in Christ*. Readaclassic.com, 2010. p. 41-43.

**WEEK TWENTY NINE**         **Confession of a Righteous Life**        **DAY 7**

Read Psalm 4

Lord, you are God, my God, the one who makes it possible to live a righteous life. You hear me when I call on you, and you provide relief in all my distress and troubles. In your mercy, you hear my prayers. The men of this world take the things that are a blessing to me and try to use them to embarrass me and put me to shame. But I know the things they set their affections on and pursue constantly are worthless. The things they think are essential are fake, counterfeits based on lies and deceit. (Pause and ponder this.) I know that the Lord separates and sets apart those who live godly lives. I am numbered among them because the Lord hears me when I call. In the stillness of the night, I will still my heart and think about what God has said to me. (Pause and ponder this.) As I live the surrendered life, I will daily make the sacrifices that righteousness requires and always put my trust in the Lord, my God. I will live in the light of your shining face and walk with gladness in my heart, happier than any holiday celebration. And at the end of the day, I will lie down and sleep in peace, knowing that you alone are the source of my safety.

**Record your insights, revelations, and meditations from this week. DATE:**

Tim Tremaine

**WEEK THIRTY**  *HYMNS and POEMS*  **DAY 1**

The Weaver

by B. M. Franklin (1882-1965)

My life is but a weaving
Between my God and me.
I cannot choose the colors
He weaveth steadily.

Behind my life, the Weaver stands,
And works His wondrous will:
I leave it in His all-wise hand,
And trust His perfect skill.

Should mystery enshroud His plan,
And my short sight be dim,
I will not try the whole to scan,
But leave each thread to Him.

Not 'til the loom is silent
And the shuttles cease to fly
Will God unroll the canvas
And reveal the reason why.

Oft' times He weaveth sorrow;
And I in foolish pride
Forget He sees the upper
And I the underside.

The dark threads are as needful
In the weaver's skillful hand
As the threads of gold and silver
In the pattern He has planned

He knows, He loves, He cares;
Nothing this truth can dim.
He gives the very best to those
Who leave the choice to Him.

[The website https://et1969.wordpress.com/2009/09/12/gods-tapestry/ lists this title and author; however, I first found a version of this poem in Paul Billheimer's book, *Adventure in Adversity*, where he attributes it to author unknown. Many websites mention that the poem was made famous by Corrie Ten Boom, who referred to it as "The Tapestry Poem." The version above is a combination of three versions of the poem with the order of the verses chosen by me.]

**WEEK THIRTY**  *INSIGHT and ENCOURAGEMENT*  **DAY 2**

The First and Last Duty

by Frank Laubach (1884-1970)

Submission is the first and last duty of man. That is exactly what I have been needing in my Christian life. Two years ago, a profound dissatisfaction led me to begin trying to line up my actions with the will of God about every 15 minutes or every half hour. Other people to whom I confessed this intention said it was impossible. I judge from what I have said that few people are trying even that. But this year I have started out trying to live all my waking moments in conscious listening to the inner voice, without ceasing, "What, Father, do you desire said? What, Father, do you desire done this minute?"

For the past few days I have been experimenting in a more complete surrender than ever before. I am taking by deliberate act of will, enough time from each hour to give God much thought. Yesterday and today I have made a new adventure, which is not easy to express. I am feeling God in each movement, by an act of will – willing that He shall direct these fingers that now strike this typewriter – willing that He shall pour through my steps as I walk – willing that He shall direct my words as I speak, and my very jaws as I eat!

You will object to this intense introspection. Do not try it, unless you feel unsatisfied with your own relationship with God, but at least allow me to realize all the leadership of God I can. I am disgusted with the pettiness and futility of my unled self. If the way out is not more perfect slavery to God, then what is the way out? I am trying to be utterly free from everybody, free from my own self, but completely enslaved to the will of God every moment of this day.

We used to sing a song in the church in Benton which I liked, but which I never really practiced until now. It runs:

> "Moment by moment, I'm kept in his love;
> Moment by moment I've life from above;
> Looking to Jesus till glory doth shine;
> Moment by moment, O Lord, I am thine."

It is exactly that "moment by moment," every waking moment, surrender, responsiveness, obedience, sensitiveness, pliability, "lost in His love," that I now have the mind-bent to explore with all my might. It means two burning passions: First, to be like Jesus. Second, to respond to God as a violin responds to the bow of the master. Open your soul and entertain the glory of God and after a while that glory will be reflected in the world about you and in the very clouds above your head.

Foster, Richard J. and Smith, James Bryan. *Devotional Classics*. New York: Harper One, 2005. Pp. 101-102. (Frank's diary entries for January 20 and 26, 1930.)

**WEEK THIRTY**     **Confession of a Victorious Warrior**     **DAY 3**

Read Psalm 9

Lord, I will praise you with my entire being. I will enthusiastically tell the story of your amazing deeds in my life. I will be so happy and full of joy that I will feel like singing your praises. Why? Because my problems melted away when I brought them into your presence. You have supported me and justified my efforts by your judgments of righteousness. Rebuke and demolish the works of the evil one. Erase even the memory of what they have done. Grant that I can face my troubles and say, "Your time is up! The days of you bringing destruction into my life are over. You will have no lasting reputation, but the fame of the Lord will last forever." You are the Righteous Judge of the world, and you will dispense justice for your righteous people. My Lord is also a refuge when I am oppressed, a safe haven in times of trouble. Because I know who you are, I can put my hope and faith in you. When I earnestly seek for you, you always let me find you. I will tell everyone about the wonderful things you have done for me. You never forget me. Your mercy is always a reason to rejoice in your salvation. When the wicked set out traps for me, you come to the rescue. You don't forget me in times of need. My desires for you are always fulfilled. Your righteousness always prevails.

**WEEK THIRTY**  *INSIGHT and ENCOURAGEMENT*  **DAY 4**

Can It Be Done?

by Frank Laubach (1884-1970)

Every waking moment of the week I have been looking toward him, with perhaps the exception of an hour or two. How infinitely richer this direct first hand grasping of God himself is, than the old method which I used and recommended for years, the endless reading of devotional books. Almost it seems to me now that the very Bible cannot be read as a substitute for meeting God soul-to-soul and face-to-face.

We cannot keep two things in mind at once. Indeed we cannot keep one thing in mind more than half a second. Mind is a flowing something. It oscillates. Concentration is merely the continuous return to the same problem from a million angles. So my problem is this: Can I bring God back in my mind-flow every few seconds so that God shall always be in my mind as an after image, shall always be one of the elements in every concept and precept? I choose to make the rest of my life an experiment in answering this question.

I do not invite anybody else to follow this arduous path. I wish much might. We need to know, for example, Can a laboring man successfully attain this continuous surrender to God? Can a man working at a machine pray for people all day long, and at the same time do his task efficiently? Can another wash dishes, care for the babies, continuously talking to God?

If you are like myself, this has been a pretty strong diet. So I will put something simpler and more attainable: "Any hour of any day may be made perfect by merely choosing. It is perfect if one looks to God that entire hour, waiting for His leadership all through the hour and trying hard to do every tiny thing exactly as God wishes it done."

If this record of a soul struggling to find God is to be complete it must not omit the story of difficulty and failure. I have not succeeded very well so far. This week, for example, has not been one of the finest in my life, but I resolve not to give up the effort. Yet strain does not seem to do good. At this moment I feel something "let go" inside, and lo, God is here! It is a heart melting "here-ness," a lovely whispering of father to child, and the reason I did not have it before was because I failed to let go. This thing of keeping constant touch with God, making him the object of my fault and the companion of my conversations, is the most amazing thing I ever ran across. I cannot do it even half a day – not yet, but I believe I shall be doing it someday for the entire day. It is a matter of acquiring a new habit of thought.

Excerpted from; Foster, Richard J. and Smith, James Bryan. *Devotional Classics*. New York: Harper One, 2005. p. 103-105. (Frank's diary entries for March 15 and 23, and April 19 and 22, 1930.)

**WEEK THIRTY**  *HYMNS and POEMS*  **DAY 5**

I Gave My Life For Thee
by Frances Ridley Havergal (1836-1879)

I gave My life for thee,
My precious blood I shed,
That thou might ransomed be,
And raised up from the dead;
I gave, I gave My life for thee,
What hast thou giv'n for Me?

My Father's house of light,
My glory-circled throne
I left for earthly night,
For wand'rings sad and lone;
I left, I left it all for thee,
Hast thou left aught for Me?

I suffered much for thee,
More than thy tongue can tell,
Of bitt'rest agony,
To rescue thee from hell;
I've borne, I've borne it all for thee,
What hast thou borne for Me?

And I have brought to thee,
Down from My home above,
Salvation full and free,
My pardon and My love;
I bring, I bring rich gifts to thee,
What hast thou brought to Me?

Sims, Walter Hines, ed. *Baptist Hymnal*, Nashville: Covington Press, 1956. p. 399.

**WEEK THIRTY**  The Lie of the Devil  **DAY 6**

Perhaps the supreme, yet most subtle, lie Satan uses to hamstring Christian converts is the idea that they can have God's way and their own way at the same time. Satan's enticing argument to Eve in the garden began with the doubt-inducing question – "Did God really say?" So it is today with the Christian convert contemplating full disciple status in the church of Jesus Christ. Satan casts dispersions on Christ's definition of a true disciple. The question, in its multitude of variations, is basically this; "Did Jesus really say that to be His disciple you must forsake everything?"

The deceiver then launches a barrage of propositions that sound logical and sensible and equitable, but in the end lead to frustration and defeat for the soul wanting to follow Jesus but looking for a justification to circumvent the only way to do so. "Surely a loving Father would want you to be happy and prosperous and enjoy good things?" the tempter whispers. He can even support his half-truths with Scriptures and a long line of proponents who concur with his thesis, which is the antithesis of the verses he knows too well will result in a self-emptied, Spirit-filled, demon-bashing disciple of the Lord Jesus Christ.

Stripped of all power and all authority through the cross, the defeated one has only one play: to attempt to pull the wool over the convert's eyes and keep him from becoming who he is – an heir of God and co-heir of Christ to all that the Kingdom of God is and means to those who are absolutely surrendered to Christ.

The instability of the struggling convert and his inability to get settled about this matter of discipleship is evidence of what James calls "double-mindedness" (James 1:8). The convert knows or at least has an inkling, what the Lord accepts from His followers but the voice of the evil one, amplified by the world, still has its allure.

The Psalmist calls it having a double heart (Psalm 12:2). The affections are divided and pulled in opposite directions. The convert can identify with, although may not understand, Paul's sentiments in Romans chapter 7 when he bemoans the fact that the things he should do, he cannot; and the things he should not do, he does. Paul discovers, as we all must, that the only solution to the problem, the only resolution to this dilemma, the only answer to our desperate plea for help, is the Cross. To live for God, we must die to self.

Three times in Luke chapter 14, the Lord says not doing this means you cannot be his disciple. Exalting any other relationship, withholding any possession, resisting every invitation to place all of the soul on the Cross so that Christ can live his life through you, disqualifies the convert, not from heaven but from heaven on earth as a full-fledged disciple whose every breath speaks; "Thy Kingdom come, Thy will be done."

**WEEK THIRTY**      **Confession of a Grateful Sinner**      **DAY 7**

Read Nehemiah 1 and Deuteronomy 30

Lord God of heaven, you are a great and awesome God. You keep your promises and covenants that you have made with your people. You are merciful and gracious to those who love you and obey your commandments. Your eyes are always attentive, and your eyes are always open to the prayers of your servants. We can come to you any time of the day or night to confess our sins, and you will hear and forgive. Even though we have sinned by acting very corruptly against you and have not kept the commandments, statutes, and ordinances found in your word, you still honor the promise you gave to Moses. "If you are unfaithful, I will scatter you among the nations; but if you return to Me, and keep my commandments and do them, though some of you were cast out to the farthest part of the heavens, yet I will gather them from there, and bring them to the place which I have chosen for a dwelling for My name." I bless your name that there is nowhere I can go that is too far for you to reach me. There is no place from which I cannot return to your obedience and find the grace and mercy of your forgiveness and restoration. Hear my continuing prayer. Make me follow you in obedience all the days of my life, for I desire to fear your name. Prosper me in your presence, O Lord my God.

**Record your insights, revelations, and meditations from this week.  DATE:**

_____

_____

_____

_____

_____

_____

_____

_____

_____

_____

_____

_____

_____

_____

**WEEK THIRTY ONE**  *HYMNS and POEMS*  **DAY 1**

Let Worldly Minds the World Pursue
                                                            by John Newton (1725-1807)

| | |
|---|---|
| Let worldly minds the world pursue, | Creatures no more divide my choice, |
| It has no charms for me; | I bid them all depart; |
| Once I admired its trifles too, | His name, and love, and gracious voice, |
| But grace has set me free. | Have fixed my roving heart. |
| | |
| Its pleasures now no longer please, | Now, Lord, I would be Thine alone, |
| No more content afford; | And wholly live to Thee; |
| Far from my heart be joys like these; | But may I hope that Thou wilt own |
| Now I have seen the Lord. | A worthless worm, like me? |
| | |
| As by the light of opening day | Yes! though of sinners I'm the worst, |
| The stars are all concealed; | I cannot doubt Thy will; |
| So earthly pleasures fade away, | For if Thou hadst not loved me first |
| When Jesus is revealed. | I had refused Thee still. |

http://www.hymntime.com/tch/htm/l/e/t/letwomin.htm


**WEEK THIRTY ONE**  *INSIGHT and ENCOURAGEMENT*  **DAY 2**

The Perfect Man
                                                            by Alexander Maclaren (1826-1910)

Read Phil 3:15. "As many as be perfect;" and how many may they be? Part of the answer to such a question may be found in observing that the New Testament very frequently uses the word to express not so much the idea of moral completeness as that of physical maturity. Clearly in such cases it means "full grown," as in contrast with "babes," and expresses not absolute completeness, but what we may term a relative perfection, a certain maturity of character and advanced stage of Christian attainment, far removed from the infantile epoch of the Christian life. In this context these "perfect" people are exhorted to cultivate the sense of not having "already attained," and to be constantly reaching forth to unattained heights, so that a sense of imperfection and a continual effort after higher life are parts of Paul's "perfect man."

The language of the New Testament has no scruple in calling men "saints" who had many sins, and none in calling men perfect who had many imperfections. It wisely considers the main thing about a character to be not the degree to which it has attained completeness in its ideal, but what that ideal is. The distance a man has got on his journey is of less consequence than the direction in which his face is turned.

If that it be wise to rank a man in their pursuits according to their aims rather than their accomplishments, is there one class of aims that to take them for one's own, and to reach some measure of approximation to them, may fairly be called the perfection of human nature? The literal force of the word in our text gives pertinence to that question, for it distinctly means "having reached the end." He who lives for God is doing what he was made and meant to do; and however incomplete may be its attainments, the lowest form of a God-fearing, God-obeying life is higher and more nearly "perfect" than the fairest career or character that glorifies God not. Better a life of Godward aspiration, and straining after purity, than one of habitual earthward grubbing, undisturbed by gross sin.

How did Paul think of himself? "Not as though I were already perfect…" So, then a leading characteristic of this true Christian perfection is a constant consciousness of imperfection. In all fields of effort, as faculty grows, consciousness of insufficiency grows with it. The measure of our perfection will be the consciousness of our imperfection – a paradox, but a great truth. The condition of all Christian progress is to be drawn by that fair vision before us, and to be stung into renewed effort to reach it, by the consciousness of present imperfection. They who are perfect are most conscious of imperfection, and most eager in their efforts after a further progress in the knowledge, love, and likeness of God in Christ.

Excerpted from, *The Secret of Power*. London: Macmillan and Co., 1882. p. 280-288.

## MONTH EIGHT

As I write this, the world is months into the Covid-19 pandemic, and the United States is about two weeks into the George Floyd protests, demonstrations, and riots. Back in 2015, we saw similar things, only not to this extent, after several high-profile deaths of black men at the hands of police. The list of names from 2014-2015 is long. What was happening in the police industry was difficult to comprehend. Why did this keep happening? Is no one paying attention? Is no one learning anything from what was going on?

I became burdened about what to do and asked the Lord to give me a way to have some input or offer up an idea that might be constructive. I began to study culture related to police culture because so many people complained that the police culture was systemically flawed and needed a significant overhaul. I started to think about what one officer could do when faced with another officer's misconduct or potential misconduct in the field in the heat of the moment. It took a few months to educate myself on the subject and begin to have some creative thoughts on the matter.

I was living alone at the time, so I had plenty of time to dedicate to the task, but it was a challenge. This was an entirely new area of study for which I had no formal background. I knew how to study and organize thoughts and write things out, but the terminology was new, the scholarship was unfamiliar, and there was a ton of it. Gradually, an idea began to take shape, and I thank the Lord for the inspiration He provided for the content of the program I developed. [See my 2016 book, *Officer Up! Creating a Climate for Appropriate Officer Behavior*.]

All that to say, this was my life in the spring of 2016. After weeks of reading and thinking, and writing, I was getting tired. I was hoping to have the project finished by summer, but everything was moving slowly, and I was running out of steam. I'm sure I asked God for help, although I don't remember that specifically, but help came in an unexpected fashion.

For some time, I had been having a problem with neuropathy in my feet and legs. There was a progressive increase in the numbness and tingling there. That was not surprising since my dad had suffered from the same thing, albeit for a different reason. I went to a neurologist who diagnosed the problem. Once the problem is tested and diagnosed, you have to go back regularly for check-ups. Mine was in April of that year. This time blood tests were ordered and, when I went in for the update, I got a rude awakening. The doctor (who shall remain nameless because his bedside manner left much to be desired) came in and bluntly told me that the results of my tests were often what he saw with people who get cancer. A few weeks later – after many more tests and a hip biopsy that was loads of fun – I got the diagnosis. I had a pre-cancerous condition for multiple myeloma, an incurable disease that was usually fatal.

When you ask God for motivation, you have to be willing to accept whatever he provides. I finished the book because I wanted to have it done for my children's sake. I am grateful that the condition is stable and may not lead to cancer, but I am also thankful God revealed it when he did and gave me the grace to accept it for what it was. I had not learned about surrender then, but when you surrender to him, you surrender to his sovereignty to do what He knows is best for you. Praise God for the "pre-surrender" grace to trust him.


**WEEK THIRTY ONE**　　　　　*HYMNS and POEMS*　　　　　**DAY 3**

Majesty Divine!

by Frederick William Faber (1814-1863)

Full of glory, full of wonders,
Majesty Divine!
Mid Thine everlasting thunders
How Thy lightnings shine!
Shoreless Ocean! who shall sound Thee?
Thine own eternity is round Thee,
Majesty Divine!

Timeless, spaceless, single, lonely,
Yet sublimely Three,
Thou art grandly, always, only
God in Unity!
Lone in grandeur, lone in glory,
Who shall tell Thy wondrous story,
Awful Trinity?

Speechlessly, without beginning,
    Sun that never rose!
Vast, adorable, and winning,
    Day that hath no close!
Bliss from Thine own glory tasting,
    Everliving, everlasting,
    Life that never grows!

Thine own Self forever filling
    With self-kindled flame,
In Thyself Thou art distilling
    Unctions without name!
Without worshipping of creatures
Without veiling of Thy features,
    God always the same!

In Thy praise of Self untiring
    Thy perfections shine;
Self-sufficient, self-admiring,
    Such life must be Thine;
Glorifying Self, yet blameless
With a sanctity all shameless
    It is so divine!

'Mid Thine uncreated morning,
    Like a trembling star
I behold creation's dawning
    Glimmering from afar;
Nothing giving, nothing taking,
Nothing changing, nothing breaking,
    Waiting at time's bar!

I with life and love diurnal
    See myself in Thee,
All embalmed in love eternal,
    Floating in Thy sea:
'Mid Thine uncreated whiteness
I behold Thy glory's brightness
    Feed itself on me.

Splendours upon splendours beaming
    Change and intertwine;
Glories over glories streaming
    All translucent shine!
Blessings, praises, adorations
Greet Thee from the trembling nations
    Majesty Divine!

Tozer, A. W. *The Christian Book of Mystical Verse: A Collection of Poems, Hymns, and Prayers for Devotional Reading.* Chicago: Moody Publishers, 2016. p. 29

**WEEK THIRTY ONE**       Confession of Improper Attachments      **DAY 4**

Read Ezra 9-10

Father, I confess that there are worldly affections in my life that I have not separated from. Thank you for revealing these attachments to me. I realize those are not the only ones. This is a process because we both know that I couldn't handle them all at once. This will not be a one-time occurrence, nor will it be completed in a day or two. But I will continue, by the Holy Spirit, to examine my affections and attachments to expose everything unholy in my life that I must separate from in my walk with you. Thank you for dealing graciously and patiently with me. I grieve that these affections displease you and hinder my relationship with you. Separating from these affections will be painful. Those attachments have been around a long time, and some have produced consequences that will have to be faced. And yet, my hope is in you. I want to be right with you more than I want to avoid the pain of separating from the things that displease you. As you reveal those things in my life from which I must separate myself, my response will be, "Yes! As you have said, so I must do."

| WEEK THIRTY ONE | *INSIGHT and ENCOURAGEMENT* | DAY 5 |

Discipleship

by G. Campbell Morgan (1863-1945)

The other great privilege to be remembered is that the school of Jesus is a technical school. He provides opportunities for us to prove in practical life the truths He has to declare. This is a great essential in His method, with which we shall deal more fully in a subsequent chapter. It is another evidence of His abounding grace, that the proving in technical details of the lessons He teaches, is just as much under His personal guidance and direction as the truth in theory is received directly from Him.

Now, upon what personal conditions may I become a disciple? I fain would have this enduement of pardon, cleansing and illumination. How may this be? No school of man was ever so strictly guarded, so select, as this yet none was ever so easy of access. No bar of race, or color, or caste, or age stands across the entrance. Humanity constitutes the essential claim. And yet, because of the importance of the truths to be revealed and of the necessity for the application of every power of the being to the understanding and realization of these truths, Jesus stands at the entrance, forbidding any to enter, save upon certain conditions. Let us hear His threefold word: (1)"If any man cometh unto Me, and hateth not his own father and mother, and wife and children, and brethren and sisters, yea and his own life also, he cannot be My disciple." (2)"Whosoever doth not bear his own cross and come after Me, cannot be my disciple." (3) "Whosoever he be of you that renounceth not all that he hath, he cannot be my disciple." (Lk 14:26-27, 33).

The new relationship must be superior, in the urgency of its claims to the claim of any earthly relationship it must be considered and answered before any claims of the self-life. The Teacher demands that we shall take up the cross and so follow on, even though the progress be through pain. More, we must take the deep spiritual vow of poverty, renouncing all as possessions, counting every word He shall speak, and every truth He shall reveal, through whatsoever methods, as our chief and only wealth. If this be our entering His school, we are ready for, and enter upon our course of instruction. If these conditions seem hard and severe, let it be remembered what depends upon them. Character and destiny depend upon this question of discipleship. Not to impart information and to satisfy curiosity, is Jesus the Teacher. It is because the truth sanctifies and makes free that He reveals it, and because, apart from the revelation He has to make, there is no possible way of realizing God's great purposes for us. Compare himself a moment's thought. They must all come from between Him and ourselves, so that we may know and do His will. Self renders it impossible to know Christ, when other loves and interests intervene, and breeds dissatisfaction with all else and makes that very self-sad and weak. Christ absolute, lights the whole being with His love, and joy and beauty and shines on other loves to their sanctification, and so, the abnegation of self is self's highest development. So, let us enter the school of Jesus, and, receiving His gifts, await His teaching.

*Discipleship.* Pathos Publishers EBook, 2015. p. 10-13 (reprint from 1897).

VICTORY THROUGH SURRENDER

**WEEK THIRTY ONE**  *INSIGHT and ENCOURAGEMENT*  **DAY 6**

Living a Lifestyle of Praise

| | |
|---|---|
| Praise You in the daylight | Praise You with an empty stomach |
| Praise You in the nighttime | Praise You in the crowd |
| Praise You in the bedroom | Praise You all by myself |
| Praise You in the kitchen | Praise You when I'm happy |
| Praise You in the living room | Praise You when I'm sad |
| Praise You in the front yard | Praise You in health |
| Praise You at the office | Praise You in pain |
| Praise You at the grocery store | Praise You when I'm on schedule |
| Praise You at the Post Office | Praise You when I'm late |
| Praise You at the convenience store | Praise You when things go right |
| Praise You at the doctor's office | Praise You when things go wrong |
| Praise You at the tax office | Praise You when I know the way |
| Praise You in the restaurant | Praise You when I'm lost |
| Praise You at the mall | Praise You at the hospital |
| Praise You at the stoplight | Praise You at the cemetery |
| Praise You on the highway | Praise You when I understand |
| Praise You with a full stomach | Praise You when I don't have a clue |

"Let everything that has breath, praise the Lord."     Psalm 150:6


**WEEK THIRTY ONE**  **Confession for Overcomers**[1]  **DAY 7**

My body is a temple for the Holy Spirit[2], redeemed[3], cleansed[4], and sanctified by the Blood of Jesus[5]. My members, the parts of my body, are instruments of righteousness[6], yielded to God for His service and His glory. The devil has no place in me, no power over me, no unsettled claims against me. All has been settled by the Blood of Jesus[7]. I overcome Satan by the Blood of the Lamb and by the word of my testimony, and I love not my life unto the death[8]. My body is for the Lord, and the Lord is for my body[9].


[1]Psalms 107:2     'Let the redeemed of the Lord say so, Whom He has redeemed from the hand of the enemy,'

[2]I Corinthians 6:19     'Or do you not know that your body is the temple of the Holy Spirit who is in you, whom you have from God, and you are not your own?'

[3]Ephesians 1:7     'In Him we have redemption through His blood, the forgiveness of sins, according to the riches of His grace'

[4]I John 1:7    'But if we walk in the light as He is in the light, we have fellowship with one another, and the blood of Jesus Christ His Son cleanses us from all sin.'

[5]Hebrews 13:12    'Therefore Jesus also, that He might sanctify the people with His own blood, suffered outside the gate.'

[6]Romans 6:13    'And do not present your members as instruments of unrighteousness to sin, but present yourselves to God as being alive from the dead, and your members as instruments of righteousness to God.'

[7]Romans 8:33-34    'Who shall bring a charge against God's elect? It is God who justifies. Who is he who condemns? It is Christ who died, and furthermore is also risen, who is even at the right hand of God, who also makes intercession for us.'

[8]Revelation 12:11    'And they overcame him by the blood of the Lamb and by the word of their testimony, and they did not love their lives to the death.'

[9]I Corinthians 6:13    'Foods for the stomach and the stomach for foods, but God will destroy both it and them. Now the body is not for sexual immorality but for the Lord, and the Lord for the body.'

**"Confession for Overcomers"** from *"Prayers and Proclamations"* by Derek Prince, p. 159-160. Available at https://www.hiskingdomprophecy.com/overcomers-confession/

**Record your insights, revelations, and meditations from this week.  DATE:**

_____

_____

_____

_____

_____

_____

_____

_____

_____

## VICTORY THROUGH SURRENDER

---
---
---
---
---
---

**WEEK THIRTY TWO**        *HYMNS and POEMS*        **DAY 1**

Peace

by George Herbert (1593-1633)

Sweet Peace, where dost thou dwell? I humbly crave,
Let me once know.
I sought thee in a secret cave,
And ask'd, if Peace were there,
A hollow wind did seem to answer, No:
Go seek elsewhere.

I did; and going did a rainbow note:
Surely, thought I,
This is the lace of Peace's coat:
I will search out the matter.
But while I looked the clouds immediately
Did break and scatter.

Then went I to a garden and did spy
A gallant flower,
The crown-imperial: Sure, said I,
Peace at the root must dwell.
But when I digged, I saw a worm devour
What showed so well.

At length I met a rev'rend good old man;
Whom when for Peace

Tim Tremaine

> I did demand, he thus began:
> There was a Prince of old
> At Salem dwelt, who lived with good increase
> Of flock and fold.
>
> He sweetly lived; yet sweetness did not save
> His life from foes.
> But after death out of his grave
> There sprang twelve stalks of wheat;
> Which many wond'ring at, got some of those
> To plant and set.
>
> It prospered strangely, and did soon disperse
> Through all the earth:
> For they that taste it do rehearse
> That virtue lies therein;
> A secret virtue, bringing peace and mirth
> By flight of sin.
>
> Take of this grain, which in my garden grows,
> And grows for you;
> Make bread of it: and that repose
> And peace, which ev'ry where
> With so much earnestness you do pursue,
> Is only there.

https://www.poemhunter.com/poem/peace-8/

**WEEK THIRTY TWO** *INSIGHT and ENCOURAGEMENT* **DAY 2**

Peace, Perfect Peace

by Charles C. Price (1887-1947)

You cannot get up in the morning and say, "This is the day in which I will be full of joy. I am going to be very happy today, for I have made up my mind to have lots of joy." Either you have it, or you don't. The worldly man can have his synthetic joy which is the plaything of environment and the slave of circumstance. But the Christian can have imparted joy in the Holy Ghost, and rejoice in its manifestation under every condition of life. It is not dependent upon surroundings; nor is it the slave of circumstance. It is the gift of God!

Then, there is peace. Oh, the sweetness of that beautiful peace which God implants in the hearts of all who love Him! What a wonderful day it was for the disciples when Jesus said, "My peace I give unto you!" It was not to be the peace that the world knows, for that peace is false, weak and flimsy, and can be lashed into a storm at any moment by the blowing of the winds of trouble.

The peace He gives passes all human understanding. It is so deep, that no surface troubles can ever affect it; so divine that no human hand can ever reach it to take it away; deep settled peace in the soul! It is the peace Jesus had when in His regal dignity He "held his peace" before the howling mob in the halls of Pilate.

Let me ask you: "Can you create that peace? Can you bring it about by a switch in mental attitude, or a change in outlook? Can you even so much as develop the Peace that He alone can give?" You and I know the answer! Just settle into the arms of love in the heart of the storm, and know: "Peace, perfect peace, though sorrows surge around. On Jesus' bosom naught but calm is found." It is His peace, imparted by the Spirit. All we have to do is to receive it. That is the beauty of the Christ-centered life—a life that is hid with Christ in God.

So it is with faith. He does not give it as a plaything to be operated for our own undoing and in things otherwise contrary to His will. He knows my need. He knows yours, too; and He has given His promise that no good thing will He withhold from them who walk uprightly. So we rest in that promise; and abide in Him, even as He abides in us.

To know that He is present—that He understands and cares—this is sufficient for me to know the joy which springs eternal in the knowledge that all things work together for good to them that love God, to them that are the called according to His purpose. Then shall we know the rest that comes from turning self-reliance into Christ-reliance, as we cast all our cares upon Him. In the development of His will in your life, let me assure you that when faith is needed, it will not be withheld; for The Giver of every good and perfect gift is the Author and Finisher of our faith.

Excerpted from *The Real Faith*. Self-published, 1941. Chapter 10. Jawbone Digital, Kindle ed.

**WEEK THIRTY TWO**　　　　**Confession of Whole-hearted Devotion**　　　　**DAY 3**

From Psalm 119

Blessed are those who keep your testimonies, who seek you with the whole heart! You have commanded us to keep your precepts diligently. With my whole heart, I have sought you. Oh, let me not wander from your commandments! Your word I have hidden in my heart, that I might not sin against you. I will delight myself in your statutes; I will not forget your word. Your testimonies also are my delight and my counselors. Make me understand the way of your precepts. So shall I meditate on your wonderful works. Give me understanding, and I shall keep your law. I shall observe it with my whole heart. Make me walk in the path of your commandments, for I delight in it. Establish your word to your servant, who is devoted to fearing you. The proud have forged a lie against me, but I will keep your precepts with my whole heart. Oh, how I love your law! It is my meditation all day long. I have inclined my heart to perform your statutes forever, to the very end. I cry out with my whole heart. I will keep your statutes. I rise before the dawning of the morning and cry for help. I hope in your word. My eyes are awake through the night watches that I may meditate on your word. The entirety of your word is truth, and every one of your righteous judgments endures forever. I rejoice at your word as one who finds great treasure. Seven times a day, I praise you because of your righteous judgments. I long for your salvation, O Lord, for your law is my delight.

**WEEK THIRTY TWO**     *INSIGHT and ENCOURAGEMENT*     **DAY 4**

Three Great Means of Peace
according to St. Francis of Assisi (c. 1182 – 1226)

In the various descriptions of his life are still preserved many a trait of Frances' fine feelings and tenderness for the Brothers and of his deep knowledge of the soul. He understood others so well because he understood himself, and the Brothers often felt that he was reading their hearts. Against various trials and temptations Francis over and over again advised his Brothers to use three remedies – the first was prayer, the second was obedience, such that one willingly did another's will, the third was the evangelical joy in the Lord, which drives away all evil and dark thoughts. In these three precepts, Francis set the best example to his Brothers.

The first great means of bringing about peace for Francis was obedience, taken as the complete abandonment of all personal will, the perfect subjection to every command and every power. "If anyone strikes thee on one cheek, then offer him the other, and if anyone takes thy cloak from thee, then do not keep thy habit from him… And if anyone takes thy property from thee, ask it not again from him… Therefore, if anyone comes to me and does not hate his own body, he cannot be my disciple. For he who will save his life shall lose it, but he who loses his life for my sake, he shall save it."

The other means of obtaining peace was prayer, constant and persevering prayer, prayers "without intermission." Francis himself, as Thomas of Celano says, was not one who now and then prayed, but "his whole being was changed to prayer." It was as if there was only a thin wall between him and eternity and he often, as it were, heard the sound of the eternal song of praise on the other side of the wall. In such moments he suddenly became silent, broke off the conversation, if he was with the Brothers, and covered his face with his hood or at least with his hands. The disciples then would hear him sigh deeply and murmur something or other, they would see him also nod his head, as if he answered someone, and they would steal away. They knew that the master did not want to be noticed when he prayed.

The third means for obtaining peace, which Francis pointed out to his disciples, was constant cheerfulness. "But those who belong to the devil hang their heads – we ought to be glad and rejoice in the Lord," he said. Francis repeated over and over again the words of the apostle: "Rejoice always!" He never wanted to see dark faces or sour visages – his Brothers should not be mournful hypocrites, but glad children of light. To those who asked how this was possible, he answered, "Spiritual joy arises from purity of the heart and perseverance in prayer!"

[The order change from peace – obedience – joy was written in the original text.]

Excerpted from Jorgensen, Johannes. *Saint Francis of Assisi: A Biography*. New York: Longmans, Green, and Co., 1912. p. 284-289.

**WEEK THIRTY TWO**  **Confession about Peace**  **DAY 5**

Read Isaiah 26

I confess and believe that you, Lord, will keep me in perfect peace because my soul is fixed and focused on you. I trust in you and will continue to trust in you at all times and in all circumstances, for you, Lord, are my firm foundation. You are the eternal, solid rock on which I stand. I know you oppose the proud and arrogant, those who think highly of themselves. But you make the path level for those who obey you. You smooth out the way for those who act righteously. I will walk in your righteous way and patiently wait for you to direct my path. The praise, honor, and glory of your good name is the desire of my heart. You are my last thought every night, and my first thought every morning. All day I am consumed with longing to know you more. Because of the grace you have shown me, I will acknowledge and hold in high esteem the majesty of your holy name. Lord, you secure and establish my peace. I cannot take credit for anything. You have accomplished everything. Any success, any increase, any benefit that has come my way is solely the result of your working in and through my life, and I give all the glory and praise to you, for you deserve it.

Tim Tremaine

**WEEK THIRTY TWO**  *INSIGHT and ENCOURAGEMENT*  **DAY 6**

Peace

by Fuchsia Pickett (1918-2004)

"For unto us a Child is born, unto us a Son is given; And the government will be upon His shoulder. And His name will be called Wonderful, Counselor, Mighty God, Everlasting Father, Prince of Peace."
Isaiah 9:6

Peace comes <u>*from*</u> God ("*To all who are in Rome, beloved of God, called to be saints: Grace to you and peace from God our Father and the Lord Jesus Christ.*" Romans 1:7) and is an evidence of the Messiah – whose character as the "Prince of Peace" waits to instill the settledness of His own rule in our souls. Just as the saving power of His death and resurrection makes it possible for us to have peace <u>*with*</u> God (being reconciled to Him, "*Therefore, having been justified by faith, we have peace with God through our Lord Jesus Christ,*" Romans 5:1), the indwelling of His life and character through the Holy Spirit's work in our lives is intended to help us learn to abide in the peace *of* God.

Jesus said to His disciples "*Peace I leave with you, My peace I give to you*" (John 14:27). Surrender to His will and submission to His Word will bring inner peace, as we allow the peace of God to "rule" in our hearts ("*And let the peace of God rule in your hearts, to which also you were called in one body; and be thankful.*" Colossians 3:15), that is, to let God's peace <u>*act as umpire*</u>;

1) making decisions that would trouble you,
2) overruling doubts that would disturb you, and
3) overthrowing the Adversary's lies that would defeat you or deter you.

Perfect peace is available when the heart and mind keep focused on God's promise, power, and presence. Trust Him. (Emphasis hers.)

"You will keep him in perfect peace, whose mind is stayed on You, because he trusts in You."
Isaiah 26:3
"These things I have spoken to you, that My joy may remain in you, and that your joy may be full."
John 15:11
"When He had called the people to Himself, with His disciples also, He said to them, 'Whoever desires to come after Me, let him deny himself, and take up his cross, and follow Me.'"  Mark 8:34

Hayford, Jack, Ed. *The Spirit-Filled Bible*. Nashville: Thomas Nelson, 2018. p. 917.

VICTORY THROUGH SURRENDER

**WEEK THIRTY TWO**  *HYMNS and POEMS*  **DAY 7**

Take Thou Our Minds, Dear Lord
by Calvin W. Laufer (1874-1938)

Take Thou our minds, dear Lord, we humbly pray,
Give us the mind of Christ each passing day;
Teach us to know the truth that sets us free;
Grant us in all our thoughts to honor Thee.

Take Thou our hearts, O Christ—they are Thine own;
Come Thou within our souls and claim Thy throne;
Help us to shed abroad Thy deathless love;
Use us to make the earth like heaven above.

Take Thou our wills, Most High! Hold Thou full sway;
Have in our inmost souls Thy perfect way;
Guard Thou each sacred hour from selfish ease;
Guide Thou our ordered lives as Thou dost please.

Take Thou ourselves, O Lord, heart, mind, and will;
Through our surrendered souls Thy plans fulfill.
We yield ourselves to Thee—time, talents, all;
We hear, and henceforth heed, Thy sovereign call.

http://www.hymntime.com/tch/htm/t/a/k/e/takethou.htm

**Record your insights, revelations, and meditations from this week.  DATE:**

_____

_____

_____

_____

_____

**WEEK THIRTY THREE**         *HYMNS and POEMS*        **DAY 1**

How Shall I Follow Him I Serve?

by Josiah Conder (1789-1855)

How shall I follow Him I serve?
How shall I copy Him I love?
Nor from those blessed footsteps swerve,
Which lead me to His seat above?

Privations, sorrows, bitter scorn,
The life of toil, the mean abode,
The faithless kiss, the crown of thorn—
Are these the consecrated road?

Lord, should my path through suff'ring lie,
Forbid it I should e'er repine;
Still let me turn to Calvary,
Nor heed my griefs, rememb'ring Thine.

O let me think how Thou didst leave
Untasted every pure delight,
To fast, to faint, to watch, to grieve,
The toilsome day, the homeless night:

To faint, to grieve, to die for me!
Thou camest, not Thyself to please;
And, dear as earthly comforts be,
Shall I not love Thee more than these?

https://www.hymnal.net/en/hymn/h/462

**WEEK THIRTY THREE**      *INSIGHT and ENCOURAGEMENT*      **DAY 2**

The True Way of Holiness

by Walter Marshall (1628-1680)

That we may acceptably perform the duties of holiness and righteousness required in the law, our first work is, to learn *the powerful and effectual means* whereby we may attain to so great an end. This is an advertisement very needful; because many are apt to skip over the lesson concerning the *means* as superfluous and useless. When once they know the nature and excellency of the duties of the law, they account nothing wanting but diligent performances; and a rush blindly upon immediate practice, making more haste than good speed. They are quick in a promising; "All that the Lord has spoken, we will do" (Ex. 19:8), without sitting down and counting the cost. They look upon holiness as only the *means* to an end, eternal salvation; not as *the end* itself, requiring any great means for attaining the practice of it. The inquiry of most, when they begin to have a sense of religion, is, "What good thing shall I do that I may have eternal life?" (Mt. 19:16). Not, how shall I be enabled to do anything that is good? Yea, many that are accounted powerful preachers, spend all their zeal in the earnest pressing the immediate practice of the law, without any discovery of the effectual means of performance; as if the works of righteousness were like those servile employments that need no skill and artifice at all, but only industry and activity. That you may not stumble at the threshold of a religious life by this common oversight, I shall endeavor to make you sensible that it is not enough for you to know the matter and reason of your duty, but that you are also to learn the powerful and effectual means of performance, before you can successfully apply yourselves to immediate practice.

The certain knowledge of these powerful and effectual means is of great importance and necessity for our establishment in holy practice: for we cannot apply ourselves to the practice of holiness with hope of success, except we have some faith concerning the Divine assistance; which we have no ground to expect, if we use not such means as God has appointed to work by. Many Christians content themselves with external performances, because they never knew how they might attain to spiritual service; and many reject the way of holiness as austere and unpleasant, because they know not how to cut off the right hand, or pluck out a right eye, without intolerable pain; whereas they would find "the ways of wisdom" (if they knew them) "to be the ways of pleasantness, and all her paths to be peace" (Pro. 3:17). Many others set upon the practice of holiness with a fervent zeal, and run very fast, but tread not a step in the right way; and, finding themselves frequently disappointed and overcome by their lusts, they at last give over the work.

Excerpted from, *Sanctification; or The Highway of Holiness*. London: James Nisbet & Co., 1884. p. 1-5. (An Abridgment of *The Gospel Mystery of Sanctification*, 1692).

| **WEEK THIRTY THREE** | *HYMNS and POEMS* | **DAY 3** |

Abide with Me
by Henry F. Lyte (1793-1847)

Abide with me; fast falls the eventide;<br>
The darkness deepens; Lord, with me abide;<br>
When other helpers fail and comforts flee,<br>
Help of the helpless, oh, abide with me.<br>
<br>
Swift to its close ebbs out life's little day;<br>
Earth's joys grow dim, its glories pass away;<br>
Change and decay in all around I see—<br>
O Thou who changest not, abide with me.<br>
<br>
I need Thy presence every passing hour;<br>
What but Thy grace can foil the tempter's pow'r?<br>
Who, like Thyself, my guide and stay can be?<br>
Through cloud and sunshine, Lord, abide with me.<br>
<br>
I fear no foe, with Thee at hand to bless;<br>
Ills have no weight, and tears no bitterness;<br>
Where is death's sting? Where, grave, thy victory?<br>
I triumph still, if Thou abide with me.<br>
<br>
Hold Thou Thy cross before my closing eyes;<br>
Shine through the gloom and point me to the skies;<br>
Heav'n's morning breaks, and earth's vain shadows flee;<br>
In life, in death, O Lord, abide with me.

Sims, Walter Hines, ed. *Baptist Hymnal*. Convention Press, Nashville: 1956. P. 295

| **WEEK THIRTY THREE** | *INSIGHT and ENCOURAGEMENT* | **DAY 4** |

"Rules" for Holy Living
by Jeremy Taylor (1613-1667)

The grace of humility is exercised in the following rules.

*First*, do not think better of yourself because of any outward circumstance that happens to you.

*Second*, humility does not consist in criticizing yourself, or wearing ragged clothes, or walking around submissively wherever you go. Humility consists in a realistic opinion of yourself, namely, that you are an unworthy person.

*Third*, when you hold this opinion of yourself, be content that others think the same of you. If you realize that you are not wise, do not be angry if someone else should agree!

*Fourth*, nurture a love to do good things in secret, concealed from the eyes of others, and therefore not highly esteemed because of them.

*Fifth*, never be ashamed of your birth, of your parents, your occupation, or your present employment, or the lowly status of any of them.

*Sixth*, never say anything, directly or indirectly, that will provoke praise or illicit compliments from others.

*Seventh*, when you do receive praise for something you have done, take it indifferently and return it to God.

*Eighth*, make a good name for yourself by being a person of virtue and humility.

*Ninth*, do not take pride in any praise given to you. Rejoice in God who gives gifts others can see in you, but let it be mixed with a holy respect, so that this good does not turn into evil.

*Tenth*, do not ask others your faults with the intent or purpose being to have others tell you of your good qualities.

*Eleventh*, when you are slighted by someone, or feel undervalued, do not harbor any secret anger, supposing that you actually deserved praise and that they overlooked your value.

*Twelfth*, do not entertain any of the devil's whispers of pride.

*Thirteenth*, take an active part in the praising of others, entertaining their good with delight.

*Fourteenth*, be content when you see or hear that others are doing well in their jobs and with their income, even when you are not.

*Fifteenth*, never compare yourself with others unless it be to advance your impression of them and lower your impression of yourself.

*Sixteenth*, do not constantly try to excuse all of your mistakes. If you have made a mistake, or an oversight, or any indiscretion, confess it plainly.

*Seventeenth*, give God thanks for every weakness, fault, and imperfection you have.

*Eighteenth*, do not expose others' weaknesses in order to make them feel less able than you.

*Nineteenth*, remember that what is most important to God is that we submit ourselves and all that we have to him. This requires that we be willing to endure whatever His will brings us, to be content in whatever state we are in, and to be ready for every change.

Excerpted from Foster, Richard J. and Smith, James Bryan. *Devotional Classics*. New York: Harper One, 2005. p. 244-248.     [This is 400-year-old advice that still has value.]


**WEEK THIRTY THREE**          *HYMNS and POEMS*          **DAY 5**

Wholehearted Service

by Charles W. Naylor (1874-1950)

I've turned from the world and its follies,
Forever forsaken all sin;
I've given myself unto Jesus
To ever and only serve Him.

*Refrain:*
*I'll put my whole heart in His service,*
*And do all he asketh of me;*
*I mean to live holy and blameless—*
*A Christian indeed will I be.*

I will not be languid or careless,
Or formal, or cold, or untrue;
But, striving with earnest endeavor,
The will of my Lord I will do.

Since Jesus gave all to redeem me,
Since only through mercy I live,
It now is my joy and my purpose
A wholehearted service to give.

Oh, help me, dear Lord, to be ready
The task that Thou givest to do,
Not shrinking from labor or duty,
Devoted and faithful and true.

https://library.timelesstruths.org/music/Wholehearted_Service/


**WEEK THIRTY THREE**          *INSIGHT and ENCOURAGEMENT*          **DAY 6**

God's Provision for Holiness

by Andrew Murray (1828-1917)

All God's teaching on holiness is comprised in three great lessons. The first a revelation, "I am holy;" the second a command, "Be ye holy;" the third a gift, of the link between the two, "Ye are holy in Christ."

First comes the revelation, "I am holy." If we are to know what *holy* is, God must reveal himself to us. The deep unholiness of our nature and all that is of that nature must be shown to us. We must confess how utterly unfit we are for the revelation or the fellowship without the cleansing of fire. Conscious of our utter impotence to know God through our own wisdom or understanding, our souls must in contrition, brokenness from ourselves and our power or efforts, yield to God's Spirit, the Spirit of holiness, to reveal God as the holy one. And as we begin to know Him in His infinite righteousness, in His fiery burning zeal against all that is sin, and His infinite self-sacrificing love to free the sinner from his sin, and to bring him to His own perfection, we shall learn to wonder at and worship this glorious God, to feel and deplore our terrible unlikeness to Him, to long and cry for some share in the divine beauty and blessedness of this holiness.

And then we come with new meaning to the command, "Be holy, as I am holy." You who profess to obey the commands of your God, give this all-surpassing and all-including command that first place in your heart and life which it claims. Be holy with the likeness of God's holiness. Be holy as He is holy. Perhaps the more you meditate and study, the less you can grasp this infinite holiness. Perhaps the more you at moments grasp of it, the more you despair of the holiness so divine. Then remember that such breaking down and such despair is just what the command was meant to work. Learn to cease from your own wisdom as well as your own goodness. Draw near in poverty of spirit to let the Holy One show you how utterly above human knowledge or human power is the holiness He demands. To the soul that ceases from self and has no confidence in the flesh, He will show and give the holiness He calls us to.

To such the great gift of holiness in Christ becomes intelligible and acceptable. Christ brings the holiness of God closer by showing it in human conduct and relationships. He brings it within reach by removing the barrier between it and us, between God and us. He brings it nigh, because He makes us one with himself. "Holy in Christ": our holiness is bestowed by God, held for us, communicated to us, working mightily in us because we are in *Christ*. That holy Son and Servant of the Father, beautiful in His life of love and obedience on earth, sanctifying Himself for us – that life of Christ is the ground in which I am planted and rooted, the soil from which I draw as my nourishment its every quality and its very nature. How that word sheds its light both on the revelation, "I am holy," and on the command, "Be ye holy," and binds them into one! In Christ I seek what God's holiness is, and what my holiness is. In Him both are one, and both are mine. In Him I am holy. Abiding in and growing up in Him, I can be holy in all manner of living, just as God is holy.

Excerpted from *The Believer's Secret of Holiness*. Minneapolis: Bethany House, 1984. p. 22-23.

**WEEK THIRTY THREE**  **Confession of an Elder Saint**  **DAY 7**

Read Psalm 71

Lord, my trust is in you and you alone. You have never let me be put to shame. I am again in need of help and look to you. You have always been my refuge and shelter. You are the strong fortress I retreat to when

I am in distress. Hear my prayer again. I know you will deliver me from the people and forces that oppose me. I have trusted in you from my youth. Although many wonder what I'm doing and why, I am convinced you will show yourself strong on my behalf and give me another reason to praise and glorify your holy name. Even though I am old, and my strength fails me, you are not through with me yet. Despite adversity and opposition, I will continue to put my hope and trust in you. No matter what comes, I will praise you more and more. I press on in the strength you provide to testify of all the wonderful things you have done for me. The things you taught me in my youth are still true and powerful today. I will declare your glorious power to the generations to come until my dying day. I never cease to be amazed at your righteousness. Even the difficulties I now face are simply another opportunity for you to display your great power and desire to save and deliver those who know to fear your name. My soul will rejoice in your redemption. People will get tired of hearing me brag about you all day long. While I wait for your deliverance, I will sing songs of your faithfulness.

**Record your insights, revelations, and meditations from this week. DATE:**

_____

_____

_____

_____

_____

_____

_____

_____

_____

_____

_____

VICTORY THROUGH SURRENDER

**WEEK THIRTY FOUR** *HYMNS and POEMS* **DAY 1**

If I Gained the World, But Lost the Savior
by Anna Olander (unknown)

If I gained the world, but lost the Savior,
Were my life worth living for a day?
Could my yearning heart find rest and comfort
In the things that soon must pass away?

If I gained the world, but lost the Savior,
Would my gain be worth the lifelong strife?
Are all earthly pleasures worth comparing
For a moment with a Christ-filled life?

Had I wealth and love in fullest measure,
And a name revered both far and near,
Yet no hope beyond, no harbor waiting,
Where my storm-tossed vessel I could steer.

If I gained the world, but lost the Savior,
Who endured the cross and died for me,
Could then all the world afford a refuge,
Whither, in my anguish, I might flee?

O what emptiness! – without the Savior
Mid the sins and sorrows here below!
And eternity, how dark without Him!
Only night and tears and endless woe!

What, though I might live without the Savior,
When I come to die, how would it be?
O to face the valley's gloom without Him!
And without Him all eternity!

O the joy of having all in Jesus!
What a balm the broken heart to heal!
Ne'er a sin so great, but He'll forgive it,
Nor a sorrow that he does not feel!

If I have but Jesus, only Jesus,
Nothing else in all the world beside –
O then everything is mine in Jesus;
For my needs and more He will provide.

https://www.hymnal.net/en/hymn/h/1079

**WEEK THIRTY FOUR** *INSIGHT and ENCOURAGEMENT* **DAY 2**

Following Jesus
by Dietrich Bonhoeffer (1906-1945)

If we would follow Jesus, we must take certain definite steps. The first step, which follows the call, cuts the disciple off from his previous existence. The call to follow at once produces a new situation. To stay in the old situation makes discipleship impossible. Levi must leave the receipt of custom and Peter his nets in order to follow Jesus. One would have thought that nothing so drastic was necessary at such an early stage. Could not Jesus have initiated the publican into some new religious experience, and leave them as they were before? He could have done so, had he not been the incarnate Son of God. But since he is the Christ, he must make it clear from the start that his word is not an abstract doctrine, but the re-creation of the whole life of man. The only right and proper way is quite literally to go with Jesus. The call to follow implies that there is only one way of believing on Jesus Christ, and that is by leaving all and going with the incarnate Son of God.

The first step places the disciple in the situation where faith is possible. If he refuses to follow and stays behind, he does not learn how to believe. He who is called must go out of his situation in which he cannot believe, into the situation in which, first and foremost, faith is possible. But this step is not the first stage of a career. Its sole justification is that it brings the disciple into fellowship with Jesus which will be victorious. So long as Levi sits at the receipt of custom, and Peter at his nets, they could both pursue their trade honestly and dutifully, and they might both enjoy religious experiences, old and new. But if they want to believe in God, the only way is to follow his incarnate Son.

Until that day, everything had been different. They could remain in obscurity, pursuing their work as the quiet in the land, observing the law and waiting for the coming of the Messiah. But now he has come, and his call goes forth. Faith can no longer mean sitting still and waiting—they must rise and follow him. The call frees them from all earthly ties, and binds them to Jesus Christ alone. They must burn their boats and plunge into absolute insecurity in order to learn the demand and the gift of Christ. Had Levi stayed at his post, Jesus might have been his present help in trouble, but not the Lord of his whole life. In other words, Levi would never have learnt to believe. The new situation must be created, in which it is possible to believe on Jesus as God incarnate; that is the impossible situation in which everything is staked solely on the word of Jesus. Peter had to leave the ship and risk his life on the sea, in order to learn both his own weakness and the almighty power of his Lord. If Peter had not taken the risk, he would never have learnt the meaning of faith. Before he can believe, the utterly impossible and ethically irresponsible situation on the waves of the sea must be displayed. The road to faith passes through obedience to the call of Jesus. Unless a definite step is demanded, the call vanishes into thin air, and if men imagine that they can follow Jesus without taking this step, they are deluding themselves like fanatics.

*The Cost of Discipleship.* New York: Simon & Schuster, 2018. p. 70-72.

**WEEK THIRTY FOUR**           **Confession about the Voice of God**          **DAY 3**

Read Psalm 29

I unite my praise with everyone in the heavens. I render praise to my Lord for the strength and majesty of His glorious voice. I will adorn my worship with holiness. The voice of the Lord is like an approaching hurricane rumbling and roaring over the waters. All the streams, rivers, and oceans combined cannot drown out your voice. Lightning flashes, thunder rolls, winds howl in an unstoppable, irresistible force. The power and majesty of your voice can disintegrate the tallest tree like a tornado strike or volcanic explosion. One word from your voice can send the largest tree hopping and skipping over the field like a tiny sliver, flicked away by a finger. Your voice is like a wildfire fueled by gale-force winds. The flames split apart and consume everything around them. Your voice shakes the ground like an earthquake sending tremblors in every direction. It shakes the very foundations of the earth and leaves in its wake a brand new terrain, an altered horizon, requiring new pathways to navigate its landscape. Even the wildlife in nature, that cannot comprehend what you say, cannot escape the impact and effect of Your voice. Everything in creation is subject to your voice. You sit in power above it all. You always have. The whole of creation is dependent on your voice for its existence and survival. Your people also rely on your voice. I rely on your voice. When problems and troubles overwhelm me like a flood, or try to blow me away like a hurricane, or burn me up like a volcano, or swallow me up like an earthquake, I depend on your voice for strength to prevail. Hearing your voice brings peace during chaos and confusion. Your voice is all I need.

**WEEK THIRTY FOUR**      *INSIGHT and ENCOURAGEMENT*      **DAY 4**

The Secret

by Hannah Whitall Smith (1832-1911)

This secret lies just here, that our will, which is the spring of all our actions, has been in the past under the control of sin and self, and these have worked in us all their own good pleasure. But now God calls upon us to yield our wills up unto Him, that He may take the control of them, and may work in us to will and to do of His good pleasure. If we will obey this call, and present ourselves to Him as a living sacrifice, He will take possession of our surrendered wills, and will begin at once to work in us "that which is well pleasing in his sight, through Jesus Christ" (Heb 13:21), giving us the mind that was in Christ, and transforming us into his image (Rom 12:1, 2).

A lady who had entered into this life hid with Christ was confronted by a great prospective trial. Every emotion she had within her rose up in rebellion against it. But she had learned the secret of the will and she did not pay the slightest attention to her emotions. She repeated over and over, "Thy will be done! Thy will be done!" asserting, in the face of all her rebelling feelings, that she did submit her will to God's, that she chose to submit it, and that His will should be and was her delight! In an incredibly short space of time every thought was brought into captivity, and she began to find even her very emotions rejoicing in the will of God.

Let me show you how to apply this principle to your difficulties. Cease to consider your emotions, for they are only the servants; and regard simply your will, which is the real king in your being. Is your will given up to God? If so, then *you* are in the Lord's hands, and you decide to believe, and you choose to obey; for your will is yourself. And the thing is done. The transaction with God is as real, when only your will acts, as where every emotion coincides. It does not seem as real to you; but in God's sight it is as real. And when you have got hold of this secret and have discovered that you need not attend to your emotions but simply to the state of your will, all the scripture commands to yield yourself to God, to present yourself a living sacrifice to Him, to abide in Christ, to walk in the light, to die to self, become possible to you.

If the feeling of unreality or hypocrisy comes, do not be troubled by it. It is only in your emotions, and not worth a moment's thought. Only see to it that your will is in God's hands, that your inward self is abandoned to His working, that your choice, your decision, is on His side; and there leave it. When God is "working in us to will," we must set our faces like a flint to carry out this will, and must respond with an emphatic "I will" to every "Thou shalt" of His. For God can only carry out His own will with us as we consent to it, and will in harmony with Him. He wills that you should be entirely surrendered to Him, and that you should trust Him perfectly. Do you will the same?

Adapted from *The Christian's Secret of a Happy Life*. Grand Rapids: Revell, 1952. p. 83-87.

**WEEK THIRTY FOUR**  **Confession about Love**  **DAY 5**

Read 1 Corinthians 13

If I could speak a hundred languages, were a gifted orator, a wordsmith beyond compare, even could speak the language of heaven, but the words did not come from a heart of love backed by loving action, I would just be making a lot of noise. And an irritating noise at that. I could be the smartest person in the world, unrivaled in wisdom and understanding, even to the point of correctly predicting the future. But if I have no love in my heart for others, what's the point? I could be the most generous person, have the most influence, be so dedicated to my beliefs that I'm willing to die for them, but it would all count for nothing without love. If a person really loves, you can tell. They are not impatient or harsh. They don't always want what someone else has or try to take credit for what someone else does. They are always polite, always thinking of others, don't have buttons that are easy to push, and don't think or say the worst about people. A loving person doesn't get happy when someone else messes up and is always happy when someone else succeeds. He is tolerant, faithful, and full of hope. Love always perseveres and ultimately wins the day. Every other ability, strength, gift, or talent comes in second place to love. I didn't think this way when I was young and immature, but I'm learning that as great as faith is, as awesome as hope is, love supersedes everything.

**WEEK THIRTY FOUR**  *INSIGHT and ENCOURAGEMENT*  **DAY 6**

The Badge of True Discipleship
by Dietrich Bonhoeffer (1906-1945)

The cross is laid on every Christian. The first Christ-suffering which every man must experience is the call to abandon the attachments of this world. It is that dying of the old man which is the result of his encounter with Christ. As we embark upon discipleship, we surrender ourselves to Christ in union with his death—we give over our lives to death. Thus it begins; the cross is not the terrible end to an otherwise Godfearing and happy life, but it meets us at the beginning of our communion with Christ. When Christ calls a man, he bids him come and die. It may be a death like that of the first disciples who had to leave home and work to follow him, or it may be a death like Luther's, who had to leave the monastery and go out into the world. But it is the same death every time—death in Jesus Christ, the death of the old man at his call. Jesus' summons to the rich young man was calling him to die, because only the man who is dead to his own will can follow Christ. In fact, every command of Jesus is a call to die, with all our affections and lusts. But we do not want to die, and therefore Jesus Christ and his call are necessarily our death as well as our life. The call to discipleship, the baptism in the name of Jesus Christ means both death and life. The call of Christ, his baptism, sets the Christian in the middle of the daily arena against sin and the devil. Every day he encounters new temptations, and every day he must suffer anew for Jesus Christ's sake. The wounds and scars he receives in the fray are living tokens of this participation in the cross of his Lord. But there is another kind of suffering and shame which the Christian is not spared. While it is true that only the sufferings of Christ are a means of atonement, yet since he has suffered for and borne the sins of the whole world and shares with his disciples the fruits of his passion, the Christian also has to undergo temptation, he too has to bear the sins of others; he too must bear their shame and be driven like a scapegoat from the gate of the city. But he would certainly break down under this burden, but for the support of him who bore the sins of all. The passion of Christ strengthens him to overcome the sins of others by forgiving them. He becomes the bearer of other men's burdens— "Bear ye one another's burdens, and so fulfil the law of Christ" (Gal. 6.2). As Christ bears our burdens, so ought we to bear the burdens of our fellow-men. The law of Christ, which it is our duty to fulfill, is the bearing of the cross. My brother's burden which I must bear is not only his outward lot, his natural characteristics and gifts, but quite literally his sin. And the only way to bear that sin is by forgiving it in the power of the cross of Christ in which I now share. Thus, the call to follow Christ always means a call to share the work of forgiving men their sins. Forgiveness is the Christ-like suffering which it is the Christian's duty to bear. But how is the disciple to know what kind of cross is meant for him? He will find out as soon as he begins to follow his Lord and to share his life. Suffering, then, is the badge of true discipleship.

The disciple is not above his master. Following Christ means *passio passiva,* suffering because we have to suffer. That is why Luther reckoned suffering among the marks of the true Church, and one of the memoranda drawn up in preparation for the Augsburg Confession similarly defines the Church as the community of those "who are persecuted and martyred for the gospel's sake." If we refuse to take up our cross and submit to suffering and rejection at the hands of men, we forfeit our fellowship with Christ and have ceased to follow him. But if we lose our lives in his service and carry our cross, we shall find our lives again in the fellowship of the cross with Christ. The opposite of discipleship is to be ashamed of Christ and his cross and all the offense which the cross brings in its train.

Discipleship means allegiance to the suffering Christ, and it is therefore not at all surprising that Christians should be called upon to suffer. In fact, it is a joy and a token of his grace. The acts of the early Christian martyrs are full of evidence which shows how Christ transfigures for his own the hour of their mortal agony by granting them the unspeakable assurance of his presence. In the hour of the cruelest torture they bear for his sake, they are made partakers in the perfect joy and bliss of fellowship with him. To bear the cross proves to be the only way of triumphing over suffering. This is true for all who follow Christ, because it was true for him.

[Often when we read or hear about Christian suffering, we think of physical pain and death. Bonhoeffer knew this reality being perhaps the most famous Christian martyr of the 20th Century, murdered by the Nazis in World War II. However, physical suffering is not the only kind and certainly not the most prevalent kind in the western world. We know that martyrdom still exists around the world to this day, but the mental and emotional suffering of discipleship is a cost just as real and just as significant as physical suffering. And it is recognized as such by the Lord as He leads us down the path of absolute surrender. When we let go of something that had value to us in the past, or that we relied on for strength or comfort; when we die to that thing, or that experience, or that relationship, there is often a real pain associated with that loss. Even if that thing is sin to us, there can still be a pain and grieving process that we must suffer through. God is just as available and present to us in that suffering as if we were facing physical pain or death. His power to heal and restore are just as necessary, just as accessible, and just as adequate. As you follow Christ on the path of discipleship through dependency, you will be required to let go of the things that are not consistent with that life, but His grace is sufficient even then – especially then.

Do not recoil from pain. Pain, especially the pain of loss, can be the doorway to a new level of joy and peace in Christ. Remember that Jesus endured the cross for the joy that was set before Him. The cross was not joyful. It was no fun to suffer as He did. But by faith, He knew what lay on the other side of that pain, and He chose to pass through it for our sake. Many people have come to the threshold of pain and turned away for fear of suffering, only to discover that the only path to the fullness of joy Jesus promised was through the cross of pain and loss. Let the Holy Spirit speak to you now about that path. It may not be fun or pain free, but it will be rewarding and worth it on the other side.]

*The Cost of Discipleship.* New York: Simon & Schuster, 2018. p. 103-106.


**WEEK THIRTY FOUR**          *HYMNS and POEMS*          **DAY 7**

Once It Was A Blessing

by A. B. Simpson (1843-1919)

Once it was the blessing,
Now it is the Lord;
Once it was the feeling,
Now it is Your Word;
Once Your gift I wanted,
Now, the Giver own;
Once I sought for healing,
Now Yourself alone.

Once 'twas painful trying,
Now 'tis perfect trust;
Once a half salvation,
Now the uttermost;
Once 'twas ceaseless holding,
Now You hold me fast;
Once 'twas constant drifting,
Now my anchor's cast.

## VICTORY THROUGH SURRENDER

Once 'twas busy planning,
Now 'tis trustful prayer;
Once 'twas anxious caring,
Now You have the care;
Once 'twas what I wanted,
Now what Jesus says;
Once 'twas constant asking,
Now 'tis ceaseless praise.

Once it was my working,
Yours it hence shall be;
Once I tried to use You,
Now You do use me;

Once the pow'r I wanted,
Now the Mighty One;
Once for self I labored,
Now for You alone.

Once I hoped in Jesus,
Now I know You're mine;
Once my lamps were dying,
Now they brightly shine;
Once for death I waited,
Now Your coming hail;
And my hopes are anchored
Safe within the veil.

https://www.hymnal.net/en/hymn/h/513  (Pronouns were changed to first person.)


**Record your insights, revelations, and meditations from this week.  DATE:**

_____

_____

_____

_____

_____

_____

_____

_____

_____

## WEEK THIRTY FIVE     *HYMNS and POEMS*     DAY 1

My Spirit, Soul, and Body
by Mary Dagworthy James (1810-1883)

My spirit, soul, and body,
Dear Lord, I give to Thee,
A consecrated offering,
Thine evermore to be.

My all is on the altar;
Lord, I am all Thine own;
Oh, may my faith ne'er falter!
Lord, keep me Thine alone.

Lord Jesus, mighty Savior,
I trust in Thy great name;
I look for Thy salvation,
Thy promise now I claim.

Now, Lord, I yield my members,
From sin's dominion free,
For warfare and for triumph,
As weapons unto Thee.

Oh, blissful self-surrender,
To live, my Lord, by Thee;
Now, Son of God, my Savior,
Live out Thy life in me.

I'm Thine, O dear Lord Jesus,
Washed in Thy precious blood,
Sealed by Thy Holy Spirit,
A sacrifice to God.

https://www.hymnal.net/en/hymn/h/447

| WEEK THIRTY FIVE | *INSIGHT and ENCOURAGEMENT* | DAY 2 |
|---|---|---|

## The Crown of Holiness

by Andrew Murray (1828-1917)

Among the many points in which the high priest typified Christ as our sanctification, perhaps none is more suggestive or beautiful than the holy crown he wore on his forehead. He was always to wear a plate of gold engraved with the words, *Holiness to the Lord.* There everyone read that the whole object of his existence, the one thing for which he lived, was to embody and bear the divine holiness, to be the chosen one through whom God's holiness might flow out in blessing upon the people. The way in which the blessing of the holy crown was to act was a most remarkable one. In bearing *Holiness to the Lord* on his forehead, he is, we read, "to bear the iniquity of the holy things… That they may be accepted before the Lord" (Ex. 28:36,38).

But how about the sin that cleaves to the very sacrifice and religious service itself? How painfully the worshipper might be oppressed by the consciousness that his penitence, his faith, his love, his obedience, his very consecration, were called imperfect and defiled! Even for this need of the worshipper, God had provided. The holiness of the high priest covered the sin and the unholiness of his holy things. The holy crown was God's pledge that the holiness of the high priest rendered the worshipper acceptable. If he was unholy, there was one who was holy, who had a holiness that could avail for him too, a holiness in which he could trust. He could look to the high priest not only to effect atonement by his blood sprinkling, but also to secure a holiness in his person that made him and his gifts most acceptable. Conscious of personal unholiness, the worshipper might rejoice in the holiness of another, the priest whom God had provided.

Have we not here a most precious lesson, leading us a step farther along in the way of holiness? How does God produce holiness? The divine answer: Through a man whom the Divine Holiness has chosen to rest upon, and whose holiness belongs to us as His brethren, the very members of His own body. Through a holiness which is of such efficacy that the insufficiency of our best intentions is cleansed, and we can enter the holy presence with the assurance of being altogether well-pleasing. Is not this precisely the lesson that many earnest seekers after holiness need? They know all that the Word teaches but when they hear of the childlike simplicity and assurance of faith, the loving obedience and blessed surrender with which the Father expects them to come and receive the blessing, their hearts fail for fear – as if the blessing were beyond their reach. As I pray or worship, and realize how much I lack that humility, fervency and faith that God has a right to demand, I may look up to the High Priest in His holiness, to the holy crown upon His forehead. The iniquity of my best intentions is born and taken away. It is the blessed truth of substitution, God's way of making us holy. The sacrifice of the worshipper is holy and acceptable in virtue of the holiness of Another.

Tim Tremaine

Adapted from *The Believer's Secret of Holiness*. Minneapolis: Bethany House, 1984. p. 65-66.

**WEEK THIRTY FIVE**  **Confession about the Name of the Lord**  DAY 3

Various scriptures

I will rejoice in you because I love your name. I will constantly sing praises to your name. Because I know and trust your name, I can seek refuge in you in times of trouble and rely on you to defend me in times of war. I will lift up the name of my God like a castle raises the standard to announce: the king is in residence. You lead and guide me for your name's sake. Through your name, I can overcome anything that rises up against me. I will wait on your name for it is good. You have given me the heritage of those who fear your name. I live in the reality of all your name represents because I love it so much. Your name shall continue to endure forever. The amazing things you do show that the power of your name is always at hand. What a privilege it is to call upon your name. The people who live in the light of your countenance rejoice in your name all day long. Truly, your name is deserving of all the glory. For the sake of your wonderful name, you have made salvation available so that your mighty power will be known to all. Holy and awesome is your name. My help is in the name of the Lord. Your name is like a fortified tower that I can run into for safety. The desire of my soul is for your name. It is my highest privilege and greatest joy to be called by your name. Your name alone is the Lord. I trust in the name of the Lord.

**WEEK THIRTY FIVE**  *INSIGHT and ENCOURAGEMENT*  DAY 4

The Way to Victory

by Charles C. Price (1887-1947)

Beneath the outstretched arms of the trees in the Garden, our Lord cried, "IF it be possible, let this cup pass from Me." And then, in complete abandonment of Himself to God and to the purpose and will of His Father, He finished, "Nevertheless, not My will but Thine be done." The only way to The Resurrection was through The Garden. The only way to His victory over the tomb was by the way of the Cross; and He has to bring us to that place! But we know full well that His resurrection life in us must be preceded by our death!

Even the seemingly good side of our Adamic nature has to be sacrificed with the acknowledged bad. Isaac was the son of promise, yet he had to be "sacrificed" in obedience to God's command. But here was the man who believed God, and IT WAS ACCOUNTED UNTO HIM FOR RIGHTEOUSNESS, for he took that good, living sacrifice and climbed with him to the top of the mountain. It was in, and through, his obedience that the revelation came! The RAM IN THE THICKET was revealed! It was the revelation of a SUBSTITUTE, provided by God and therefore acceptable unto Him. The redemptive plan of our Blessed Lord, to cleanse humanity for His indwelling, is not by some "get-well-quick" system! There is only one way! That way is CHRIST!

In the days of Jesus' earthly walk, the Pharisees cried, "Lo, here is truth!" and the Sadducees, in contradiction said, "No, it is here." Grecian philosophers had long proclaimed that they had the truth. However, our Blessed Lord silenced them all in His declaration, "I am the Way, the Truth, and the Life. No man cometh unto the Father but by Me." There is no difference today. He is our Way. He is our Truth. He is our Life! There is no other way! There is no other Life! There is no other Truth!

Flesh dies; and the Adamic nature must be crucified. It may hurt a bit to come to complete surrender, but that is where our Lord would bring us in Spirit and in Truth before He Himself can condescend to indwell this vessel of clay.

What a privilege it is to surrender! How blessed it is to be invited to lay our all at the Master's feet! How poor our understanding — in comparison with His! How faulty our Adamic wills are in the light of the Divine Will which was fulfilled in Christ Himself. Beloved, there can be no short-cuts! The inspired Word declares that if any man try to climb up any other way, the same is a thief and a robber; for the Lord Jesus Christ is the only door to God! No man can come to the Father but by Him! How sweet it is to reminisce as well as testify.

Excerpted from *The Real Faith*. Self-published, 1941. Chapter 12. Jawbone Digital, Kindle ed.

## MONTH NINE

This will surprise many people, but my wife and I have been married three times to each other. The first time was in 1983. We divorced in 2005, and after thirteen years of divorce, we remarried in 2018 – twice. We planned to get married in September and bring our children from Nashville back to Arlington, Texas, for the ceremony. Along the way, we were spending time with our old pastor in preparation for the event, and he mentioned, almost in passing, that he didn't have a problem with people getting married earlier than planned if they couldn't or did not want to wait. Ceremonies are nice, but relationship is the issue. We thought about that for a while and decided we did not want to wait any longer. I asked a Justice of the Peace friend if he would marry us, and he agreed. We were married the second time a few weeks earlier than planned and had the third wedding as scheduled, which was a fantastic time with friends and family. We spent our honeymoon in San Jose, California, attending the annual Transform Our World (TOW) International Conference.

There is more to the story behind our visit to the 2018 Conference in San Jose. 2017 was a pivotal year for me. While there were many blessings and much to be grateful for, a disagreement developed between myself and my youngest son. That conflict went on for months. The rift in our relationship was the impetus for my desperation cry for more of the Lord. There were many difficult discussions and cathartic experiences along the way. The culmination began with the 2017 TOW conference, also held in San Jose. The Lord spoke clearly about the need for restoration in the relationship with my son. I had a week of vacation scheduled, so I drove to Tennessee to try and fix things with my son.

What happened the day I drove to Tennessee has been the pivot point of my life so far. I had an all-day encounter with the Lord, which included streaming the conference on my phone during the drive. I listened to sermons, played worship music, worshipped, and prayed. Everything came to a head at a mountain top rest stop in Tennessee, just outside Nashville, where I finally came to understand what absolute surrender meant and gave myself to it.

That week was good and started the healing process. When I got home, the Lord brought some strategic books my way to help me understand what to do. Those resources, and the ones that followed, are used in this book. I developed a prayer out of that process that I have prayed every day since (mentioned in the Introduction). Getting re-married was one of the many demonstrable effects of that process. I learned that surrender meant giving up many things, but I also learned that the things God was asking me to give up were not the things I needed in my life to be an honest disciple of Jesus Christ. Of all the people in the world to re-connect me with, he chose my ex-wife. This was something I never thought would happen. But in God's providence, we started meeting again due to our oldest son's impending wedding. Meetings became dates, and the dates rekindled the relationship. I began to think about how beautiful she was and how much I enjoyed being with her. Then one day, while I was driving to work, God said as clear as a bell, "You love her." So here we are, married for the better part of thirty-eight years (more or less). God's a funny guy.

**WEEK THIRTY FIVE**  *HYMNS and POEMS*  **DAY 5**

I Could Not Do Without Thee
by Frances Ridley Havergal (1836-1879)

I could not do without Thee
O Savior of the lost,
Whose precious blood redeemed me
At such tremendous cost.
Thy righteousness, Thy pardon
Thy precious blood, must be
My only hope and comfort,
My glory and my plea.

I could not do without Thee,
I cannot stand alone,
I have no strength or goodness,
No wisdom of my own;
But Thou, belovèd Savior,
Art all in all to me,
And perfect strength in weakness
Is theirs who lean on Thee.

I could not do without Thee,
For, oh, the way is long,
And I am often weary,
And sigh replaces song.
How could I do without Thee?
I do not know the way;
Thou knowest, and Thou leadest,
And wilt not let me stray.

I could not do without Thee,
O Jesus, Savior dear!
E'en when my eyes are holden,
I know that Thou art near.
How dreary and how lonely
This changeful life would be,
Without the sweet communion,
The secret rest with Thee.

## VICTORY THROUGH SURRENDER

| | |
|---|---|
| I could not do without Thee! | I could not do without Thee, |
| No other friend can read | For years are fleeting fast, |
| The spirit's strange deep longings, | And soon in solemn loneness |
| Interpreting its need; | The river must be passed; |
| No human heart could enter | But Thou wilt never leave me, |
| Each dim recess of mine, | And though the waves roll high, |
| And soothe, and hush, and calm it, | I know Thou wilt be near me, |
| O blessèd Lord, but Thine. | And whisper, It is I. |

Lyrics first published in *Home Words* in 1873 according to http://www.hymntime.com/

**WEEK THIRTY FIVE**     *INSIGHT and ENCOURAGEMENT*     **DAY 6**

Mysteries in Religion to be Expected
by Alexandre Vinet (1797-1847)

To expect that there should be no mysteries in religion, is in the highest degree unreasonable. What is religion? It is the belief that God places Himself in relation with man, the Infinite with the finite. This is a mystery common to all religion, and in itself impenetrable.

It is impossible that true religion should not present a great number of mysteries. How can it be otherwise in religion, when it is so in nature? The more God gives us there to contemplate, the more He gives us to wonder at. To every creature is attached an enigma. If therefore the display which God has made of Himself in nature gives rise to many questions which we cannot answer, how will it be when another revelation is given; when God the Creator reveals himself as God the reconciler and Savior?

With new discoveries must not mysteries multiply? Christianity then must be mysterious, even more so than any other religion, precisely because it is true and sublime. Shall we murmur because we do not comprehend everything in the Gospel? We might as well complain that we cannot grasp the ocean in the hollow of our hand, as that we cannot comprise uncreated Wisdom within the bounds of our intellect.

Every day we admit facts which we understand not. The union of body and soul, the action of thought and will, our very existence itself, all are mysteries. Nor would the explication of these, or of the mysteries of religion, be very valuable or useful to us. It concerns us infinitely to know that Christ is the Son of God and Savior of men: but do we need to know precisely in what *manner* that divine and human nature are in His adorable person united?

We shall not comprehend everything in the doctrines of the gospel. We must be saved therefore by what we do not fully comprehend. But is this a calamity? Is our salvation the less? Are we to find fault that the Most High ordains a remaining darkness which we cannot penetrate, when for all that is essential, He grants us abundant light? Let us embrace with love the truths which never could have entered into the heart of man, but which, though mysterious, will avail to save us. Let us learn to love, and we shall know hereafter.

Shepperd, John (1785-1879). *Chosen Words from Christian Writers.* London: Hodder & Stoughton, 1869. p. 115-116.

**WEEK THIRTY FIVE**       **Confession about Warrior God**       **DAY 7**

Read Psalm 35

You are the salvation of my soul, oh Lord my God. You counter the arguments of those who strive with me. You come to the fight dressed and armed for battle to stop the enemy in his tracks. Those who seek to destroy me will be completely ashamed and forced to retreat in utter confusion. They planned to lure me into a trap, making me fall into the pit they had dug for me. But you chased them back on themselves and made them slide into the very pit they prepared for me. The destruction they intended for me will come upon them suddenly when they get caught in their own traps. Words cannot express the joy and relief I feel at your victory. Without you, I would have been at their mercy. They wanted nothing but bad things for me even though I treated them as friends. I stood by them when they were in need. I grieved within them through sad times. I prayed and cared for them in sickness as I cared for my own family, which is how they reward me. They constantly gossiped and spread lies about me. They plot my demise with others behind my back. But you came to my rescue. You exposed their schemes and frustrated their plans. You have vindicated me and caused them to be swallowed up in shame and dishonor. I will constantly sing your praises for what you have done for me.

**Record your insights, revelations, and meditations from this week. DATE:**

**WEEK THIRTY SIX**  *HYMNS and POEMS*  **DAY 1**

Speak, Lord, In the Stillness
by Emily May Grimes Crawford (1864-1927)

Speak, Lord, in the stillness,
While I wait on Thee;
Hushed my heart to listen,
In expectancy.

Speak, O blessed Master,
In this quiet hour;
Let me see Thy face, Lord,
Feel Thy touch of power.

For the words Thou speakest,
They are life indeed;
Living bread from heaven,
Now my spirit feed!

All to Thee is yielded,
I am not my own;
Blissful, glad surrender,
I am Thine alone.

Speak, Thy servant heareth,
Be not silent, Lord;
Waits my soul upon Thee
For the quickening word.

Fill me with the knowledge
Of Thy glorious will;
All Thine own good pleasure
In Thy child fulfill.

Like a watered garden,
Full of fragrance rare,
Lingering in Thy presence,
Let my life appear.

https://www.hymnal.net/en/hymn/h/809

**WEEK THIRTY SIX**  *INSIGHT and ENCOURAGEMENT*  **DAY 2**

Holding Ourselves Accountable
by Henry Blackaby (1935-present)

I am deeply convinced that praying for revival is an offense to God if we do not have a clean heart. It is almost blasphemy to come into the presence of a holy God and ask Him to bless us when our hearts are not clean before Him. Praying for revival has a prerequisite. Who can stand in His holy place? The Scripture says that when our lives are what God wants them to be, there will be an obvious open blessing of God.

I talk with so many pastors who describe their churches as being rebellious and disoriented to God. I ask them, "How long have you been there?" Many reply 5, 10, 15 years. I reply, "Then the people in the church are the product of your walk with God. You ought not to have been with the people for five years or more and the holiness of God not absolutely come over the people. The holiness of God should be so real in your own heart that when you get up to speak, there is a sense of holy awe that you have been in the presence of God."

Do you hold yourself accountable as the servant of God? Do you look at the scriptures and then say, "If God says this, then this is what will come when a person walks with God?" Do you know what I believe to be one of our greatest dangers? We have all the truths in our heads, but it has never touched our hearts. According to Jesus it is spiritually impossible to have your heart in one condition and the fruit of your life in another condition. If we can say that we believe the Truth from the Word of God and yet see no evidence of the implementing of those Truths in our lives, then the Scripture has just been in our heads and it has never struck our hearts.

All through the Scriptures God says the highway over which He goes, the highway over which God's people travel is the *way of holiness.* That is especially true when God brings to our hearts what He wants us to do in prayer. When we pray as God initiates us to and our lives are clean to receive His Word, then He will respond. But if He does not respond, it is at that point that we should hold ourselves accountable.

The Scripture says we need to pursue holiness. That is, we need to let the full measure of the nature of God become the pattern for our character. We need to let Him form in us the full measure of the righteousness of Christ. We need to let him take every part of our minds and our hearts and keep them holy unto Himself. When the one who walks consistently in his relationship to God stands in God's presence, the character and holiness of God absolutely overwhelms him. Does the holiness of God overwhelm you?

Excerpted from *Holiness*. Nashville: Thomas Nelson, 2003. p. 78-98.

**WEEK THIRTY SIX**  **Confession about Wisdom**  **DAY 3**

Various scriptures

One of the most important things for me, and one of the biggest challenges, is simply paying attention to you. Wisdom, knowledge, and understanding come only from you. I cannot expect to live successfully without it. Walking the right path and making the right decisions require a firm grasp of the instructions only you can give. I have known many people who have not sought after or refuse to accept your instruction and have ended up in one of life's ditches. I have ditched my own life a few times, and I'm tired of it. I don't want to follow my opinion or have to make decisions based on my own thoughts. The only way to succeed in life is to follow your wise instruction. Disregarding divine wisdom only leads to wickedness, failure, and misery. Not only do I need to pay attention to what you are about to say, I need to pay attention to what you have already said. I need to review and remind myself of the truth you have already revealed and entrusted to me. I am responsible for walking in the light I already have. I must set your truth before my eyes constantly, and I will. I must take your instruction and your correction to heart and let it direct my life in the way that pleases you, and I will. I must diligently consider all my ways and words and seek your thoughts on everything, and I will. Only you can conform my heart, mind, and will to your purpose, and you will.

**WEEK THIRTY SIX** *INSIGHT and ENCOURAGEMENT* **DAY 4**

Spiritual Strongholds made up of Good Thoughts and Intentions
by Ed Silvoso (1945-present)

This characteristic of strongholds greatly contributes to their ability to go undetected. We seldom suspect our good thoughts. Satan uses this very cleverly. Our own good thoughts create a blockage for the excellent thoughts of God to come in. Such a case in point is Peter's thinking in Matthew 16:21–23. What was the strongest word Jesus ever used to rebuke a human being? It is the word *Satan*, when Jesus called Peter by that name. Never before then and never again after did Jesus use that term to refer to another human being. Why would Jesus denounce him so harshly? Peter had just given Jesus well-meaning, compassionate advice. When Jesus predicted that He would suffer and die, Peter said, "God forbid it, Lord! This shall never happen to You" (verse 22). To which Jesus replied, "Get behind Me, Satan!" (verse 23).

Why did Jesus identify Peter with Satan? Because Peter was setting his mind on man's interests rather than God's. In other words, Jesus was saying, *You are looking at this from man's point of view rather than God's.* By calling Peter *Satan*, Jesus identified man's perspective with Satan's. Being the Son of God, He was able to see through the wall of speculation present in Peter's mind, and He called it as He saw it. This is why I say that strongholds are often made up of good thoughts. The enemy of the *best* is not the *worst*. The enemy of the *best* is *good*, because *good* and *best* can be easily confused. Satan knows this, and he uses it to his advantage. This is why we are exhorted to take "every thought captive to the obedience of Christ" (2 Corinthians 10:5)—not just the evil thoughts, but all of them, the good ones included.

The church of Laodicea was not cold (evil), but lukewarm (good). This prevented it from realizing that it was not hot (excellent). To understand this more fully, we must look deeper into the context of the Matthew 16 passage. One of the tragedies of modern-day Bible translations is the well-meaning addition of subtitles, paragraph headings and so on to the original text. Many chapter divisions are located in the wrong place. Many times, a new chapter or section begins with the words *likewise*, *therefore* or *moreover*, which clearly refer the reader to the preceding chapter or section. Matthew 16:23–24 is a classic example of the confusion created by man's additions to the Word of God. *But He turned and said to Peter, "Get behind Me, Satan! You are a stumbling block to Me; for you are not setting your mind on*

God's interests, but man's." Then Jesus said to His disciples, "If anyone wishes to come after Me, he must deny himself, and take up his cross and follow Me."

This subtitle divider leads the reader to believe that verse 23 was the end of Jesus' explanation, and that verse 24, with its reference to self-denial and picking up the cross, is a different subject—in essence, a call to discipleship. In Matthew 16:24, however, Jesus begins with what amounts to a precursor of 2 Corinthians 10:5. Denial of self is what "taking every thought captive to the obedience of Christ" is all about. Taking up the cross implies dying to ourselves, and this spells death for our speculations as well. Following Jesus means leaving behind our own understanding and submitting to His guidance. (Emphasis his.)

Excerpted from *Strongholds*. Bloomington, MN: Chosen Books, 2018. p. 22-24.

**WEEK THIRTY SIX**  Confession about the Fear of the Lord  **DAY 5**

Various scriptures

Teach me to fear you all the days of my life; to fear you and always keep all your commandments and statutes. This is what you have always required of your people: that we fear your name, walk in your ways, serve you wholeheartedly, and keep your commandments. This I do as I love and serve my Savior, Christ Jesus the Lord. To walk after you and fear you requires that I hear your voice. Tune my ears to hear your voice. I will constantly be in the Word to learn how to fear you more by observing everything you tell me to do. My primary task is to hear and learn to obey your voice. In obedience, I will worship you. The secret of the Lord is with those who fear you. Great goodness is in store for me because I fear your name. Your eyes are focused on those who obey you. Your word says there is no want to those who fear you. Your salvation is near to those who fear you. My heart has a single desire, one purpose, to live obediently in the fear of the Lord. You will not withhold any good thing from me when I live uprightly in the fear of the Lord. Great is your mercy for those who fear you. Wisdom begins with fearing God. Blessing flows from fearing God. I desire those things so I can walk in fear, not in the fear of an angry or mean god but in the reverence and awe of a good and forgiving God that leads to surrender and obedience. I know this pleases you. I will be zealous for the fear of the Lord because it leads to life. Indeed, the abundant life comes to those who follow the Lord in spirit and in truth.

| WEEK THIRTY SIX | *INSIGHT and ENCOURAGEMENT* | DAY 6 |

The Path to Victory

by Ed Silvoso (1945-present)

With the battlefront at the cosmic and heavenly levels under control, Revelation 12:11 explains in specific detail the three arenas in which the earthly struggle takes place. The first one has to do with *the act of redemption*. The saints who do the overcoming have understood what it was that "the blood of the Lamb" purchased, and we know very clearly from the Scriptures that it was much more than souls. It was indeed the whole of creation (including the nations of the world), which is now waiting with bated breath for the manifestation of the sons of God (see Rom. 8:19).

The second arena involves *the act of reclamation*. The phrase "the word of their testimony" is much more than a testimony about "how I came to know of the Lord" or about "what Jesus did for me." It certainly should include that, but what is depicted here is not a word about something that has happened in the past. Rather, it is a public declaration about the present and the future by which Christians make it known that they understand that they are empowered to reclaim what the blood of the Lamb has already redeemed.

For instance, in Luke 10:2, Jesus said to the 70, "The harvest is plentiful…" How many of us have heard it said, or have been ourselves guilty of saying, "My city is hard to reach." That statement does not reflect what God's perspective is; rather it plays into the devil's schemes. We need to know that what we speak is not only heard by humans but also by the forces of darkness, and when we declare the redemptive purpose that God has already declared, our declaration is paramount to serving an eviction notice on those usurpers to move off the premises that has been purchased by Christ's blood, because the property has been turned over to his deputies, the Church.

The third arena is *the total denial of self*. "They did not love their lives to the death" (Rev. 12:11 NKJV). When we are able to say with the Apostle Paul, "I have been crucified with Christ; and it is no longer I who lives, but Christ lives in me; and the life which I now live in the flesh I live by faith in the Son of God, who loved me and gave himself up for me" (Gal. 2:20), then we have trumped Satan's best hand when it comes to spiritual power. It is the equivalent of renouncing our citizenship in the Babylonian system, placing us outside of its jurisdiction. We no longer live by its standards. Having no life but Christ's, we are fearless, we are operating completely by faith, and we have the backing of the King of the nations upon us for victory.

*Transformation.* Ventura, CA: Regal Books, 2007. Pp. 210-211.

VICTORY THROUGH SURRENDER

**WEEK THIRTY SIX**  *HYMNS and POEMS*  **DAY 7**

In Heavenly Love Abiding

by Anna Laetitia Waring (1820-1910)

In heavenly love abiding,
No change my heart shall fear;
And safe is such confiding,
For nothing changes here:

The storm may roar without me,
My heart may low be laid;
But God is round about me,
And can I be dismayed?

Wherever He may guide me,
No want shall turn me back;
My Shepherd is beside me,
And nothing can I lack.

His wisdom ever waketh,
His sight is never dim:
He knows the way He taketh,
And I will walk with Him.

Green pastures are before me,
Which yet I have not seen;
Bright skies will soon be o'er me,
Where the dark clouds have been.

My hope I cannot measure:
My path to life is free:
My Saviour has my treasure,
And He will walk with me.

Tozer, A. W. *The Christian Book of Mystical Verse: A Collection of Poems, Hymns, and Prayers for Devotional Reading.* Chicago: Moody Publishers, 2016. p. 133.

**Record your insights, revelations, and meditations from this week.  DATE:**

___
___
___
___
___
___
___

## WEEK THIRTY SEVEN     *HYMNS and POEMS*     DAY 1

Savior, While My Heart is Tender

by John Burton, Jr. (1803-1877)

Savior, while my heart is tender,
I would yield that heart to Thee;
All my powers to Thee surrender,
Thine and only Thine to be.

Take me now, Lord Jesus, take me;
Let my youthful heart be Thine;
Thy devoted servant make me;
Fill my soul with love divine.

Send me Lord, where Thou wilt send me,
Only do Thou guide my way;
May Thy grace through life attend me,
Gladly then shall I obey.

Let me do Thy will or bear it;
I would know no will but Thine;
Shouldst Thou take my life or spare it,
I that life to Thee resign.

May this solemn consecration
Never once forgotten be;
Let it know no revocation,
Registered and confirmed by Thee.

Thine I am, O Lord, forever
To Thy service set apart;
Suffer me to leave Thee never,
Seal Thine image on my heart.

http://www.hymntime.com/tch/htm/s/w/m/swmhiten.htm

VICTORY THROUGH SURRENDER

**WEEK THIRTY SEVEN**  *INSIGHT and ENCOURAGEMENT*  **DAY 2**

The Highest Activity of Man

by Andrew Murray (1828-1917)

There is a view of the Christian life that regards it as a sort of partnership, in which God and man have each to do their part. It admits that it is but little that man can do, and that little defiled with sin; still he must do his utmost – then only can he expect God to do his part. To those who think thus, it is extremely difficult to understand what Scripture means when it speaks of our being still and doing nothing, of our resting and waiting to see the salvation of God. It appears to them a perfect contradiction, when we speak of this quietness and ceasing from all effort as the secret of the highest activity of man. And yet this is just what Scripture does teach. The explanation of the apparent mystery is to be found in this, that when God and man are spoken of as working together, there is nothing of the idea of a partnership between two partners who each contribute their share to work. The relation is a very different one. The true idea is that of cooperation founded on subordination. As Jesus was entirely dependent on the Father for all His words and all His works, so the believer can do nothing of himself. What he can do of himself is altogether sinful. He must therefore cease entirely from his own doing, and wait for the working of God in him. As he ceases from self-effort, faith assures him that God does what He has undertaken and works in him. And what God does is to renew, to sanctify, and waken all his energies to their highest power. As he yields himself a truly passive instrument in the hand of God, will he be wielded of God as the active instrument of His almighty power. The soul in which the wondrous combination of perfect passivity with the highest activity is most completely realized, has the deepest experience of what the Christian life is.

Among the lessons to be learned by those who are studying the blessed art of abiding in Christ, there is none more needful and more profitable than this one of stillness of soul. In it alone can we cultivate that teachableness of spirit, to which the Lord will reveal His secrets, that meekness to which he shows His ways. It is the spirit exhibited so beautifully by His mother Mary whose only answer to the most wonderful revelation ever made to a human being was, "Behold the handmaid of the Lord; be it unto me according to Thy word"; and of whom, as mysteries multiplied around her, it is written: "Mary kept all these things and pondered them in her heart." And in another Mary who "sat at Jesus' feet, and heard His word," and who showed, in the anointing of Him for His burial, how she had entered more deeply into the mystery of His death than even the beloved disciple. It is a soul silent unto God that is the best prepared for knowing Jesus, and for holding fast the blessings He bestows. It is when the soul is hushed in silent awe and worship before the Holy Presence that reveals itself within, that the still small voice of the blessed Spirit will be heard. Cultivate quietness as a means to the abiding in Christ; expect the ever deepening quietness and calm of heaven in the soul as the fruit of abiding in Him.

Excerpted from *Abide in Christ*. Readaclassic.com, 2010. p. 67-69.

**WEEK THIRTY SEVEN**  *HYMNS and POEMS*  **DAY 3**

Lord, Speak to Me that I may speak
by Frances Ridley Havergal (1836-1879)

Lord, speak to me that I may speak
In living echoes of Thy tone;
As Thou has sought, so let me seek
Thine erring children lost and lone.

O lead me, Lord, that I may lead
The wandering and the wavering feet;
O feed me, Lord, that I may feed
Thy hungering ones with manna sweet.

O strengthen me, that while I stand
Firm on the rock, and strong in Thee,
I may stretch out a loving hand
To wrestlers with the troubled sea.

O teach me, Lord, that I may teach
The precious things Thou dost impart;

And wing my words, that they may reach
The hidden depths of many a heart.

O give Thine own sweet rest to me,
That I may speak with soothing power
A word in season, as from Thee,
To weary ones in needful hour.

O fill me with Thy fullness, Lord,
Until my very heart overflow
In kindling thought and glowing word,
Thy love to tell, Thy praise to show.

O use me, Lord, use even me,
Just as Thou wilt, and when, and where,
Until Thy blessèd face I see,
Thy rest, Thy joy, Thy glory share.

Originally set to music of Robert Schumann in 1872 according to http://www.hymntime.com/

---

**WEEK THIRTY SEVEN**  **Confession about Blessing**  **DAY 4**

Read Psalm 67

Father, you say in your word that I can ask for your blessing. I can ask for your mercy in the situations that I face. I can ask for your face to shine upon me and be gracious unto me. I depend on all those things. Every day I surrender myself to you again for that day so that I am in a position to receive those blessings. I know if I regard iniquity in my heart, you will not hear me. My requests will fall on deaf ears, even though you desire to bless your children. But I also confess that in my requests, my heart, my motives must be right. The purpose of your blessing is not just to help me, although it certainly does; it is not just to make things better for me, although it certainly does. I see in your Word a different purpose; a different motivation is required. Your blessing me is not just for me or about me. You bless your children so that your way may be known on earth. You bless me so that your salvation may be known among all nations. Our blessings should result in all peoples singing praise to you and coming under the government of your Kingdom through salvation and surrender to you. Your purpose in blessing us is that the whole world will see your goodness and kindness and mercy and love and will begin to fear your name and live in obedience to your Word.  I will continue to ask for all these things but now will understand and acknowledge that your hand of blessing is not simply for my benefit but the benefit of others, that they may come to know you as I know you and love and praise and serve you as I do.  Bless the Lord, for your way is a good way.  I will walk in it.

**WEEK THIRTY SEVEN**  *HYMNS and POEMS*  **DAY 5**

Sweet the Moments, Rich in Blessing
by Walter Sheely et al. (1725-1786)

Sweet the moments, rich in blessing,
   Which before the Cross I spend;
Life and health and peace possessing
   From the sinner's dying Friend.

Truly blessed is this station,
   Low before His Cross to lie;
While I see divine compassion
   Beaming in His languid eye.

Love and grief my heart dividing,
   With my tears His feet I'll bathe;
Constant still in faith abiding,
   Life deriving from His death.

For Thy sorrows we adore Thee
For the griefs that wrought our peace
Gracious Saviour! we implore Thee,
   In our hearts Thy love increase.

Tozer, A. W. *The Christian Book of Mystical Verse: A Collection of Poems, Hymns, and Prayers for Devotional Reading.* Chicago: Moody Publishers, 2016. p. 60.

**WEEK THIRTY SEVEN**  *INSIGHT and ENCOURAGEMENT*  **DAY 6**

The Certainty of Blessing
by Andrew Murray (1828-1917)

O, that our hearts might learn to wait before Him, until He Himself reveals to us what His promises mean, and in the promises reveals Himself in His hidden glory!  We shall be irresistibly drawn to wait on Him alone.  God increase the company of those who say: "Our soul waiteth for the Lord: He is our help and our shield."

This waiting upon God on behalf of His church and people will depend greatly upon the place that waiting on Him has taken in our personal life.  The mind may often have beautiful visions of what God has promised to do, and the lips may speak of them in stirring words, but these are not really the measure of our faith or power.  No; it is what we really know of God in our personal experience, conquering the enemies within, reigning and ruling, revealing Himself in His holiness and power in our inmost being. *It is this that will be real measure of the spiritual blessing we expect from Him, and bring to our fellow man*. It is as we know how blessed the waiting on God has become to our own souls, that we shall confidently hope in the blessing to come on the Church around us, and the keyword of all our expectations will be, He hath said: "All they that wait on me shall not be ashamed." From what He has done in us, we shall trust him to do mighty things around us. "Blessed are all they that wait for him." Yes, blessed even now in the waiting. The promised blessings for ourselves, or for others, may tarry; the unutterable blessedness of knowing and having Him who has promised, the divine Blesser, the living fountain of the coming blessings, is even now ours. *Do let this truth get full possession of your souls, that waiting on God is itself the highest privilege of the creature, the highest blessedness of his redeemed child.* (Emphasis mine)

Even as the sunshine enters with its light and warmth, with its beauty and blessing, into every little blade of grass that rises upward out of the cold earth, so the everlasting God meets, in the greatness and the tenderness of His love, each waiting child, to shine in his heart "the light of the knowledge of the glory of God in the face of Jesus Christ." Read these words again, until your heart learns to know what God waits to do to you. Who can measure the difference between the great sun and a little blade of grass? And yet the grass has all of the sun it can need or hold. Do believe that in waiting on God, His greatness and your littleness suit and meet each other most wonderfully. Just bow in emptiness and poverty and utter impotence, in humility and meekness, and surrender to His will before his great glory, and be still. As you wait on Him, God draws nigh. He will reveal Himself as the God who will fulfill mightily His every promise. And let your hearts ever again take up the song: "Blessed are all they that wait for Him." (Isaiah 30:18; 49:23)

*Waiting On God*. Chicago: Moody Press. p. 109-113 (reprint from 1905).

**WEEK THIRTY SEVEN**  **Confession about the Offering**  **DAY 7**

Read Malachi 1 and 3

How can I expect or even hope for the windows of heaven to open and pour out an overflowing blessing if I am not willing first to offer to you what rightfully belongs to you? I acknowledge that you are the source of everything I have and everything I am. I will not rob you of what lawfully belongs to you. You graciously grant me stewardship over wealth and resources, not just money or property but time, strength, abilities, gifts, and influence. I will not just bring you the scraps. I will not give only what I can live without. I will not dedicate only that which I cannot otherwise use. I will not show up only when I have nothing better to do. If I were a government official or a company employee, would they accept that? Would they accept some of my time, the leftovers of my energy, or the lowest level of my dedication?

Hardly! And you are the Great King! The King of Kings to whom I have pledged my eternal devotion. How could I bring such an insulting offering to the altar of sacrifice? The scraps, the leftovers, the worn-out and useless, only what I can spare? Heaven forbid! You deserve the first and the best, and the most of who I am and what I have. Take pleasure in my offering Lord. My offering is myself.

[I always had difficulty with the tithe. Money was often short, and there was always something for the children or the house that needed doing. I gave a little to the church and other worthy causes but never enough, never regularly, and never consistently. When I look back at this journey to live the surrendered life, I can trace the origins to the time I finally made a commitment to be faithful in my stewardship. Once I made that decision, things began to change, doors began to open, opportunities appeared, and the direction I needed came, leading to the life of absolute surrender to the Lord. I can highly recommend it.]

**Record your insights, revelations, and meditations from this week. DATE:**

_____

_____

_____

_____

_____

_____

_____

_____

_____

_____

_____

Tim Tremaine

| WEEK THIRTY EIGHT | *HYMNS and POEMS* | DAY 1 |

Soul, What Return Has God, Thy Savior
by Karl Friedrich Lockner (1634-1697)

Soul, what return has God, thy Savior,
  For all He gives thee day by day?
  Oh, hast thou in thy gift a favor
That can delight and please Him?—Say!

  The best of offerings He requires:
  Thy heart it is that He desires.
  Give unto God thy heart's affection;
  Who else can claim thee as His own?

Should Satan hold thee in subjection?
With him but pangs of hell are known.
  To Thee alone, O Lord divine,
  My heart and all I now resign.

Accept the gift which Thou requirest,
  My heart and soul, O gracious God,
The first-fruits Thou so much desirest,
For which Thy Son paid with His blood.

  To Thee I willingly assign
  My heart, dear Lord, for it is Thine.
  Whom should I give my heart's affection
  But Thee, who gavest Thine to faith?

Thy fervent love is my protection;
Lord, Thou hast loved me unto death.
  My heart with Thine shall ever be
  One heart throughout eternity.

http://www.hymntime.com/tch/htm/s/o/u/soulwhat.htm

| WEEK THIRTY EIGHT | The Importance of Testimony | DAY 2 |

I listened to a pastor preach once about the importance of testimonies and how testimony creates culture, not our personal salvation testimony, but the testimonies we give about what we have seen God do in our lives. At the same time, I was reading through the book of Malachi, and I came across this verse: *"Then those who feared the Lord spoke to one another, and the Lord listened and heard them; so a book of remembrance was written before Him for those who fear the Lord and who meditate on His name"* (Malachi 3:16). I was impressed by something I saw here. The phrase "the fear of the Lord" often is synonymous with obedience. So, the verse says, 'When the obedient ones spoke to one another, God heard them.' They were testifying to one another, not talking to God. That is a testimony. The result was a book of remembrance which also was "for" them, not for God. So, the testimonies of obedient ones create a memory that benefits those who continue to obey and focus on who God is ("His Name.") You can build a culture of obedience and faithfulness through testimony.

Everyone knows the Great Commission, but the second part of that equation comes in Acts 1:8 when the Lord says before He ascends, "…you shall be witnesses to Me…" (Acts 1:8). I wonder if we have not shortcut the meaning of "witness" in this verse? We have historically referred to this verse as meaning we will be witnesses in terms of giving a witness to the lost. Perhaps there is also the sense in which we will be witnesses to what God will do in all the regions of the world so that we can bring a word of testimony to the Church that will promote obedience?

The writer of Hebrews connected living by faith (which equates to obedience) with obtaining a good testimony. "Now faith is the substance of things hoped for, the evidence of things not seen. For by it the elders obtained a good testimony" (Heb 11:1-2; also Heb 11:39). While it can be translated, 'they received a good report,' could it be that it was a good report or testimony about what God had done? David demonstrated this in Psalm 106. The first few verses and the last few are directed to God, but the large middle section is directed toward the people. He was recounting the memory of God's mighty deeds. So, living by faith should result in a testimony of the power of God that promotes obedience in the faithful. Testimonies are important.

I am writing this in the middle of the Coronavirus Crisis of 2020. I am reminded of Jesus' prophecy in Luke 21:11-13: "And there will be great earthquakes in various places, and famines and pestilences… But it will turn out for you as an occasion for testimony." Faithful obedience in the face of things like pestilence can create opportunities for us to gain a testimony of God's mighty deeds that not only can be a witness to salvation for the lost but a powerful benefit that promotes further obedience in the Church. Testimonies are important.

In Revelation, John gives us the key to spiritual victory over satan. "And they overcame him by the blood of the Lamb and by the word of their testimony, and they did not love their lives to the death" (Rev 12:11). The blood was shed and remains available. When we add not just the fact that we are saved, but that we have witnessed God's mighty deeds and that we will be faithfully obedient, even unto death, we can overcome in any situation. Testimony is important. If we live lives of faithful obedience, we can expect to witness God's mighty deeds in our lives. Share your testimonies if you have them. If you don't have them, find out why.

**WEEK THIRTY EIGHT**  **Confession of Presentation**  **DAY 3**

Read Romans 6 and 8

God, you did a marvelous thing by sending your one and only Son to this earth as a man so that I can be free from the law of sin and death. I am no longer under condemnation as long as I live according to the Spirit and not according to the flesh. Now it is not I who stands condemned but sin because of the death and resurrection of my Lord Jesus Christ. Because of Christ, the righteous requirement of the law, which the law was powerless to effect in me, can be fulfilled in me as I live according to the Spirit and not according to the flesh. The person who lives according to the flesh has a mindset that always considers the things of the flesh. But I want to be a person who lives according to the Spirit, with a mindset that always considers the things of the Spirit. The mind set on the flesh is hostile towards God and refuses to subject itself did anything God says. The person with this mindset cannot please God. I am not that person. Spirit of God dwell in me. Spirit of Christ, make your habitation in my heart. Spirit of life, make yourself at home in my spirit. I no longer have to live according to the flesh because Jesus has set me free, and God has adopted me as his son. I submit to the leadership of God's Spirit. I will no longer present the members of my body as instruments of unrighteousness, enslaved by filthiness and lawlessness, but I now and forever present myself to God as a servant of righteousness looking forward to seeing the fruit of holiness in my life.

## WEEK THIRTY EIGHT — INSIGHT and ENCOURAGEMENT — DAY 4

The Face of God

by Alexander Maclaren (1826-1910)

Psalm 27:8-9  There may be some difficulties about the rendering of our text, which, however, need not concern us now. Our English version is sufficient for our present purpose, and, according to it, we have here, summed up in a kind of dialogue of two phrases, the whole speech of God to us men, and the inmost meaning of all that devout souls say to God. "Seek my face" – such is the essential meaning of all God's words and works. "Thy face, Lord, will I seek" – such is the essential meaning of all prayer, worship, and obedience.

But let us observe a little more closely what the Psalmist means by that phrase, "Seeking God's face." It needs to be translated into a more modern dialect, in order to convey much meaning to some of us. We may begin then by asking the significance of that expression, "the face of God."

It is one of those strong Scripture phrases which escape any danger of misconstruction by the very boldness of their corporeal metaphors. The highest and most spiritual conception of God is reached, not by a pedantic scrupulosity in avoiding material representations, but by an unhesitating use of these, and the remembrance that they *are* representations.

The face of the Lord is that aspect or side of the divine nature which is turned to man and is perceptible by him. It is, roughly speaking, almost equivalent to "the name of the Lord." That expression has a much profounder meaning than is ordinarily felt to belong to it. It means the manifested character of God, the net result of all his self-revelation by word and work. And these two phrases – *the face of the Lord* and *the name of the Lord*, come to nearly the same thing. Both of them are worth noting for one reason besides others, that there is that in God which may be known, and also that which cannot be.

While "the face of God" is used in the Old Testament to express the dazzling brightness of His essential being, which no man can look on, it more usually means the knowable part of the divine nature. The simple expression of our text keeps us from the twin errors of supposing that we can know nothing of

God, and not forgetting that we can know but an aspect and a side of His nature. Another idea is usually connected with the expression, namely that of light.

To seek God's face is no long, dubious search, nor is He hard to be found. We have only to desire to possess and we shall walk all the day in the light of His countenance. Endeavour to keep vivid the consciousness of that face as looking always in on you. Make Him your companion. Let Him be the object of your thoughts, and more and more of your whole nature.

Adapted from, *The Secret of Power*. London: Macmillan and Co., 1882. p. 222-227.

**WEEK THIRTY EIGHT**  **Confession about Openness**  **DAY 5**

John Baillie prayer

O DIVINE Love, as you stand outside the closed doors of human hearts and knock, grant me the grace to throw open all the doors of my heart. Tonight let me draw back every bolt and bar that until now has robbed my life of air and light and love. Open my ears, O God, so that I can hear your voice calling me to attempt great things. Too often when you have spoken to me I have been deaf to your appeals; but now give me the courage to answer, Here I am; send me. Help me to hear when any of my human brothers and sisters, your children, call out in need. Help me to hear your voice in their cry. Open my mind, O God, so that I may welcome any new insights or knowledge that you wish to give me. May I not cling to the past so tightly that I limit the life ahead of me. Give me courage to change my mind when that is needed. Help me to be tolerant to the thoughts of others and open to the truths they may teach me. Open my eyes, O God, so that I may see you in your wonderful creation around me. Let all lovely things fill my heart with joy, and may they turn my mind to your everlasting loveliness. Forgive me for the times when I have been blind to the grandeur and glory of creation, the charm of little children, and the beauty of human lives, and so have failed to see you in all these reminders of your presence. Open my hands, O God: hands ready to share with others all the blessings you have so richly given me. Deliver me from all mean and selfish instincts. All my money is yours and all my possessions belong to you; help me to be a faithful steward of your generosity. All honor and glory be to you forever. Amen.

*A Diary of Private Prayer*. New York: Scribner, 1949. p. 60-61.

**WEEK THIRTY EIGHT**  *INSIGHT and ENCOURAGEMENT*  **DAY 6**

The Refiner's Fire

by A. W. Tozer (1897-1963)

Some have the idea that God's purpose is to make our lives more tolerable here on earth. That rather cheapens what Christ did on the cross. If all He wanted to do was make our lives tolerable, then He could have done it in a variety of other ways. God's supreme purpose for us is to make us like His son, Jesus Christ. If we understand that everything happening to us is to make us more Christlike, it will solve a great deal of anxiety in our lives. If, on the other hand, we have the idea that God's purpose is to make this life heaven on earth, then God has a lot of explaining to do. It is not happening. The way is rough, and the pathway is littered with all kinds of distractions and disturbances along the way.

I have referred to the cross as an instrument to accomplish God's purpose, His ultimate purpose in our life. I now want to refer to another tool that goes along with this: the Refiner's Fire. Let me point out the difference between the two. The cross deals with our self-life; to put self on the cross and have it absolutely crucified under Christ. But the Refiner's Fire takes a different approach. The purpose of the Refiner's Fire is to burn away all the bondage imposed on us by the world. When I talk about "the world," I am not referring to the mountains and valleys and the meadows and the forest. I'm talking about the spirit of this world that is diametrically opposed to everything that God represents.

Even as God the Father did not spare His own son the pains and the sufferings of the cross, so too God will not spare us any pain in bringing us to that ultimate place of Christlikeness. The Refiner's Fire is simply an instrument by which God accomplishes His purposes in our lives. We are never to worship fire. Remember that Israel fell into idolatry by worshipping the brazen servant that stopped the death angel. The brazen serpent was only to remind them of what God had done, but they became more enamored with the object than the God behind the object. We are to allow God to use whatever instrument or tool He chooses to accomplish His purpose. Again, that purpose is to bring us to a point of absolute Christlikeness, because it is through the Son that He is glorified.

To understand God and His nature is to understand that nothing impure can stand before Him. Therefore, in dealing with us as sons and daughters, we must meet His standard of purity. Nothing impure, nothing from this world, nothing contrary to the nature and character of God can be left in our lives. Some aspects of our lives are so resistant to God's grace that it necessitates fire to burn it completely out of our lives.

Excerpted from, *The Crucified Life: How to Live Out a Deeper Christian Experience*. Minneapolis: Bethany House, 2017. p. 199-201.

**WEEK THIRTY EIGHT** *HYMNS and POEMS* **DAY 7**

He Will Never Fail to Help

by Charles W. Naylor (1874-1950)

Brother, on the holy way
Lift your heart to God today,
He will never fail to help you if you trust Him;
Look with confidence above,
See His hand outstretched in love,
For it is His joy to help all those who trust Him.

*Refrain::*
*He will never fail to help you if you trust Him,*
*Only trust Him, fully trust Him;*
*In the dark and trying hour,*
*He'll sustain you by His pow'r,*
*He will never fail to help you if you trust Him.*

Should a trial press your soul,
Or the darkness hide your goal,
He will never fail to help you if you trust Him;
When for grace and help you pray,
Do not think Him far away,
He is ever near to help all those who trust Him.

Should a sorrow fill your heart,
Do not from the Lord depart,
He will never fail to help you if you trust Him;
Should your burden heavy grow,
Only trust and you shall know
That His hand is strong to help all those who trust Him.

Strong and many are your foes,
But your need the Savior knows,
He will never fail to help you if you trust Him;
He will shield you by His might,
He will put your foes to flight,
He will never fail to help you if you trust Him.

https://library.timelesstruths.org/music/He_Will_Never_Fail_to_Help/

**Record your insights, revelations, and meditations from this week. DATE:**

# VICTORY THROUGH SURRENDER

**WEEK THIRTY NINE**  *HYMNS and POEMS*  **DAY 1**

Sensitiveness

by John Henry Newman (1801-1890)

Time was, I shrank from what was right
From the fear of what was wrong;
I would not brave the sacred fight,
Because the foe was strong.

But now I cast that finer sense
And sorer shame aside;
Such dread of sin was indolence,
Such aim at Heaven was pride.

So, when my Saviour calls, I rise
And calmly do my best;
Leaving to Him, with silent eyes
Of hope and fear, the rest.

I step, I mount where He has led;
Men count my haltings o'er –
I know them; yet, though self I dread,
I love His precept more.

Eitel, Lorraine, ed. *The Treasury of Christian Poetry*. Old Tappan, NJ: Revell, 1982. p. 157.

**WEEK THIRTY NINE**  *INSIGHT and ENCOURAGEMENT*  **DAY 2**

The School of Patience

by Andrew Murray (1828-1917)

The word patience is derived from the Latin word for suffering. It suggests the fault of being under the constraints of some power from which we fain would be free. At first we submit against our will. Experience teaches us that when it is vain to resist, patient endurance is our wisest course. In waiting on God it is of infinite consequence that we not only submit, because we are compelled to, but because we lovingly and joyfully consent to be in the hands of our blessed Father. Patience then becomes our highest blessedness and our highest grace. It honors God, and gives Him time to have His way with us. It is the highest expression of our faith in His goodness and faithfulness. It brings the soul perfect rest in the assurance that God is carrying on His work. It is the token of our full consent that God should deal with us in such a way and time as He thinks best. True patience is the losing of our self-will in His perfect will.

Such patience is needed for the true and full waiting on God. Such patience is the growth and fruit of our first lessons in the school of waiting. To many a one it will appear strange how difficult it is truly to wait upon God. The great stillness of soul before God that sinks into its own helplessness and waits for Him to reveal Himself; the deep humility that is afraid to let its own will or own strength work aught except as God works to will and to do; the meekness that is content to be and to know nothing except as God gives his light; the entire resignation of the will that only wants to be a vessel in which His holy will can move and mold – all these elements of perfect patience are not found at once.  But they will come in measure as the sole maintains its position, and ever again says: "Truly my soul waiteth upon God; from Him cometh my salvation: he only is my rock and my salvation."

Have you ever noticed what proof we have that patience is a grace for which very special grace is given, in these words of Paul: *"Strengthened with all might, according to his glorious power, unto all"* – what? *"patience and longsuffering with joyfulness."* Yes, we need to be strengthened with all God's might, and that according to the measure of His glorious power, if we are to wait on God in all patience.  It is God revealing Himself in us our life and strength, that will enable us with perfect patience to leave all in His hands.  If any are inclined to despond, because they have not such patience, let them be of good courage.  It is in the course of our feeble and very imperfect waiting that God Himself by His hidden power strengthens us and works out in us the patience of the saints, the patience of Christ himself.  (Emphasis his.)

*Waiting on God.*  Chicago: Moody Press, unk. p. 72-75 (reprint from 1895).

**WEEK THIRTY NINE**      **Confession about the Christian Life**      **DAY 3**

Romans 12

I will...
- Love without hypocrisy
- Abhor what is evil
- Cling to what is good
- Be kindly affectionate to others with brotherly love
- In honor, give preference to others
- Not lag behind regarding diligence
- Serve the Lord with spiritual fervency
- Rejoice in hope
- Be patient in tribulation
- Continue steadfastly in prayer
- Demonstrate hospitality for other believers in need
- Bless those who persecute me and not curse them
- Rejoice with those who rejoice and weep with those who weep
- Have the same attitude towards others as I expect towards myself
- Not be a snob but associate with those humbled by life's circumstances
- Not think too highly of myself
- Not repay evil for evil

Live at peace with everyone to the extent that it depends on me
Let everyone see my appreciation for the good things that happen
Not take revenge for anything that happens to me (that is Your job)
Treat my enemy as a friend
Not be overcome with evil but will overcome evil with good

**WEEK THIRTY NINE**  *INSIGHT and ENCOURAGEMENT*  **DAY 4**

Patient in Affliction

by Richard Allestree (1621-1681)

Surely you will not think that child hath due humility to his parent, or that servant to his master, that when they are corrected, shall fly in the father's or master's face. But this do we, whenever we grudge and repine at that which God lays upon us. But besides the want of humility in our so doing, there is also a great want of justice in it; for God hath, as we are his creatures, a right to do with us what he will; and therefore for us to resist that right of his, is the highest injustice that can be. It is also the greatest folly in the world; for it is only our good that God aims at in afflicting us; that heavenly Father is not like our earthly ones, who sometimes correct their children only to satisfy their own angry humor, not to do them good. But this is subject to no such frailties; *He doth not afflict willingly, nor grieve the children of men*, (Lam. 3:33). They are our sins, which do not only give him just cause, but even force and necessitate him to [discipline] us. Now, when a father sees his child stubborn and rebellious, and running on in the course that will certainly undo him, what greater act of fatherly kindness can he do, than chasten and correct him, to see if by that means he may amend him? He could not be said to have true kindness to him if he should not. And thus it is with God, when he sees us run on in sin; either he must leave off to love us, and so leave us to ourselves to take our own course, and that is the heaviest curse that can befall any man, or else, if he continue to love us, he must correct and [discipline] us, to bring us to amendment: therefore, whenever he strikes us, we are, in all reason, not only patiently to lie under his rod but (as I may say) kiss it also; that is, be very thankful to him that he is pleased not to *give us over to our own hearts' lusts*, (Ps. 81:12) but still continues his care of us; sends afflictions as so many messengers to call us home to himself. You see, then, how gross the folly is to murmur at those stripes which are meant so graciously; it is like that of a froward patient, which reproaches and reviles the physician that comes to cure him; and if such a one is left to die of his disease, everyone knows whom he is to thank for it.

But it is not only quietness, no, nor thankfulness neither, under afflictions that is the full of our duty in this matter: we must have fruitfulness also, or all the rest will stand us in no stead. By fruitfulness I mean bringing forth that which the afflictions were sent to work in us, *viz.* the amendment of our lives. To which purpose, in time of afflictions, it is very necessary for us to call ourselves to an account, to examine our hearts and lives, and search diligently what sins lie upon us, which provoked God thus to smite us: and whatsoever we find ourselves guilty of, humbly to confess to God, and immediately to forsake for the rest of our time; whether our suffering be from God's hand, or whether it be men that are the instruments of afflicting us. For when any man doth us hurt, he could not do it without God's permission and sufferance; and God may as well make them the instruments of [chastening] us, as do it directly by himself: and it is but a counterfeit patience that pretends to submit to God and yet can bear nothing from man.

Adapted from *The Whole Duty of Man*. London: Society for Promoting Christian Knowledge, 1841. p. 42-44.

**WEEK THIRTY NINE**         **Confession about the Precepts of God**        **DAY 5**

From Psalm 119

I have chosen to follow and obey your precepts. No matter what state I am in, happy, healthy, and content, or humbled, sickly, and in need, I will not forget your precepts. In the face of trials and temptations, I will not turn from obeying your precepts. Though spoken evil love, made fun of, and ridiculed in public, I will continue to keep your precepts. They will be on my mind and in my thoughts constantly. Daily I will review and meditate on them. I will give attention to their complete obedience. The more I consider your precepts, the more I come to understand how your Kingdom works. There is freedom in following your precepts. The more I obey, the greater freedom I experience. As I consider your ways, I appreciate more and more how wonderful your deeds are on my behalf. Your precepts are good and right and keep me on the path that you approve. My life is preserved when I faithfully follow your precepts. They help me escape the snares and traps the enemy sets for me. My commitment is never to forget your precepts. I will meditate on them day and night. I will never stop seeking to learn them and obey them with all my heart. I will express my love for you by demonstrating my love for your word.

**WEEK THIRTY NINE**        *INSIGHT and ENCOURAGEMENT*        **DAY 6**

Wait Patiently

by Andrew Murray (1828-1917)

"So then it is not of him who wills, nor of him who runs, but of God who shows mercy." (Romans 9:16). We have as little power to increase or strengthen our spiritual life, as we had to originate it. We "were born not of the will of the flesh, nor of the will of man, but of the will of God." Even so, our willing and running, our desire and effort, avail nought; all is "of God who shows mercy." All the exercises of the spiritual life, our reading and praying, our willing and doing, have their very great value. But they can go no farther than this, that they point the way and prepare us in humility to look to and depend alone upon God Himself, and in patience to wait His good time and mercy. The waiting is to teach us our absolute dependence upon God's mighty working, and to make us in perfect patience place ourselves at his disposal. They that wait on the Lord shall inherit the land; the promised land and its blessing. The heirs must wait.

## VICTORY THROUGH SURRENDER

"Rest in the Lord, and wait patiently for Him. It is resting in the Lord, in His will, His promise, His faithfulness, and His love, that makes patience easy. And the resting in Him is nothing but being silent unto Him, still before Him. Having our thoughts and wishes, our fears and hopes, hushed into calm and quiet in that great peace of God which passes all understanding. That peace keeps the heart and mind when we are anxious for anything, because we have made our request known to Him. The rest, the silence, the stillness, and the patient waiting, all find their strength and joy in God Himself.

The need for patience, and the reasonableness, and the blessedness of patience will be opened up to the waiting soul. Our patience will be seen to be the counterpart of God's patience. He longs for more to bless us fully than we can desire it. But as the husbandman has long patience till the fruit be ripe, so God bows himself to our slowness and bears long with us. Let us remember this, and wait patiently. Of each promise and every answer to prayer the word is true: "I the Lord will hasten it *in its time*."

"Rest in the Lord, and wait patiently for Him." Yes, *for* Him. Seek not only the help, the gift, seek Himself; wait for Him. Give God his glory by resting in Him, by trusting Him fully, by waiting patiently for Him. This patience honors Him greatly; it leaves Him, as God on the throne, to do His work; it yields self wholly into His hands. It lets God *be God*. If your waiting be for some special request, wait patiently. If your waiting be more the exercise of the spiritual life seeking to know and have more of God, wait patiently. Whether it be in the shorter specific periods of waiting, or as the continuous habit of the soul, rest in the Lord, be still before the Lord, and wait patiently. "They that wait on the Lord shall inherit the land." (Emphasis his)

*Waiting on God.* Chicago: Moody Press, unk. p. 60-62 (reprint from 1895).

**WEEK THIRTY NINE**  *HYMNS and POEMS*  **DAY 7**

Press On

by Barney E. Warren (1867-1951)

Press on, my brother, sister,
And face the deadly foe;
Through Jesus Christ we'll conquer,
While trav'ling here below.

*Refrain:*
*Press on, press on,*
*Says Christ, our loving Friend;*
*Press on, press on,*
*"I'm with thee to the end."*

Press on, and let thy failings
A blessing to thee prove;
No wave of care or sorrow
Thy trusting soul shall move.

Press on, though raging tempests
And fiery billows roll;
While crossing life's rough rapids,
He'll safely guide thy soul.

Press on, 'mid strong temptation,
　Tell Satan he must flee;
　In Jesus' name resist him,
　And vict'ry thine shall be.

　Press on, forever trusting,
　In faith believing, too;
In spite of doubt or feeling,
　God's word will take you through.

　Press on to what's before us,
　Forgetting all the past;
　The light of heav'n so glorious
　Eternally shall last.

https://library.timelesstruths.org/music/Press_On/

**Record your insights, revelations, and meditations from this week.  DATE:**

_____
_____
_____
_____
_____
_____
_____
_____
_____
_____
_____
_____

# MONTH TEN

*Journal entry from April 16, 2018*
I had breakfast with Ron at Jay Jay's. The "woman of peace" there (a la Luke 10:6) is a waitress named Erica. Last week she shared that her ex-boyfriend of four years, Orlando, contracted the flu, which worsened. He was now in ICU with pneumonia and kidney failure. We prayed for him with her last week. Today she said Orlando had gotten worse still to the point where the doctors have given up hope and told the family to begin thinking about taking him off life support. We prayed for Orlando again. I asked where he was, and she said MCA hospital, ICU room 26. I must have had that look on my face because she asked me if I was going to go see him. I think I said, "Maybe." After we finished, I did feel that I should go and went straight there from the restaurant. On the way, the Lord showed me how to think about doing these prayer assignments, because not getting proud has been a concern of mine. Not having the right attitude has been a hindrance in the past. The Holy Spirit said, "You are the Gardener's helper." God is the Gardener (Vine-dresser, Husbandman), and He decides what needs to be done and when and how. But I get to be the Gardener's helper. I'm a tool (in the positive sense of the word). That's all, and that's it. That was a major revelation to me.

While I was preparing myself in the car, I felt the Lord give four instructions: read Proverbs 4:20-22, anoint Orlando with oil, pray for him, and play "Heal Me" by Terry McAlmon. I said to the Lord, "If anyone stops me or challenges me at all, I'm going to take that as a sign that I am not supposed to go in, and I will leave." No one did.

When I entered the hospital, I walked down a long hall, up the elevator, into the ICU back doors, which I expected to be locked, and right up to his room. There was a team in the room running tests, so I had to wait for a minute. After the team left, only a female friend of Orlando's and a nurse were there. The nurse acted like she did not see me. I asked the friend if it was OK to pray for him, and she graciously said yes. It was a weak effort. I read the scripture, put the smallest amount of oil possible on his forehead (I am not sure why I had oil with me that day), and then prayed. I was afraid to play the music with the nurse there, so I left. I made it back to the car but knew I had not completed the assignment, so I went back in. The nurse was gone this time. I just told the friend I forgot to do something. I played the song quietly on my phone. I sat the phone on the pillow by Orlando's head, sat down in the chair next to his friend, and waited. When the song was over, I left. I am anxious to get a report back next week.

*Journal entry from April 20, 2018*
Today, we learned from Erica that Orlando had come out of the coma and was out of ICU. That was great news because I went to the hospital on Wednesday, and his ICU room was empty.

[Orlando recovered, and I went to his house a couple of weeks later to pray with him. He remains in good health to this day. When we have surrendered our lives to the Father and seek to walk in the Spirit every day, we must be willing to do what He says, when He says to do it, how He says to do it, no matter what it feels or sounds like. Surrender means He gets to decide.]

**WEEK FORTY**         *HYMNS and POEMS*         **DAY 1**

I'll Go Where You Want Me To Go

by Mary Brown (1856-1919)

It may not be on the mountain's height,
Or over the stormy sea;
It may not be at the battle's front,
My Lord will have need of me;
But if by a still, small voice He calls,
To paths that I do not know,
I'll answer, dear Lord, with my hand in Thine,
I'll go where You want me to go.

*Refrain:*
*I'll go where You want me to go, dear Lord,*
*O'er mountain, or plain, or sea;*
*I'll say what You want me to say, dear Lord,*
*I'll be what You want me to be.*

Perhaps today there are loving words
Which Jesus would have me speak;
There may be now in the paths of sin,
Some wand'rer whom I should seek;
O Savior, if Thou wilt be my guide,
Though dark and rugged the way,
My voice shall echo Thy message sweet,
I'll say what You want me to say.

There's surely somewhere a lowly place,
In earth's harvest fields so white,
Where I may labor through life's short day,
For Jesus the Crucified;
So trusting my all to Thy tender care,
And knowing Thou lovest me,
I'll do Thy will with a heart sincere,
I'll be what You want me to be.

https://library.timelesstruths.org/music/Ill_Go_Where_You_Want_Me_to_Go/

| WEEK FORTY | *INSIGHT and ENCOURAGEMENT* | DAY 2 |

The Kingdom of God
by B. F. Westcott (1825-1901)

This thought of the kingdom was, indeed, the moral of the Old Testament, the issue to which all the training of God's chosen people tended. From the first call of their Father Abraham to their last struggle with foreign invaders the same lesson was being enforced upon them in many ways. By bondage and wondering, by conquest and oppression, by brilliant triumphs, by heroic sufferings, by desolate exile, by painful return, the Jews were taught to lift their thoughts to the contemplation of a divine sovereignty. They were brought into contact with the great nations of the east, and so they learned to field the essential weakness of the powers beneath which they had fallen for a time only to rise again still stronger. They themselves received a dynasty, in answer to their prayers, which in its first glory seemed to realize by the ways of earth all for which they hoped. But the kingdom of David rapidly descended to the level of human monarchies and served only to furnish the imagery in which the aspirations of later prophets were clothed. So the hope which had been brought home to the mind of the people, became, in its promise and in its failure, fruitful in greater hopes. Step by step the full majesty of the divine ideal was realized in thought, while the organization of material forces was pressed forward with relentless vigor by Roman conquest. At last, in the fullness of time, the contrast between "the kingdom of heaven," founded on the eternal basis of truth and justice, and the kingdom of the world, which was the final expression of force and self-will, stood revealed. The one was recognized in the sovereignty of love welcomed by faith and seen in the person of *the Word became flesh*: the other stood out in the isolation of victorious might, with a deified man as the supreme object of human devotion.

Thus the Gospel of Christ was in its announcement and in its preparation, as it is in its essence, *the Gospel of the Kingdom*. To seek *the Kingdom [of God] and His righteousness* is enjoined upon the believer as his first duty; and we ourselves at least in word acknowledge the obligation (Matt. 6:23, 33). Morning and evening we all pray in Christ's own words that "our Father's Kingdom may come, on earth as in heaven": that it may "come," not that we may be carried away to it far off, out of this stormy tumult of common cares as to some tranquil haven of rest: that it may come to us "on earth as in heaven." For the Kingdom of God is at once spiritual and historical: eternal and temporal: outward and inward: visible and invisible: a huge system and an energy. It is an order of things in which heavenly laws are recognized and obeyed. It depends both for its origin and for its support upon forces which are not of earth. It is inspired by the principles and powers of a higher sphere. It implies a harmonious relation between man and the beings of an unseen universe (*the Kingdom of Heaven*). It places its members in a social and personal relationship to a Divine Head, as citizens to a King, as children to a Father ("*the Kingdom of God,*" "*the Kingdom of your father which is in heaven*").

But at the same time, though it is not limited by the conditions of our present existence, it is manifested under them. It is in the world though it is not of the world. The scene on which it is shown to be realized is the scene of human life. The Lord speaks habitually of His coming again, of His Presence, and in one sense he fixes that time of his coming in the generation of those whom he addressed (Matt. 15:28). He points forward, if I may gather up what I would say in one sentence, to a transfiguration of human society which corresponds to the Resurrection of the individual.

Yes, this is Christ's teachings; and we believe the fullness of His promise: we acknowledge the universality of his work. He did not come to found a school by unfolding new forms of intellectual truth: He did not come to mold a sect by the imposition of an outward rule. He came to deal with the whole of life, with thought, action, feeling, with life in its largest and noblest forms, with life in every phase of its progressive activity. He came to bring a message to the strong and the wealthy and the gay, as well as to the weary and heavy-laden. He came to found a Kingdom into which *the Kings of the earth should bring their glory*. And for to us that Kingdom, the Kingdom of Heaven, the Kingdom of God, the Kingdom of the Son of man, is a present reality. We live in it, and yet we look for it. We live in it as recognizing the supremacy of a Divine law, the rule of a Divine sovereign, the constitution of a Divine church. We look for it, as we wait for *the redemption of our own bodies* (Rom. 8:23). Meanwhile we are bound by the obligations of its citizenship, heirs of its glories, sharers in its destiny.

*Social Aspects of Christianity*. London: Macmillan and Co., 1900. p. 86-90.

---

**WEEK FORTY**     *HYMNS and POEMS*     **DAY 3**

Aspirations of the Soul After Christ
by Jeanne Marie De La Motte-Guyon (1648-1717)

My Spouse! in whose presence I live,
Sole object of all my desires,
Who know'st what a flame I conceive,
And canst easily double its fires;
How pleasant is all that I meet!
From fear of adversity free,
I find even sorrow made sweet,
Because 'tis assign'd me by Thee.

Transported I see Thee display
Thy riches and glory divine;
I have only my life to repay,
Take what I would gladly resign.
Thy will is the treasure I seek,
For Thou art as faithful as strong;
There let me, obedient and meek,
Repose myself all the day long.

My spirit and faculties fail;
Oh finish what Love has begun!
Destroy what is sinful and frail,
And dwell in the soul Thou hast won!
Dear theme of my wonder and praise,
I cry, who is worthy as Thou!
I can only be silent and gaze;
'Tis all that is left to me now.

Oh glory, in which I am lost,
Too deep for the plummet of thought!
On an ocean of Deity toss'd,
I am swallow'd, I sink into nought.
Yet lost and absorb'd as I seem,
I chant to the praise of my King;
And though overwhelm'd by the theme,
Am happy whenever I sing.

Tozer, A. W. *The Christian Book of Mystical Verse: A Collection of Poems, Hymns, and Prayers for Devotional Reading.* Chicago: Moody Publishers, 2016. p. 174.

**WEEK FORTY**  *INSIGHT and ENCOURAGEMENT*  **DAY 4**

The Gospel of the Kingdom

by Ed Silvoso (1945-present)

When the church as we know it today fails to make the transition from the Law and the Prophets to the Gospel of the Kingdom, it ends up preaching a message that is relevant only to the past (Christ died on the cross to redeem us) and the future (He will return in Glory), but it fails to present its relevance for today. This, in turn, can easily give room to legalism and to falling out of sync with God's timing.

Let me expand on this. Contemporary legalism, like the legalism practiced by the Pharisees, leads us to focus on the forms: the temple (building), the liturgy, the traditions and the creeds. Falling out of sync with God's timing paralyzes us spiritually because it causes us to relegate our expectations to something that we believe will happen only in the future, when in reality it is already here. The consequence of all this is inactive believers who hover around a temple and live innocuously inside a religious system, at best. Or at worst, they become prisoners in a doctrinal POW camp, hoping to be liberated when their Commander in Chief returns.

Right after John the Baptist's ministry came to an end, Jesus announced the advent of the Kingdom: "Now after John had been taken into custody, Jesus came into Galilee, preaching the gospel of God, and saying, 'the *time is fulfilled, and the kingdom of God is at hand*; repent and believe the gospel'" (Mark 1:14-15, emphasis added [Silvoso]). Jesus' Gospel from the very beginning consisted in the proclamation of God's Kingdom as being present now in the midst of people.

Consequently, His Ekklesia is not the Ekklesia of the Law and the Prophets, which can only remind us of what He did in the past and what He will do in the future. That outlook would leave us with just the temple, the forms, and a resignation to wait for better days. Not at all! Jesus' intention is that the Ekklesia's proclamation of the Gospel of the Kingdom would confront the Gates of Hades now, in the present, until those gates collapse so that people, and eventually nations, are transformed.

It is evident that a new season requiring a new message was at hand "lift up your eyes and look on the fields, that they are white for harvest" (John 4:35). The Gospel of the Kingdom was that new message.

The law and the prophets can be summarized in one phrase: "He will come." The Gospel of the Kingdom is expressed in this: "He is here! That truth snatches us out of a passive escapism mindset and puts us on a path of personal victory and transformation.

Excerpted from *Ekklesia*. Bloomington, MN: Chosen Books, 2018. p. 55-57.

## WEEK FORTY — Confession about Worship — DAY 5

Read Psalm 95

"Oh, come." It's an invitation. Come and sing. How often this worship draws out my voice to sing your praise. Singing to you, I can feel your presence. There's nothing like the sound of hundreds or thousands of voices singing your praise in united harmony. No wonder you delight in it. Sometimes your joy makes me shout because I cannot contain the happiness you make me feel. I'm happy because my salvation is secure on solid ground. I'm happy and grateful to be in your presence, the presence of my Lord, the great God, and King above all. I gladly recite my psalms and songs of praise to you. In one hand, you cup the depths of the ocean. In the other, you cover the highest mountains. Every sea is yours by the right of creation. You own the title to every inch of land because you formed it all. How can I not humble myself and bow before you in worship and adoration? On bended knee, I raised my hands in worship and surrender to you. You could have treated me like a beast of burden set on rocky, unlevel terrain. But instead, you put me in a place of abundance with access to everything I need. You gently lead and guide me because you know my sight is limited, and I'm easily frightened. Even though I can be stubborn and rebellious, when I respond to you with a soft heart, you lead me into a place of rest and peace.

## WEEK FORTY — *INSIGHT and ENCOURAGEMENT* — DAY 6

Job #1 in Evangelism

by Ed Silvoso (1945-present)

The best way to pray intelligently for the unsaved, and especially for those in authority, is to get to know them and to maintain contact with them in order to pray for their felt needs. We must become aware of the difference between the most important need a person has [salvation] and what that person feels is his most important need – what is known as the "felt need." The felt needs of the lost are defined by the lost themselves; it is what they feel is most important to them. When we pray for their felt needs and God answers, their eyes are opened to the reality and the power of God, and this in turn leads them to recognize their need for salvation.

Jesus was in the habit of meeting men's felt needs first in order to draw them to salvation. Meeting the felt needs of the lost opens their eyes to the reality of God and allows them to make a vital connection between His power and His love for them. The main factor that keeps us from praying consistently for the felt needs of the lost is our inability to distinguish between acceptance and approval. Through our verbal and nonverbal communication, we demonstrate judgment and condemnation, rather than love and acceptance. Though Christ died, the ultimate sacrifice for us when we were still sinners, we, His followers, refuse to extend grace to those in the same condition.

Our selfish preoccupation with our cosmetic needs at the expense of the eternal life of the lost is the ultimate expression of the religious spirit that controls many Christians today. Not once did Jesus compromise His holiness because He was able to accept the sinner without approving of his lifestyle in an atmosphere overflowing with compassion. By feeling good for the sins, we do not commit, we fail to see the crucial need we have for the grace of God on account of the sins we *do* commit. Spiritual pride is the greatest obstacle to genuinely and lovingly accepting sinners. We must accept the lost and graciously minister to their felt needs so that their eyes will be opened to the reality of the power and the love of God. Like Jesus, we must accept them as they are so we can show them the way to change.

Why should God answer prayers on behalf of people who are living in sin, cut off from the glory of God and following the prince of the power of the air? Such desperate conditions trigger His grace. Prayers for the felt needs of the lost have a higher priority than the prayers for the needs of the saved. To believers, a crisis is a temporary problem affecting their comfort level this side of heaven. To unbelievers, it is either heaven or hell. God's heartbeat is for the lost. He loves them to the point of having given the very best for them: his Son. [Absolute surrender is essential for effective prayer evangelism because it deals with the issues of spiritual pride and functioning under a religious spirit.]

Adapted from *That None Should Perish*. Ventura, CA: Regals Books, 1994. Pp. 77-84.

**WEEK FORTY**  *HYMNS and POEMS*  **DAY 7**

Full Surrender

by Sharla Sensenig (unknown)

Lord, Almighty Father, take my will;
Let Thy righteousness my being fill;
Let Thy Holy Spirit reign within,
Crucifying carnal self and sin.

Savior, Lamb of God, who died for me—
Whispered, "Not my will," to set me free—
Thou dost lead e'en as Thou seest fit;
Grant me strength to willingly submit.

Tim Tremaine

Holy Spirit, Comforter divine,
All my fleshly sins I now resign;
Move within my being, touch my soul,
Crucify my will, and take control.

Blessed Trinity, I give to Thee
All that I have ever hoped to be;
The pursuit of selfishness I cease,
For in full surrender lieth peace.

https://library.timelesstruths.org/music/Full_Surrender/ from 2014.

**Record your insights, revelations, and meditations from this week. DATE:**

_____
_____
_____
_____
_____
_____
_____
_____
_____
_____
_____
_____
_____

VICTORY THROUGH SURRENDER

**WEEK FORTY ONE**  *HYMNS and POEMS*  **DAY 1**

Living For Jesus
by Thomas O. Chisholm (1793-1847)

Living for Jesus, a life that is true,
Striving to please You in all that I do;
Yielding allegiance, glad-hearted and free,
This is the pathway of blessing for me.

*Refrain:*
*O Jesus, Lord and Savior, I give myself to Thee,*
*For Thou, in Thy atonement, didst give Thyself for me;*
*I own no other Master, my heart shall be Thy throne;*
*My life I give, henceforth to live, O Christ, for Thee alone.*

Living for Jesus Who died in my place,
Bearing on Calv'ry my sin and disgrace;
Such love constrains me to answer Your call,
Follow Your leading and give You my all.

Living for Jesus, wherever I am,
Doing each duty in Your holy Name;
Willing to suffer affliction and loss,
Deeming each trial a part of my cross.

Living for Jesus through earth's little while,
My dearest treasure, the light of Your smile;
Seeking the lost ones You died to redeem,
Bringing the weary to find rest in You.

Sims, Walter Hines, ed. *Baptist Hymnal*. Nashville: Convention Press, 1956. p. 352.

**WEEK FORTY ONE**  *INSIGHT and ENCOURAGEMENT*  **DAY 2**

The Fourth Conversation
by Brother Lawrence (c. 1614-1691)

He told me [speaking of himself] that all consists in one hearty renunciation of everything which we are sensible does not lead to God; that we might accustom ourselves to a continual conversation with Him, with freedom and in simplicity. That we need only to recognize God intimately present with us, to address ourselves to Him every moment, that we may beg His assistance for knowing His will in things doubtful, and for rightly performing those which we plainly see He requires of us, offering them to Him before we do them, and giving Him thanks when we have done.

That, without being discouraged on account of our sins, we should pray for His grace with a perfect confidence, as relying upon the infinite merits of our Lord Jesus Christ. That God never failed offering us His grace at each action; that he distinctly perceived it, and never failed of it, unless when his thoughts had wandered from a sense of God's Presence, or he had forgotten to ask His assistance. That God always gave us light in our doubts, when we had no other design but ask to please Him.

That our sanctification did not depend upon changing our works, but in doing that for God's sake, which we commonly do for our own. That it was lamentable to see how many people mistook the means for the end, addicting themselves to certain works, which they performed very imperfectly, by reason of their human or selfish regards.

That the most excellent method he had found of going to God, was that of doing our common business without any view of pleasing men, and (as far as we are capable) purely for the love of God. That it was a great delusion to think that the times of prayer ought to differ from other times: that we are as strictly obliged to adhere to God by action in the time of action, as by prayer in the season of prayer.

That his prayer was nothing else but a sense of the presence of God, his soul being at that time insensible to everything but Divine love: and that when the appointed times of prayer were past, he found no difference, because he still continued with God, praising and blessing Him with all his might, so that he passed his life in continual joy; yet hoped that God would give him somewhat to suffer, when he should grow stronger.

That we ought, once for all, heartily to put our whole trust in God, and make a total surrender of ourselves to Him, secure that He would not deceive us. After this we should not wonder that troubles, temptations, oppositions and contradictions happen to us from men. We ought, on the contrary, to submit ourselves to them, and bear them as long as God pleases, as things highly advantageous to us. That the greater perfection a soul aspires after, the more dependent it is upon Divine grace.

Adapted from *The Practice of the Presence of God*. Grand Rapids: Revell, 1958 (eBook). p. 19-22.

**WEEK FORTY ONE**  **Confession about the Word of God**  **DAY 3**

Read Psalm 119:97-104

I have to confess that I love to think about the Word of God. I meditate on it all day long. Because I read and think about the Word so much, it always comes to mind. I can tell I make better decisions because I remember God's Word. The more I meditate on your Word, the more insight into the Word you give me.

The more I obey what I know of your commands, the more understanding of your will I get. I am not forgetting or departing from your Word because you are teaching me these truths yourself. Your teachings are more delightful than the finest delicacies and more precious than the purest gold. Learning your laws and commands helps me understand how to think and what to do. The more I understand your will and your Word, the more I despise the thought of not obeying your Word and of not following your will. I will follow the right path as you give me revelation and understanding to know it.

## WEEK FORTY ONE — *INSIGHT and ENCOURAGEMENT* — DAY 4

Wonderful Passion for God

by Oswald Chambers (1874-1917)

*'Forasmuch then as Christ hath suffered for us in the flesh, arm yourselves likewise with the same mind: for he that hath suffered in the flesh hath ceased from sin; That he no longer should live the rest of his time in the flesh to the lusts of men, but to the will of God.'* 1 Peter 4:1-2

Steady contemplation of the Passion of our Lord will 'do to death' everything that is not of God. It is only after a long while of going on with God and steady contemplation of the Cross that we begin to understand its meaning. "Today you will be with Me in paradise" is said only in one place, viz. at the Cross.

This is not a message about our salvation and sanctification, but about the outcome of salvation and sanctification in our implicit life, i.e. where we live it and cannot speak it. Jesus said, 'If any man would be My disciple…' not, 'If any man would be saved and sanctified…' 'If any man would be My disciple – those are the conditions.' Jesus Christ always talked about discipleship with an 'If.' We are at perfect liberty to toss our spiritual head and say, 'No, thank you, that is a bit too stern for me,' and the Lord will never say a word, we can do exactly what we like. He will never plead, but the opportunity is there – 'If…'.

After all, it is the great stern call of Jesus that fascinates men and women quicker than anything. It is not the gospel of being saved from hell and enjoying heaven that attracts men, saving in a very shallow mood; it is Christ crucified that attracts men; Jesus said so – "I, if I be lifted up from the earth, will draw all men unto Me." Jesus Christ never attracts us by the unspeakable bliss of Paradise; He attracts us by the ugly beam. We talk about getting down to the depths of a man's soul: Jesus Christ is the only One who ever did. If once a man had heard the appeal of Jesus from the cross, he begins to find there is something there that answers the cry of the human heart and the problem of the whole world. What we have to do as God's servants is to lift up Christ crucified. We can either do it as gramophones, or as those who are in fellowship with Him.

Many of us have heard Jesus Christ's first 'Follow Me' – to a life of liberty and joy and gladness; how many of us have heard the second 'Follow Me' – 'deny your right to yourself and "do to death" in yourself everything that never was in Me?'

*If Thou Wilt Be Perfect*. Fort Washington, PA: Christian Literature Crusade, 1941. p. 60-61.

**WEEK FORTY ONE**           **Confession about Surrender**           **DAY 5**

Read Mark 8 and 10

I confess that it's hard for me to find the 3-year-old inside me who lived life in total faith, total trust, total wonder, and complete fearlessness. When I come to the Word, when I seek your face, when I touch the world, I want to be that child. Take me in your arms and bless me. I long to exchange smile for smile. I am willing to be made willing to begin to say no to the things I have wanted and desired. I am willing to identify with the life you lived, no matter the consequences. I trust that your Holy Spirit will come and live your life in and through me. I will lose my life, the things that make up the life I now live; people, places, thoughts, activities, possessions, dreams, and desires, for the sake of the gospel of Christ. Despite the opinions of others, I refuse to be ashamed of you or your Word because I don't want you to be ashamed of me. Daily, I will keep my mind concentrated on the things of God and keep my eyes focused on the footsteps of Jesus so that I will always enter and remain in the Kingdom of God.

**WEEK FORTY ONE**           *INSIGHT and ENCOURAGEMENT*           **DAY 6**

Saturday, 12 January 1723, in the morning
by Jonathan Edwards (1703-1758)

I have this day solemnly renewed my baptismal covenant and self-dedication, which I renewed when I was received into the communion of the church. I have been before God; and have given myself, all that I am and have to God, so that I am not in any respect my own. I can claim no right in myself, no right in this understanding, this will, these affections that are in me; neither have I any right to this body or any of its members; no right to this tongue, these hands nor feet; no right to the senses, these eyes, these ears, this smell or taste. I have given myself clear away. This I have done. And I pray God, for the sake of Christ, to look upon it as a self-dedication; and to receive me now as entirely His own, and deal with me in all respects as such; whether He afflicts me or prosper me, or whatever He pleases to do with me, who am His. Now henceforth I am not to act in any respect as my own. I shall act as my own, if I ever make use of any of my powers to anything that is not to the glory of God, or do not make the glorifying of Him my whole and entire business; if I murmur in the least at afflictions; if I grieve at the prosperity of others; if I am any way uncharitable; if I am angry because of injuries; if I revenge my own cause; if I do anything purely to please myself, or avoid anything for the sake of my ease, or omit anything because it is great self-denial; if I trust to myself; if I take any of the praise of any good that I do, or rather God does by me; or if I am in any way proud.

Baillie, John. *A Diary of Readings*. New York: Macmillan Publishing Co., 1955. p. 132.

VICTORY THROUGH SURRENDER

**WEEK FORTY ONE**   *INSIGHT and ENCOURAGEMENT*   **DAY 7**

A Plea in Prayer

by Andrew Murray (1828-1917)

"Let integrity and uprightness preserve me; for I wait on thee." – Psalm 25:21

For the third time in this psalm we have the word *wait*. As before in verse 5, "On thee do I wait all the day," so here too, the believing supplicant appeals to God to remember that he is waiting on Him, looking for an answer. It is a great thing for a soul not only to wait on God, but to be filled with such a consciousness that its whole spirit and position is that of a waiting one, that it can, in childlike confidence, say, "Lord, Thou knowest, I wait on Thee!" It will prove the mighty plea in prayer, giving ever-increasing boldness of expectation to claim the promise: "They that wait on Me shall not be ashamed!"

The prayer in connection with which the plea is put forth here is one of great importance in the spiritual life. If we draw nigh to God, it must be with a true heart. There must be perfect integrity, wholeheartedness in our dealing with God. As we read in the next psalm (26:1, 11): "Judge me, O Lord; for I have walked in mine integrity... As for me, I will walk in mine integrity," there must be perfect uprightness or single-heartedness before God, as it is written: "His righteousness is for the upright in heart."

If at our first attempt truly to live the life of fully and always waiting on God, we begin to discover how much that perfect integrity is wanting, this will just be one of the blessings which the waiting was meant to work. The soul cannot seek close fellowship with God, or attain the abiding consciousness of waiting on Him all the day, without a very honest and entire surrender to all His will.

It is not only in connection with the prayer of our text but with every prayer that this plea may be used. It must be clear to us *what we are waiting for*. It may be waiting for God. It may be a special petition, to which we are expecting an answer. It may be our whole inner life, in which we are on the lookout for God's putting forth of His power. It may be the whole state of His church and saints, or some part of His work. It must also be clear to us, *on whom we are waiting*. Not an idol but the living God, such as He really is in His great glory, holiness, power, wisdom, and goodness. And let it be clear too that *we are waiting*. Let that become so much our consciousness that the utterance comes spontaneously, "On thee I do wait all the day." This will indeed imply sacrifice and separation, the soul entirely given up to God as its all, its only joy. If it be true that Christ made a life of continual abiding in his presence possible, nothing less ought to satisfy then to be ever breathing this blessed atmosphere, "I wait on thee."

Excerpted from *Waiting on God*. Chicago: Moody Press. p. 39-43 (reprint from 1905).

**Record your insights, revelations, and meditations from this week.  DATE:**

VICTORY THROUGH SURRENDER

**WEEK FORTY TWO** *HYMNS and POEMS* **DAY 1**

Take Thou Our Minds, Dear Lord
by William H. Foulkes (1877-1961)

*(The pronouns have been converted from third person to first person. Speak this out to the Lord.)*

Take Thou my mind, dear Lord, I humbly pray;
Give me the mind of Christ each passing day;
Teach me to know the truth that sets me free;
Grant me in all my thoughts to honor Thee.

Take Thou my heart, O Christ, it is Thine own;
Come Thou within my soul and claim Thy throne;
Help me to shed abroad Thy deathless love;
Use me to make the earth like heaven above.

Take Thou my will, Most High! Hold Thou full sway;
Have in my inmost soul Thy perfect way;
Guard Thou each sacred hour from selfish ease;
Guide Thou my ordered life as Thou dost please.

Take Thou myself, O Lord, heart, mind, and will;
Through my surrendered soul Thy plans fulfill.
I yield myself to Thee – time, talents, all;
I hear, and henceforth heed, Thy sovereign call.

Modified from *Hymns for the Family of God*. Nashville: Paragon Associates, Inc. 1976. p. 467.

**WEEK FORTY TWO** **Confession about Difficulties** **DAY 2**

Read Psalm 119:169-176

When I am troubled or confused or distressed, I will cry out to you, Lord. My prayers will come before you. I will speak praise to your name, loud and long. I will raise my voice to sing of your glory and worship your holy name. I confess my utter dependence on you for everything. I know I can't do anything in my own strength or understanding. I yield myself to your total and complete Lordship over my life. I know you can help me and are ready to help me. How I long for your salvation and am desperate for your deliverance. Allow me to live so that I can continue to praise your name, and others will give you praise because of your mercy and grace to me. Even when I stray from the path, come and get me, Lord. Bring me back. Your Word gives me true understanding. I trust in your promises of deliverance. Continue to teach me your good and righteous commands, and I will continue to obey and follow your will. The law of the Lord is my delight. Your Word sustains me through the darkest and most difficult times. As I live in Christ and through the power of the Holy Spirit, I will not forget your word or fail to live in the light of your truth forever.

**WEEK FORTY TWO**        *INSIGHT and ENCOURAGEMENT*        **DAY 3**

Take Up Your Cross

by Daniel Kolenda (1981-present)

The Kingdom of God is greater than any earthly kingdom and infinitely greater than any personal ambition. A wise person will realize it is futile and dangerous to "kick against the goads," as God said to Saul on the road to Damascus (Acts 26:14). A quick surrender is the most reasonable thing to do.

This book is about spiritual warfare. We are talking about being part of God's army. Indeed, the Christian life is a warring life in the Spirit. But here Jesus gives us a much more precise metaphor. Joining the army of the Lord is not simply a matter of going down to our recruitment office and enlisting. We are not by nature citizens of this kingdom. We are natural enemies of God. We cannot begin by merely joining Christ. We must first surrender!

Read Ephesians 2:3 and Colossians 1:21.

Listen to Paul's language. He is talking about the "cravings of the flesh," "its desires and thoughts," and how we were "enemies in [our] minds." He is referring to the demonic zeitgeist I have been describing. In order to be a part of God's army, we have to surrender this old way of thinking and living. This is why repentance is necessary for salvation. To repent is to revolutionize the way we think and therefore live!

I have used a number of metaphors in this chapter. Allow me to call on one more. This is not my metaphor, but one used by Jesus Himself. He said that if we want to follow Him, we must deny ourselves, take up our cross, and follow Him (Matt 16:24). Earlier we talked about the wisdom of the cross – how it contradicted all worldly wisdom and dealt a fatal blow to the demonic zeitgeist. Here Jesus instructs us that if we want to be His disciples, we carry that same cross. But what does it mean to take up the cross?

The cross is a symbol of suffering and death. A person who carries a cross is on his way to be crucified. He is a dead man walking. The old, carnal, demonic way of thinking cannot simply be changed. It must be killed.

## VICTORY THROUGH SURRENDER

Jesus requires us to lay aside the person we used to be and to take up a new identity, a new pattern of thinking, and a new way of living. We may live in the same physical body but our old self is dead. We have been transformed by the renewing of our minds. This is precisely what is required for effective spiritual warfare. Any soldier without a cross on his back is fighting for Satan. The battle rages not only in the world but also within us. We are where the change must begin.

*Slaying Dragons.* Lake Mary FL: Charisma House, 2019. p. 75-76

**WEEK FORTY TWO**  *HYMNS and POEMS*  **DAY 4**

Truehearted, Wholehearted, Faithful and Loyal
by Frances Ridley Havergal (1836-1879)

Truehearted, wholehearted, faithful and loyal,
King of our lives, by Thy grace we will be!
Under Thy standard, exalted and royal,
Strong in Thy strength we will battle for Thee.

Truehearted, wholehearted! Fullest allegiance
Yielding henceforth to our glorious king;
Valiant endeavor and loving obedience
Freely and joyously now would we bring.

Truehearted! Savior, Thou knowest our story,
Weak are the hearts that we lay at Thy feet,
Sinful and treacherous! yet, for Thy glory,
Heal them, and cleanse them from sin and deceit.

Wholehearted! Savior belovèd and glorious,
Take Thy great power and reign Thou alone,
Over our wills and affections victorious—
Freely surrendered and wholly Thine own.

Half-hearted, false-hearted! Heed we the warning!
Only the whole can be perfectly true;
Bring the whole offering, all timid thought scorning,
Truehearted only if wholehearted too.

Half-hearted! Savior, shall aught be withholden,
Giving Thee part who hast given us all?

Blessings outpouring, and promises golden
Pledging, with never reserve or recall.

Half-hearted? Master, shall any who know Thee
Grudge Thee their lives, who has laid down Thine own?
Nay; we would offer the hearts that we owe Thee—
Live for Thy love and Thy glory alone.

Sisters, dear sisters, the call is resounding,
Will ye not echo the silver refrain,
Mighty and sweet, and in gladness abounding—
Truehearted, wholehearted! ringing again.

Jesus is with us, His rest is before us,
Brightly His standard is waving above,
Brothers, dear brothers, in gathering chorus,
Peal out the watchword of courage and love!

*Refrain:*
*Peal out the watchword! Silence it never!*
*Song of our spirits, rejoicing and free!*
*Truehearted, wholehearted, now and forever,*
*King of our lives, by Thy grace we will be!*

Lyrics first published in *Loyal Responses* in 1878 according to http://www.hymntime.com/

**WEEK FORTY TWO**  *INSIGHT and ENCOURAGEMENT*  **DAY 5**

Spiritual Authority

by Daniel Kolenda (1981-present)

We may not always walk in perfect victory over sin, self, and the devil, as Jesus did. But as God's children we are called to grow constantly under Christ's authority. There must be "no end to the increase of His government" in our daily lives (Isa. 9:7, AMP). Jesus' victory over the forces of darkness cannot merely remain a theological or positional truth. It must become practical. It must become a lifestyle. We must actually walk in authority over sin and the devil as our Christian characters grow into Christ's image. The bottom line: we are called to live lives of discipline and holiness.

Then this authority over darkness in our own practical lives will extend into the world around us. When we are confronted with demons in others, we have authority over them as well. But when we yield to Satan in our lives, we will find it extremely difficult to take authority over his influence on someone else's life. This is both a spiritual and a practical matter. If we yield to something, we agree with it. This agreement then manifests in our actions, even if our words declare God's truth. Such disparity between our words and lives will carry no weight against satanic forces.

But it's important to understand the distinction I am making. I am not saying we have authority over demons in our own strength – when we are good enough or disciplined enough. Our authority does not come from an adequate amount of religious works or random acts of self-discipline. Our authority comes from our submission to God's authority. In fact, submission to God contradicts human pride, self-confidence, and religious works. Submission to God recognizes our deep and desperate need for His grace. But such humble surrender to God must still occur practically. Therefore, if we do *not* submit to God in our lifestyle, we actually *resist* His authority. How can we possess God's authority while simultaneously resisting it? Without submission we have no authority to confront satanic forces. When we submit to God, we receive His authority, which therefore enables us to release it to others.

"Submit yourselves therefore to God. Resist the devil, and he will flee from you" (Jas. 4:7, ESV). Our ability to resist Satan is contingent on our submission to God and for good reason: all spiritual authority comes from God. We have no authority over Satan in ourselves. In order to release *God's* authority, we must submit to it. In fact, Jude tells us that even Michael, the great archangel, said in a dispute with Satan, "The Lord rebuke you!" (v. 9). Not even mighty warrior angels possess authority within themselves over demonic forces. It comes from God alone. Likewise, our authority comes from being under His authority. (Emphasis his.)

*Slaying Dragons*. Lake Mary FL: Charisma House, 2019. p. 103-104.

**WEEK FORTY TWO**  **Confession about Attitude**  **DAY 6**

Read Philippians 2

I confess and believe that God's will for me is to be united with Christ, to have the same mind as Christ, the same love as Christ, the same spirit and purpose as Christ. My aim and my goal are to do nothing out of selfishness or conceit but to, in all humility, consider others better than myself. I will put the interests of others before my own interests and the interests of Jesus Christ before them all. I will take the attitude of Christ and make it my own, that of a humble, obedient servant. In obedience to God's Word, I will continue daily to let the life of Christ within me have its full effect with all reverence and respect. I know that God is working in me to create the desire and successfully perform the things that are according to his will and good purpose. When I obey without complaining or arguing with God, based on his Word, it becomes possible for me to be pure and blameless and without fault in this wicked world, demonstrating like a shining star that the Word of life is true. All this is possible because of Jesus, whose name is above every name and at whose feet every knee will bow, and every voice in every language in all the universe will confess with me that Jesus is Lord to the glory of Almighty God.

**WEEK FORTY TWO**  *INSIGHT and ENCOURAGEMENT*  **DAY 7**

Your Mountains Are Moved

by Charles C. Price (1887-1947)

You are trying to do the impossible. Your faith would never be strong enough or pure enough for that, though you were to struggle for a million years. What a mistake it is to take our belief in God and call it faith. How my heart has bled when I have seen some of God's dear children (and so have you) struggling to believe for victory over sickness, because they have not discerned the difference between belief in the power of God to heal (which belief even the devils have) and the faith of God which brings the victory. There is a great deal of difference between what we call the faith of man in God, and the faith of God that is imparted to man. Such faith is not the child of effort, neither is it born of struggle.

If it is the faith of God, then we get it from Him, and not from our mental attitudes or affirmations. Jesus did not say, "If you have the power to believe that God will remove that mountain, then He will do it." Neither did He say, "If you can believe hard enough that it is done, then it will be done." But He did say, "Have the faith of God." In other words, get some of God's faith; and then when you have that, you will have the only power with which mountains can be moved and cast into the sea.

But you tell me that in the second part of His statement He talks about believing with the heart and having no doubts. The second is impossible without the first. You simply cannot believe without the alloy of doubt until you have the faith of God. It takes God's faith to clean up these human hearts of ours of all the debris, the fears, misgivings and doubts. The groans and the struggles we have heard come from people who have tried to believe it is done without having God's faith! They might have confidence in His power, and belief in His promise; but to possess His faith is something else.

All this has led me to believe that it is far more important that we seek the Healer than healing. In the secret of His presence there is a hiding place for the soul. As the life empties itself of the world and its contacts, it makes room for the things which God can impart. Have you noticed that at the end of the statement our blessed Lord made to His disciples about the faith that would move mountains, He tells them to be sure to forgive everybody against whom they might have some grudge or feeling? Why does He say that in connection with this great lesson on mountain-moving faith? Is it not because of the fact that, when God would impart His faith to us, He does not want to find a channel which is choked by hate and an unforgiving spirit?

A God of infinite and eternal love wants no malice in the hearts of His children. How can we, who have been forgiven so much, refuse to forgive those who perchance have transgressed against us? The meaning of the Lord is clear. He is saying that if we are to become the recipients of the faith which is the faith of God, then we must forgive all. It is into such a yielded heart that the benediction of His faith comes; and with it the consciousness that it is there.

Excerpted from *The Real Faith*. Self-published, 1941. Chapter 6. Jawbone Digital, Kindle ed.

**Record your insights, revelations, and meditations from this week. DATE:**

Tim Tremaine

**WEEK FORTY THREE**　　　　　　*HYMNS and POEMS*　　　　　　**DAY 1**

Hymn #9　　"*That I may know Him, and the power of His resurrection.*"　Phil. 3:10
by Ann Griffiths (1776-1805)

O! for deeper meditation
On my Living, Loving Lord,
As I read the revelation
Of His Everlasting Word!
Endless death had been the sinner's
Recompense and righteous doom,
But for My Divine Redeemer's
Resurrection from the tomb.

God is terrible in power,
Though He be a God of love,
And no wonder sinners cower
At the thought of Him above.
Yet when with humiliation
We bow down before His Face,
He reveals His great Salvation
And the riches of His Grace.

To be under His protection
Is my soul's security,
While to share in His Refection
Is both meat and drink to me.
By His Own Right Hand directed
I am safe where ere I go,—
By His panoply protected
I need never fear a foe.

God, My Father, is My Tower,
And what more can I desire
In temptation's trying hour,—
In the flood, and in the fire?
By His Providence protected
I am safe in time of need:
But, if by My God rejected,
I am destitute indeed.

*The Hymns of Ann Griffiths*. Translated by George R. G. Pughe. Geo. H. Durham, Exchange Works, Blackburn, 1900. pp. 12-13

**WEEK FORTY THREE**　　　　　　*INSIGHT and ENCOURAGEMENT*　　　　　　**DAY 2**

School of Full Obedience
by Andrew Murray (1828-1917)

Exodus 19:4-6

Here are God's first words to the people; He speaks of redemption and its blessing, fellowship with Him: "You have seen how I brought you unto Myself." He speaks of holiness as His purpose in redemption: "You shall be unto me a holy nation." And as the link between the two He places obedience: "If you will indeed obey my voice, you shall be unto me a holy nation." God's will is the expression of His holiness; as we do His will, we come into contact with His holiness. The link between Redemption and Holiness is Obedience.

Obedience is the path to holiness, because it is the path to union with God's holy will. It is not itself holiness: but as the will opens itself to accept and to do the will of God, God communicates Himself and His holiness. To obey His voice is to follow Him as He leads in the way to the full revelation and communication of Himself and His blessed nature as the Holy One.

Obedience. Not knowledge of the will of God, not even approval, not even the will to do it, but the doing of it. Knowledge, and approval, and will must lead to action; the will of God must be done. Action alone proves whether the object of my interest has complete mastery over me. God wants his will done. This alone is obedience. In this alone it is seen whether the whole heart, has given itself over to the will of God; whether we live it, and are ready at any sacrifice to make it our own by doing it. God has no other way for making us holy.

To all seekers after holiness this is a lesson of deep importance. Obedience is not holiness; holiness is something far higher, something that comes from God to us, or rather, something of God coming into us. But obedience is *indispensable* to holiness: it cannot exist without it. While, therefore, your hearts seeks to follow the teaching of God's word, and looks in faith to what God has done, as he has made you *holy in Christ*, and to what God is still to do through the Spirit of Holiness as he fulfills the promise, "The very God of peace sanctify you wholly," never for one minute forget to be obedient. Begin by doing at once whatever appears right to do. Give up at once whatever conscience tells that you dare not say is according to the will of God. It is nothing less than the surrender to such a life of simple and entire obedience that is implied in becoming a Christian. The secret of gospel obedience is hearing the voice and following the lead of Jesus as a personal friend, the living Saviour. It is being led by the Spirit of God, having Him to reveal the Presence, and the Will, and the Love of the Father, that will work in us that personal revelation which the New Testament means when it speaks of doing everything unto the Lord, as pleasing God. (Emphasis his.)

Excerpted from *Holy in Christ*. Minneapolis: Bethan Fellowship, [original 1887]. p. 64-70.

**WEEK FORTY THREE**  **Confession about the Law**  **DAY 3**

From Psalm 119

Oh, how I love your law. I will meditate on it day and night. I will walk according to the law of the Lord and be blessed with those who are counted blameless. Open my eyes that I may see wonderful things in your law. Graciously teach me your law and help me understand it, and I will keep it and obey it forever. Even in the night, I will remember your name, that I may keep your law. When I am tied up in adversity and affliction, I will not forget your law. When the arrogant mock me unmercifully and set snares to trap me, I will not turn from your law. I will depend on your compassion for my very life. If your law had not been my delight, I would have perished in my affliction. You looked on my suffering and delivered me because I stayed faithful and did not forsake your law. Your law will be my delight, more precious to me than wealth or fame. Every day your law is broken by double-minded people who act like they believe and trust you but secretly devise wicked schemes because they are far from your law. My heart is broken when I see your law despised, rejected, and ignored. I detest the falsehood of the wicked and arrogant. I long for your salvation every day. Your law will be my delight all the days of my life.

**WEEK FORTY THREE**  *INSIGHT and ENCOURAGEMENT*  **DAY 4**

On Learning Obedience

by Andrew Murray (1828-1917)

Wholehearted obedience is not the end, but the beginning of our school life. The end is fitness for God's service, when obedience has placed us fully at God's disposal. A heart yielded to God in unreserved obedience is the one condition of progress in Christ's school of obedience, and of growth in the spiritual knowledge of God's will.

Young Christian, do get this matter settled it once. Remember God's rule: all for all. Give him all: He will give you all. Consecration avails nothing unless it means presenting yourself as a living sacrifice to do nothing but the will of God. The vow of entire obedience is the entrance fee for him who would be enrolled by no assistant teacher, but by Christ himself, in the school of obedience.

This unreserved surrender to obey, as it is the first condition of entering Christ's school, is the only fitness for receiving instruction as to the will of God for us. There is a general will of God for all his children, which we can, in some measure, learn out of the Bible. But there is a special individual application of these commands – God's will concerning each of us personally, which only the Holy Spirit can teach. And he will not teach it, except to those who have taken the vow of obedience.

This is the reason why there are so many unanswered prayers for God to make known His will. Jesus said, "If any man wills to do His will, he shall know of the teaching, whether it be of God." If a man's will is really set on doing God's will, that is, if his heart is given up to do, and he as a consequence does it as far as he knows it, he shall know what God has further to teach him.

It is simply what is true of every scholar at the art he studies, of every apprentice with his trade, of every man in business – doing is the one condition of truly knowing. And so obedience, the doing of God's will as far as we know, and the will and the vow to do it all as he reveals it, is the spiritual organ, the capacity for receiving the true knowledge of what is God's will for us.

Obedience to God's will shows itself in tender regard for the voice of conscience. Conscience is the guardian or monitor God has given you, to give warning when anything goes wrong. Up to the light you have, give heed to conscience. Ask God, by the teaching of his will, to give it more light. Seek the witness of conscience that you are acting up to the light. Conscience will become your encouragement and your helper, and give you the confidence, both that your obedience is accepted, and that your prayer for ever increasing knowledge of the will is heard.

Excerpted from, *The School of Obedience*. Chicago: Moody Press, no date. p. 96-101 (reprint from 1898).

**WEEK FORTY THREE**      Confession about Waiting      **DAY 5**

Read Isaiah 30

Lord, I will always seek to follow you and refuse to follow any plan that is not from you. I pledge the allegiance of my spirit to you alone. I accept and believe your Word that seeking refuge in the world only compounds sin and ends in shame and disgrace. I will always keep my ears open to hear the Lord's instruction. I cherish, respect, and honor the ministries of godly preachers and teachers who continue to confront me with the holiness of God. I hear, accept, and receive the message of truth. My goal and desire is for truth to have its full effect in my life, to expose and tear down every stronghold of sin and rebellion and resistance to your holy decrees in my heart and mind. I know that in repentance and rest, I will find salvation; in quietness and trust, I will find strength. I will wait for all of it. Sometimes it's hard to imagine that you would raise a finger to help someone like me, but your Word says, you long to be gracious to me, you rise to show your compassion. How great are you, Lord, that the just and righteous and holy God would care enough for me to rise to my aid? Blessed are those who wait for the Lord. I will wait for the Lord. When I cry for help, you answer. Adversity and affliction will be my teachers, and I will hear your voice behind me saying, "This is the way. Walk in it."

**WEEK FORTY THREE**      *INSIGHT and ENCOURAGEMENT*      **DAY 6**

Entrance to a Life of Full Obedience
by Andrew Murray (1828-1917)

*Christ spoke much of self-denial.* Self is the root of all lack of love and obedience. Our Lord called his disciple to deny himself and to take up his cross! to forsake all, two hate and to lose his own life, to humble himself and become a servant of all. He did so, because self, self-will, self-pleasing, self-seeking, is simply the source of all sin.

When we indulge the flesh in such a simple thing as eating and drinking; when we gratify self by seeking or accepting or rejoicing in what indulges our pride, when self-will is allowed to assert itself, and we make provision for the fulfillment of its desire, we are guilty of disobedience to His command. This gradually clouds the soul and makes the full enjoyment of His light and peace an impossibility.

*Christ claimed for God the love of the whole heart.* For Himself He equally claimed the sacrifice of all to come and follow Him. The Christian who has not definitely at heart made this his aim, who has not determined to seek for grace so to live, is guilty of disobedience. There may be much in his religion that appears good and earnest, but he cannot possibly have the joyful consciousness of knowing that he is doing the will of his Lord, and keeping His commandments.

When the call is heard to come and now begin anew a true life of obedience, there are many who feel the desire to do so, and tried quietly to slip into it. They think that by more prayer and Bible study they will grow into it – it will gradually come. They are greatly mistaken. The word God uses in Jeremiah might teach them their mistake: "Turn, ye backsliding children, turn to me" (Jer. 3:22).

A soul that is in full earnest and has taken the vow of full obedience may grow out of a feeble obedience into a fuller one. But there is no growing out of disobedience into obedience. A turning back, a turning away, a decision, a crisis, is needed. And that only comes by the very definite insight into what has been wrong, and its confession with shame and penitence. Then alone will the soul seek for that divine and mighty cleansing from all its filthiness which prepares for the consciousness of the gift of the new heart, and God's Spirit in it causing us to walk in His statutes.

If you would hope to lead a different life, to become a man or woman of Christlike obedience unto death, do begin by beseeching God for the Holy Spirit of conviction, to show you all your disobedience and to lead you in humble confession to the cleansing God has provided. Rest not until you have received it. (Emphasis his)

*The School of Obedience.* Chicago: Moody Press, no date. p. 72-74 (reprint from 1898).

**WEEK FORTY THREE**          *HYMNS and POEMS*          **DAY 7**

The Praises To Be Said at All the Hours
by St. Francis of Assisi (c. 1182 – 1226)

Holy, holy, holy Lord God Almighty,
Who is, and Who was, and Who is to come
*And let us praise and glorify Him forever.*

## VICTORY THROUGH SURRENDER

O Lord our God, You are worthy to receive
praise, glory and honour and blessing.
> *And let us praise and glorify Him forever.*

The Lamb Who was slain is worthy to receive
power and divinity, wisdom and strength, honour and glory and blessing.
> *And let us praise and glorify Him forever.*

Let us bless the Father and the Son with the Holy Spirit:
> *And let us praise and glorify Him forever.*

Bless the Lord, all you works of the Lord.
> *And let us praise and glorify Him forever.*

Sing praise to our God, all you His servants
and you who fear God, the small and the great.
> *And let us praise and glorify Him forever.*

Let heaven and earth praise Him Who is glorious.
> *And let us praise and glorify Him forever.*

Every creature in heaven, on earth and under the earth;
and in the sea and those which are in it.
> *And let us praise and glorify Him forever.*

Glory to the Father and to the Son and to the Holy Spirit.
> *And let us praise and glorify Him forever.*

As it was in the beginning, is now, and will be forever.
> *And let us praise and glorify Him forever.*

All-powerful, most holy, most high, supreme God:
all good, supreme good, totally good,
You Who alone are good,
may we give You all praise, all glory, all thanks,
all honour, all blessing, and all good. So be it! So be it!
Amen.

The Prayers of St. Francis of Assisi. https://ofm.org/wp-content/uploads/2017/01/Prayers.pdf p. 9-10.

**Record your insights, revelations, and meditations from this week. DATE:**

VICTORY THROUGH SURRENDER

**WEEK FORTY FOUR**      *HYMNS and POEMS*      **DAY 1**

Thou Art All My Life, Lord

by Witness Lee (1905-1997)

Thou art all my life, Lord,
In me Thou dost live;
With Thee all God's fulness
Thou to me dost give.
By Thy holy nature
I am sanctified,
By Thy resurrection
Vict'ry is supplied.

Now Thy flowing life, Lord,
Doth enlighten me,
Bringing in the spirit
Fellowship with Thee;
All my need supplying,
Making Thy demand,
Leading me to cleansing
And in Thee to stand.

Thy anointing Spirit
Me shall permeate,
All my soul and spirit
Thou wouldst saturate;
Every part transforming
Till conformed to Thee,
Till Thy life shall bring me
To maturity.

Lord, Thy life abundant,
Flowing, rich and free,
Constantly refreshes
And empowers me
Death by life is swallowed,
Weakness is made strong,
All my bonds are broken,
Gloom is turned to song.

I would give myself, Lord,
Fully unto Thee,
That Thy heart's desire
Be fulfilled in me.
I no more would struggle
To myself reform,
Thus in me to hinder
What Thou wouldst perform.

I would cease completely
From my efforts vain,
Let Thy life transform me,
Full release to gain;
Build me up with others
Till in us Thou see
Thy complete expression
Glorifying Thee.

http://www.witness-lee-hymns.org/hymns/H0841.html


**WEEK FORTY FOUR**      *INSIGHT and ENCOURAGEMENT*      **DAY 2**

Faith is the Victory

by J. Edwin Orr (1912-1987)

In the opening verses of the twelfth chapter [of Romans], he takes up again the main argument of his brief, and, indeed, comes to the climax. It is truly significant that the Apostle uses the inclusive pronoun "we" in his first argument concerning sin, his second concerning justification, his third concerning carnality, but switches to the pronoun "I" and "you" in the exhortation:

"I appeal to you therefore, brethren, by the mercies of God, to present your bodies as a living sacrifice, holy and acceptable to God, which is your spiritual worship. Do not be conformed to this world but be transformed by the renewal of your mind, that you may prove what is the will of God, what is good and acceptable and perfect" (Romans 12:1-2).

The only possible conclusion is that the Apostle Paul had already presented his whole personality to God, but implied that the Roman Christians had not so surrendered.

However, the common interpretation of Romans 12:1 seems to make of the infinitive "to present" a sort of daily consecration of one's life to God, whereas the Greek text makes clear that the action suggested in that case is instantaneous or punctiliar or eventual. In other words, the verb "to present" in this case means to make a clean sweep or full surrender, and the continuing consecration is indicated in the verb "transformed" in the second verse.

The appeal, therefore, in the opening verse of Romans 12 is for a full surrender, the surrender of the intellect, will and emotions to God at a given moment rather than gradually, though the second verse urges the continual yielding of the personality day by day. The degree of yieldedness is governed by the degree of light, and the believer is expected to surrender his life to God only as he has light on the subject. Further light means further surrender, but a believer cannot surrender more than his all at any given time, therefore the first experience of full surrender is unique, often renewed but never again the same.

It may be argued, against the crisis significance of Romans 12:1, that the believer's life is full of crises. That is undeniable. But there must occur in the life of a believer a first time when, according to his light, he yields his life completely to God and finds himself proving what it is to know and follow the "good and acceptable and perfect will of God".

Full surrender, the higher Christian experience, may be nullified by sin or disobedience. It is a crisis with a view to a process, and the moment the believer resists the work of the Spirit in lifting him to still higher ground, he is in need of renewal of surrender, whether it be intellectual, volitional, or emotional in nature. However, the appeal of Romans 12:1 is for the initial yielding, and there is a truth hidden in the general outline of the Epistle concerning the method. An unbeliever proceeds from the lower level of sin to the level of Justification by faith and not by works: a believer proceeds from the lower level of Carnality to the level of Spirituality by faith. Faith is the Victory.

*Full Surrender*. London: Marshall, Morgan & Scott, 1951. p. 46-47.

## MONTH ELEVEN

*Journal entry from Latvia, June 28, 2018*

Each American counselor at the Latvian summer camp leads a small group that meets every morning and afternoon. This morning, Elizabeth, Linda, and I gave our testimonies in my small group then I asked for the group to give their responses to the question, "What do you want God to do for you?" There were four public and four private responses. I asked the Holy Spirit to give me a prayer and a strategy to impart blessing to each of them in the afternoon session.

We held the afternoon session outside. I asked Linda to bring the guitar, and we worshipped for a few minutes. After she sang a song, I explained that even if we don't know the words or the tune, we can still give attention to the Lord and speak our love and praise to him. It's not about sitting and listening to the music. I encouraged them to try, and we sang again. I am not sure what happened with them, but the Lord showed up for me. I wept into worship before him and saw a picture of him, in my spirit, standing in front of me. I hope to discover that some of them had a similar experience.

Elizabeth asked how to tell the difference between our voice or thoughts and the voice of God. I meditated on that for a while, and God gave me this: Practice – Differentiate - Follow through (PDF). Then I talked about the requests, how they were very similar, and they are all answered by Isaiah 11. We walked through that briefly, and then I asked Linda to play the guitar as I went to each one individually and prayed for them. I felt the Spirit welling up, and I was able to pray and prophecy over each one of them. Sanija was last. As I stood up, I saw her weeping to the Lord. I had encouraged her not to worry and to wait for the Lord to answer. It was a sweet time in the Lord. After they left, I sat down on the bench and saw, in my spirit, the Lord sit down on the bench beside me and put His arm around me. I don't think I have ever felt the comfort and the pleasure of the Lord like that before. I was spent. The prayer time took everything out of me. He let me impart something to those kids, by the laying on of hands and prayer, that He can take and bless. Then He filled my emptiness with himself.

Afterward, as I was walking down the hall of our dorm, I saw Elizabeth playing the guitar and singing to an open window. When she turned, the glory of God was on her face, although I did not know that's what it was at the time. She just smiled and stared at me. I whispered, "God is good," and she said, "God is very good." I replied, "Stay in that place." I did not realize until I got outside that I had seen the glory of the Lord on her face. I have been praying to see the glory all these years but had never really known what I was looking for. I didn't realize the glory of the Lord is seen in the faces of transformed people. Just like when Moses was in God's presence and came down and his face shown. It was in Elizabeth's face and in Sanija's face earlier.

The last group time was good. Elizabeth brought snacks, and I gave out the gifts I brought from home. Goodbyes were sweet, especially with Elze. She had not smiled all week. After service that night, I went to the impromptu student-led worship in the school hallway. Elze was singing and swaying and smiling the whole time. The glory of God found her face.

| WEEK FORTY FOUR | Confession about Divine Protection | DAY 3 |

Read Psalm 91

I will live in the secret shelter of the Most High God, a place built with the spiritual stones of divine truth, so close to you that your presence overshadows it completely. There I will find your shalom rest. You are my strong and secure refuge. I can and will put my trust in you alone. You will rescue me when I am trapped by the enemy's snare and protect me and my house from the deadly pestilence. You shelter me like the outstretched wings of an eagle cover her young. Your faithful promises are a shield of protection for me. I do not have to be afraid of the fears that attack my heart by night or angry words that attack my mind by day or invisible diseases that attack my body, or unforeseen circumstances that attack my possessions and resources. Those things may touch others around me, but I will only witness how those who do not trust you suffer. Because I make you my refuge and shelter, no evil can conquer me, and no plague can invade my home. You have dispatched your angels to protect me. They are holding me up and keep me from even tripping over a stone. I will trample and crush underfoot every spiritual enemy that seeks to deceive and destroy me. You will rescue me because I love you. You will protect me because I trust in you. You will answer me when I call and will not be silent. When I am in trouble, you will be there to deliver me in recognition of my faithfulness. My satisfying reward will be long life and the gift of salvation.

| WEEK FORTY FOUR | *INSIGHT and ENCOURAGEMENT* | DAY 4 |

The Holy Spirit and the Believer

by J. Edwin Orr (1912-1987)

The teaching of the letter to the Romans makes clear that each true Christian is assured by the Holy Spirit. The Spirit Himself bears witness with our spirit that we are the children of God (Romans 8:16). Each true Christian is sealed by the Holy Spirit (Ephesians 4:30). The Greek word for seal is commonly used as a legal mark of ownership or closure to prevent tampering. Each true Christian is guaranteed by the Holy Spirit (2 Corinthians 1:22; 5:5, Ephesians 1:14). The Greek word for guarantee has the same significance as the modern business term down-payment. Each true Christian has been baptized by the Holy Spirit in the body of Christ. (1 Corinthians 12:13). But there has been great confusion in the minds of Christians regarding this baptism by the Holy Spirit into the body of Christ and the enduement of power or filling of the Holy Spirit.

It is clear that the reference in 1 Corinthians refers to the experience of the believer at regeneration which I call baptism *by* the Spirit. The prediction of John the Baptist that the one coming after him will baptize with the Holy Spirit and fire has a somewhat different emphasis and expression. In water baptism, the agent is the minister, the subject is the believer, and the element is water. In the baptism into the body of Christ, of which water baptism is a symbol, the agent is the Spirit, the subject is the believer, and the element is Christ. In the enduement of power, the agent is Christ, the subject is the believer, and the element the Spirit, reversing the order of baptism. I refer to this as baptism *with* the Spirit.

It is significant to note that nowhere in the Acts or Epistles is the phrase baptized with the Spirit used to describe the experience of an individual Christian. The word used in all post-Pentecostal cases is the word *filled* or *full*. Hence, the better term to use to describe the enduement of power is the term filling rather than baptism. Every true Christian is regenerated, indwelt, assured, sealed, guaranteed, and baptized by the Spirit automatically when they are born again. To be endued with power, baptized with the Spirit or filled with the Spirit requires an experience of full surrender.

Adapted from *Full Surrender*. London: Marshall, Morgan & Scott, 1951. p. 110-113.

**WEEK FORTY FOUR**  *INSIGHT and ENCOURAGEMENT*  **DAY 5**

A Mighty Infilling

by A. W. Tozer (1897-1963)

Although it happened unintentionally, the Scriptures have become, for some, a substitute for God. The Bible has become a barrier between them and God. "We have our Bible," they say with a certain amount of pride, "and we need nothing more." Examine their lives, and you may discover that the Bible has not really made an impact on their lifestyles. Remember, it is one thing to believe the Bible but something else altogether to allow the Bible, through the ministry of the Holy Spirit, to impact and change your life.

One problem some have is to believe that if they read it in the Bible, they have already experienced it. It is one thing to read about the new birth in the Bible and quite another thing to be born from above by the Spirit of the living God. It is one thing to read about being filled with the Holy Spirit and quite another thing to experience the mighty infilling of the Holy Spirit that radically changes our life to a life of adoring wonder and amazement at the things of God. Reading and experiencing are two quite different things.

Apart from the Holy Spirit breathing upon it, the Bible can be a useless thing, just another book of literature. It may be fine literature, but there is something infinitely more valuable than the Bible.

We might remember singing a little Sunday School chorus that says, "Every promise in the Book is mine." But we neglect to realize that it is one thing to believe a promise and quite another thing to appropriate it into our lives. It is like a man stumbling in the darkness of the night, not able to see his hand in front of his face. His companion asks, "How can you see in this darkness?"

"It's all right," the man might say, "I have a flashlight in my pocket." Simply having a flashlight in your pocket does not light your way until you pull it out and turn it on. Simply believing the Bible does no good until we pull those promises of God out of the Bible and by faith appropriate them into our lives.

One little saying that goes around in evangelical circles is, "God said it, I believe it, that settles it." The problem with that is that if you do not believe something to the extent that you appropriate it in your life, do you really believe?  The Bible exhorts us to "walk in the light." But the light has no value whatsoever unless we are walking in it.

*The Crucified Life: How to Live Out a Deeper Christian Experience.*  Minneapolis: Bethany House, 2017. p. 50-51.


**WEEK FORTY FOUR**  *HYMNS and POEMS*  **DAY 6**

Lord, Take the First Place in My Heart
by Barney E. Warren (1867-1951)

I yield to Thee, Savior, forsaking my all,
From sinful things now I will part;
To Thee I surrender, for mercy I call,
Come, take the first place in my heart.

*Refrain:*
*Oh, take the first place in my heart,*
*Oh, take the first place in my heart;*
*I open the door, come in, I implore;*
*Lord, take the first place in my heart.*

Oh, come, gentle Spirit, don't leave me, I pray,
From Thee I will never depart;
I come to Thee now, for I cannot delay,
Lord, take the first place in my heart.

I cannot be lost, Lord, for Thee I will live,
Forgiveness, O Savior, impart;
If I will confess, Thou wilt freely forgive,
And take the first place in my heart.

The joybells of heaven will ring in my soul,
My Savior, Redeemer, Thou art;
To Thee I surrender, wilt Thou make me whole?
Take now the first place in my heart.

https://library.timelesstruths.org/music/Lord_Take_the_First_Place/

VICTORY THROUGH SURRENDER

**WEEK FORTY FOUR**  *HYMNS and POEMS*  **DAY 7**

Oh, How the Thought of God Attracts
by Frederick William Faber (1814-1863)

Oh, how the thought of God attracts
  And draws the heart from earth,
And sickens it of passing shows
  And dissipating mirth! *

'Tis not enough to save our souls,
  To shun th' eternal fires;
The thought of God will rouse the heart
  To more sublime desires.*

God only is the creature's home,
  Though rough and straight the road;
Yet nothing less can satisfy
  The love that longs for God. *

Oh, utter but the Name of God
  Down in your heart of hearts,
And see how from the world at once
  All tempting light departs. *

A trusting heart, a yearning eye,
  Can win their way above;
If mountains can be moved by faith,
  Is there less power in love? *

How little of that road, my soul!
  How little hast thou gone!
Take heart, and let the thought of God
  Allure thee further on. *

The freedom from all willful sin,
  The Christian's daily task;
Oh! these are graces far below
  What longing love would ask! *

Dole not thy duties out to God,
  But let thy hand be free;
Look long at Jesus, - His sweet love
  How was it dealt to thee? **

The perfect way is hard to flesh;
  It is not hard to love;
If thou wert sick for want of God,
  How swiftly wouldst thou move! *

And only this perfection needs
  A heart kept calm all day,
To catch the words the spirit there
  From hour to hour may say. **

Then keep thy conscience sensitive
  No inward token miss,
And go where grace entices thee,-
  Perfection lies in this. *

Be docile to thine unseen Guide
  Love him as he loves thee,
Time and obedience are enough,
  And thou a saint shall be. **

* From https://www.hymnal.net/en/hymn/h/606.  ** Additional verses quoted by Hannah Whitall Smith in *The Christian's Secret of a Happy Life*. Revell, 1952. p. 104.

This poem is listed as "The Way of Perfection" in Tozer, A. W. *The Christian Book of Mystical Verse: A Collection of Poems, Hymns, and Prayers for Devotional Reading*. Chicago: Moody Publishers, 2016. p. 93-94.

**Record your insights, revelations, and meditations from this week. DATE:**

VICTORY THROUGH SURRENDER

**WEEK FORTY FIVE**  *HYMNS and POEMS*  **DAY 1**

A Good Confession
by Frederick William Faber (1814-1863)

The chains that have bound me are flung to the wind,
By the mercy of God the poor slave is set free;
And the strong grace of heaven breathes fresh o'er the mind,
Like the bright winds of summer that gladden the sea.

There was nought in God's world half so dark or so vile
As the sin and the bondage that fettered my soul;
There was nought half so base as the malice and guile
Of my own sordid passions, o' Satan's control.

For years I have borne about hell in my breast;
When I thought of my God it was nothing but gloom;
Day brought me no pleasure, night gave me no rest,
There was still the grim shadow of horrible doom.

But the word had gone forth, and said, Let there be light,
And it flashed through my soul like a sharp passing smart;
One look to my Saviour, and all the dark night,
Like a dream scarce remembered, was gone from my heart.

I cried out for mercy, and fell on my knees,
And confessed, while my heart with keen sorrow was wrung;
'Twas the labor of minutes, and years of disease
Fell as fast from my soul as the words from my tongue.

And now, blest be God and the sweet Lord who died!
No deer on the mountain, no bird in the sky
No bright wave that leaps on the dark bounding tide,
Is a creature so free or so happy as I.

All hail, then, all hail, to the dear Precious Blood,
That hath worked these sweet wonders of mercy in me;
May each day countless numbers throng down to its flood,
And God have His glory, and sinners go free.

Adapted from Tozer, A. W. *The Christian Book of Mystical Verse: A Collection of Poems, Hymns, and Prayers for Devotional Reading.* Chicago: Moody Publishers, 2016. p. 79.

**WEEK FORTY FIVE**  *INSIGHT and ENCOURAGEMENT*  **DAY 2**

A Heart Open to God
by John Henry, Cardinal Newman (1801-1890)

Do you habitually thus unlock your hearts and subject your thoughts to almighty God? Are you living in this conviction of His presence? And have you this special witness that that Presence is really set up within you unto your salvation, namely, that you live in the sense of it? Do you believe, and act on the belief, that his light penetrates and shines through your heart, as the sun's beams through a room? You know how things look when the sun's beams are on it – the very air then appears full of impurities which, before it came out, were not seen. So it is with our souls.

We are full of stains and corruptions, we see them not, but they are like the air before the sun shines; but though we see them not, God sees them: he pervades us as the sunbeam. Our souls, in his view, are full of things which offend, things which must be repented of, forgiven, and put away. He, in the words of the Psalmist, "has set our misdeeds before Him, our secrets sins in the light of his countenance." This is most true, though it be not at all welcome doctrine to many.

We cannot hide ourselves from Him; and our wisdom, as our duty, lies in embracing this truth, acquiescing in it, and acting upon it. Let us then beg Him to teach us the Mystery of His Presence in us, that, by acknowledging it, we may thereby possess it fruitfully.

Let us confess it in faith, that we may possess it unto justification. Let us so own it as to set Him before us in everything. "I have set God always before me," says the Psalmist, "for He is on my right hand, therefore I shall not fall." Let us in all circumstances thus regard Him. Whether we have sinned, let us not dare keep from Him, but, with the prodigal son, rise up and go to Him. Or, if we are conscious of nothing, still let us not boast in ourselves or justify ourselves, but feel that "He who judgeth us is the Lord." Let us have no secret apart from him.

Baillie, John. *A Diary of Readings.* New York: Macmillan Publishing Co., 1955. p. 111.

**WEEK FORTY FIVE**  *INSIGHT and ENCOURAGEMENT*  **DAY 3**

The Prayer of Fénelon (in modern English)
by François Fénelon (1651-1715)

My God, men do not know You. They do not discern who You are and what You are! The light shines in darkness and the darkness does not comprehend it. By You we exist, we think, we taste pleasures, then forget Him who caused all this. We see nothing except by You, the universal light, the Sun of souls, who shines more clearly than our material sun, and seeing nothing but by You we yet do not behold You. You alone impart everything; to the stars their splendor, to the fountains their streams and currents, to the earth plants, to fruits their flavors, to flowers their beauty and perfumes, to all nature its riches, to man health, reason, virtues, graces; You give, do, rule all. I see You, Lord, only. All else disappears as a shadow to the eyes of him who beholds You; but the world discerns You not. Alas, he who does not discover You, has seen nothing: he has spent his life in the illusions of a dream! As for me, oh my God, I have found You everywhere; even within myself. It is You who causes whenever I do that is good. A thousand times I have felt that I could not subdue my wrong tempers or destroy my habits, that I could not subdue my pride, nor follow my reason, nor continue to will the good I have once willed. It is You who gives a right will, and who maintains it uncorrupted. Without you I am but a reed shaken by the wind. I leave myself, O God, in your hands: mold and remold this clay; give it right form, then break it, if that is Your will: it is Yours; it is sufficient that Your counsel be fulfilled, and that nothing opposes Your good pleasure, for which I was created.

Shepperd, John (1785-1879). *Chosen Words from Christian Writers*. London: Hodder & Stoughton, 1869. p. 296-297.

**WEEK FORTY FIVE**　　　　　　*INSIGHT and ENCOURAGEMENT*　　　　　　**DAY 4**

　　　　　　　　The Shadow of a Mighty Rock
　　　　　　　　　　　　by Charles L. Culpepper, Sr. (1895-1986)

In the days that followed Ola's healing, the tension in the interior began to subside, and we prepared to return to our mission station. After returning home, the question that Miss Monsen had asked me, "Have you been filled with the Holy Spirit?" continued to disturb me. That day in her apartment, I had not known the answer. Now, alone at home, I decided I must search the Scriptures to see what the Bible teaches about the fullness of the Holy Spirit. Thus I began a great spiritual quest that was to last four years.

The hunger to know more about the deeper spiritual life was common among the missionaries in China. It influenced every moment of every day and led us through a spiritual wilderness of internal turmoil and crisis. The local wars, the Communist-inspired unrest, bandit raids, and other incidents showed us how little progress had actually been made in evangelizing China by Sun Yat-sen or by missionaries.

We realized the foundations needed to be re-examined, and in the days following the 1927 crisis, we did so. First, we probed deeply into our own spiritual lives. Then we looked with disillusionment upon the Chinese churches. We discussed our concern in detail when the North China Mission (an organization of Southern Baptist missionaries) met in Chefoo in 1930. Three Chinese evangelists made discouraging reports of work among "dead" churches. A note of despair and spiritual hunger permeated their messages.

A missionary reminded the group that in the North China Association, at least seventy churches had "died." Another missionary related her fears for the Chinese Christians. Many, she felt, had accepted God's grace as an outside coating of whitewash but had only "covered" their sins, not been forgiven for them.

Our best-known Chinese evangelist, at the point of despair because of the seeming hopelessness of the work, echoed these fears. He told the group he felt more than 1,000 church members had been converted to Christianity, not to Christ. If foreign missions had been merely a human project, the end of the North China Mission would have been in sight that day. But we realized that God had sent Marie Monsen to point us toward the right way.

She had spent her first missionary years mainly as a Bible teacher to church members. But after 14 years, she became convinced that most church members had never experienced the second birth. She also recognized her own shallowness and longed for the spiritual power necessary to witness effectively. Focusing her hope on Galatians 3:14, she prayed all day and far into the night for the promised Holy Spirit. Each time she prayed, she felt the power of Satan mocking her request, telling her she was not worthy of such a blessing. Finally, near midnight, her eyes fell on verse 13, "Christ hath redeemed us from the curse of the law, being made a curse for us."

As she read that reassurance, she opened her heart to God, and the Holy Spirit flooded her soul! Overcome with joy, she began singing and praising God, continuing until she had exhausted her voice. Then she went to a small organ and played hymns for the rest of the night.

Strengthened by this experience, Miss Monsen rooted her life in the center of God's will and battled the drift toward spiritual shallowness. With Miss Monsen's encouraging example, other men and women began to find strength. It became apparent that God had raised her up to expose the spiritual apathy and weakness that existed among the Christians of North China.

Spiritual power continued to deepen. Many of the Southern Baptist missionaries attended the Peh Ta Ho Conferences and heard Dr. Jonathan Goforth, esteemed missionary in China, and others speak on the subject of prayer and the deeper spiritual life. After this, missionaries toured China leading conferences and trying to stoke spiritual fires. Seeking and finding deeper personal commitment to Christ, they then challenged the churches with a series of messages entitled, "Christ Is My Life," based on Colossians 3:3,4. It was more and more evident that many of the people had become dissatisfied with the spiritual coldness and the apathy of the churches and the mission.

Everywhere they went they encouraged their co-workers to engage in soul-searching prayer. In the fall of 1931, a missionary began teaching the Book of Acts to a high school class. The emphasis, dealing with the person and power of the Holy Spirit in soul winning, made her acutely conscious of her own lack of power. She sought and found God's strength. When news reached the other missionaries that one of their co-workers had received the fullness of the Holy Spirit, they too became eager for the new experience. The drought was broken, and God's Spirit poured out just as He had promised. By June 1932, 24 missionaries and many Chinese Christian leaders had experienced the personal presence of the Holy Spirit and rejoiced in the new life they saw developing in the once spiritually dead churches.

*The Shantung Revival.* https://www.gospeltruth.net/shantung.htm. 1968. Chapter One.
(Based on the book of the same name by Mary K. Crawford in 1933.)

# VICTORY THROUGH SURRENDER

**WEEK FORTY FIVE** — *INSIGHT and ENCOURAGEMENT* — **DAY 5**

Surrendering Self

by Andrew Murray (1828-1917)

The death of Christ on the cross is the highest and the holiest that can be known of Him even in the glory of heaven. And the highest and the holiest that the Holy Spirit can work in us is to take us up and to keep us in the fellowship of the cross of Christ. We need to enter deeply into the truth that Christ the beloved Son of the Father could not return to the glory of heaven until He had first given Himself over unto death. As this great truth opens up to us, it will help us to understand how in our life, and in our fellowship with Christ, it is impossible for us to share His life until we have first surrendered ourselves every day to die to sin and to abide in the unbroken fellowship with our crucified Lord.

Christ had for the first time definitely announced that he would have to suffer much and would be killed and raised again. "Peter rebuked him saying, 'Be it far from Thee, Lord: this shall never be unto Thee.'" Christ's answer was, "Get thee behind Me, Satan." The spirit of Peter, seeking to turn Him away from the cross and its suffering, was nothing but Satan tempting Him to turn aside from what God had appointed as our way of salvation.

Christ then adds the words of our text, in which He uses for the second time the words "take up the cross." Along with them He uses a significant expression revealing what is implied in the cross: "If any man come after Me, let him deny himself, and take up his cross." When Adam sinned, he fell out of the life of Heaven and of God into the life of the world and of self. When Jesus Christ came to restore man to his original place, "being in the form of God, He emptied himself, taking the form of a servant, and humbling Himself even to the death of the cross." What He has done Himself He asks of all who desire to follow Him: "If any man will come after me, let him deny himself."

Peter denied his Lord: "I know not the Man." When a man learns to obey Christ's commands, he says of himself: "I know not the man." It is the secret of true discipleship, to bear the cross, to acknowledge the death sentence that has been passed on self, and to deny any right that self has to rule over us. The surrender to Christ is to be so entire, to live for those around us so complete, that self is never allowed to come down from the cross to which it has been crucified, but is ever kept in the place of death.

Let us listen to the voice of Jesus: "Deny self;" and ask that by the grace of the Holy Spirit we may ever live as those in whom self has been crucified with Christ, and in whom the crucified Christ in our lives is Lord and Master.

Excerpted from *Growing in Christ*. Westchester, IL: Good News Publishers, 1979. p. 24-27.

**WEEK FORTY FIVE**  *HYMNS and POEMS*  **DAY 6**

Thou Art All My Life, Lord

by Alfred C. Snead (1884-1961)

Fully surrendered—Lord, I would be,
Fully surrendered, dear Lord, to Thee.
All on the altar laid,
Surrender fully made,
Thou hast my ransom paid;
I yield to Thee

Fully surrendered—life, time, and all,
All Thou hast given me held at Thy call.
Speak but the word to me,
Gladly I'll follow Thee,
Now and eternally
Obey my Lord.

Fully surrendered—silver and gold,
His, who hath given me riches untold.
All, all belong to Thee,
For Thou didst purchase me,
Thine evermore to be,
Jesus, my Lord.

Fully surrendered—Lord, I am Thine;
Fully surrendered, Savior divine!
Live Thou Thy life in me;
All fullness dwells in Thee;
Not I, but Christ in me,
Christ all in all.

https://www.hymnal.net/en/hymn/h/442

**WEEK FORTY FIVE**  **Confession about the Promises of God**  **DAY 7**

Read Psalm 119:49-56

I know that you have made a promise to me, and I put my hope in the assurance that you will remember what you have promised me. Especially during times of affliction, I take comfort in your life-giving promise. Even when I am insulted and ridiculed for trusting in you, I will not turn away from your Word. Your laws never change, and that, too, gives me comfort. Your Word sets the boundaries of safety and blessing for me. I am horrified at the wickedness of those around me who rebel against and reject your Word. In desolate places and on difficult journeys, I can still sing because of your steadfast Word. At night, I remember your name and obey your Word. During dark times, I will still remember your name and continue to keep your laws, for they are precious to me. I have learned that your Word can be trusted. I know that I have been blessed, I am blessed, and I will be blessed because I follow, am faithful to, and obey the laws and commandments in Your word.

**Record your insights, revelations, and meditations from this week. DATE:**

Tim Tremaine

**WEEK FORTY SIX**  *HYMNS and POEMS*  **DAY 1**

My Heart Longs for Absolute Surrender

by Anonymous

My heart longs for absolute surrender
That I'd wholly consecrated be,
Not in word alone but all my being
Would be fully given unto Thee.

There is little willingness within me
To place all I am before Thy feet,
So I lay my hands on Thy dear head, Lord
As the burnt off'ring, perfect, complete.

Lord, You are the only One who offered
Yourself without reluctance unto God;
Full obedience to the Father given,
Absolute, You sacrificed Your all.

As this One, You're dwelling in my spirit;
Moving, spreading outward day by day.
There's a whisper of Amen within me
In response to all that You would say.

I say Yes and give You full permission
To touch every corner of my heart;
Break through all the barriers in my being;
Do not let me withhold any part.

'Tis my joy to give You all the ground, Lord;
Make my heart a dwelling place for You;
I want You to be at home within me;
Come and settle down in every room.

Lord, do cleanse my heart from all self-seeking
That I'd truly want nothing but Thee;
Let my soul be occupied, possessed, Lord,
That You would be magnified in me.

https://www.hymnal.net/en/hymn/ns/366

**WEEK FORTY SIX**  *INSIGHT and ENCOURAGEMENT*  **DAY 2**

Seven Steps in The Consecrated Life

by James Smith (1802-1862)

Mark 1:9-15 This little portion is one of those garden plots so common in Mark's gospel, and fragrant with many a precious flower. Let us follow the footsteps of the Master. He was –

I. **Decided**. "In those days Jesus came and was baptized of John" (v.9). What did this step involve for him? It was the most decisive and important step in the life of our Lord. It implied the forsaking of all the earthly ties of human relationship, the perfect surrender of Himself to the will of His Father as His Son, the public declaration of His character as a teacher come from God, and as the Lamb that taketh away the sin of the world. From Nazareth to Jordan was a solemn journey for Jesus. Have we yielded ourselves unto God that His will may be done in us?

II. **Accepted**. "And straightway He saw the heavens opened" (v.10). He offered Himself, and was immediately accepted of the Father, through the opened heavens. As sinners, we yield ourselves to be saved; as sons, we yield ourselves to Him for service. Don't say your life is not worth offering when it has been redeemed by the precious blood of God's Son. If you wish the heavens to open above you, present yourselves unto God.

III. **Anointed**. "The Spirit, like a dove, descended upon Him" (v.10). The holy anointing for service is sure to come when the life has been wholly devoted to God. All Christ's words and works were spoken and wrought in the power of the Spirit. This same baptism every serving son of God needs and may have (Acts 1:8; 19:2).

IV. **Assured**. "There came a voice from heaven, saying, Thou art my beloved son, in whom I am well pleased" (v.11). Like Enoch, He walked with God, and also had this testimony that He *pleased* God. This is another blessing that belongs to the path of the consecrated. The anointing of the Holy Ghost always brings with it the sweetest assurance in the soul that the life is accepted and sanctified, and pleasing to Him. Without *faith* this is impossible.

V. **Impelled**. "Immediately the Spirit driveth into the wilderness" (v.12). This word "*driveth*" is very strong, it is the same word used in John 2:15, "He drove them all out of the temple." The leading of the Spirit in the consecrated life is an inscrutable but mighty controlling impulse.

VI. **Tested**. "He was in the wilderness tempted of Satan" (v.13). It was not till Christ was anointed with the Holy Spirit that the tempter came. This is most suggestive to us. The kingdom of Satan is not in much danger by us until we are baptized with the Spirit of Power. But "greater is he that is in us than all that can be against us" (1 John 4:4).

VII. **Testified**. "Jesus came preaching the Gospel of the Kingdom of God" (v.14). Luke tells us, "He *returned* in the power of the Spirit." He came from the conflict a victor, through the anointing of the Holy Ghost, preaching the gospel of the Kingdom. If the power of the Holy Ghost has come upon us, it is that we might be witnesses unto Him. Go and preach the gospel.

Excerpted from *Handfuls on Purpose II*. London: Pickering & Inglis, 1923. p. 131-133.

Tim Tremaine

**WEEK FORTY SIX**  *INSIGHT and ENCOURAGEMENT*  **DAY 3**

The New Man

by Johann Arndt (1555-1621)

Oh! how blessed is the man in whom Christ does all and is all; whose will, thoughts, mind, and words, are the will, thoughts, mind, and words of Christ! It was thus the apostle who said, "We have the mind of Christ" (1 Cor. 2:16). And so indeed it must be with the believer; because the life of Christ is the new life, yea, the new man in him; and whoever lives in Christ after the Spirit, hath really put on the new man, and all the graces with which he is adorned. His meekness and obedience are the meekness and obedience of Christ; his patience and humility are the patience and humility of Christ; and his life itself is the life of Christ, by whom and in whom he lives. This is the "new creature" which is created after God (2 Cor. 5:17); and that life of Christ in us, of which St. Paul experimentally says, "I live, yet not I, but Christ liveth in me" (Gal. 2:20). This is to follow Christ truly. This is to walk in the light of his life, and to bring forth "fruits meet for repentance;" for, by this means, the "old man" is destroyed, the carnal life gradually declines, and the new and divine life is established in the soul. He who has this life is not a *nominal*, but a *real* Christian; not in word and in appearance only, but in deed and in truth. He is a true child of God, begotten of Him, and quickened and renewed by faith after the image of Jesus Christ.

Although we cannot attain to a state of perfection, while encompassed with so many infirmities that obstruct our progress in the divine life, we ought not, therefore, to be discouraged, but rather to be inspired with more fervor in seeking after a consummation so much to be desired. We ought ardently to wish and pray, to endeavor and study, that the kingdom of Christ be established within us, and the kingdom of Satan destroyed (1 John 3:9; Eph. 2:5). The object of our cares and efforts, of our groans and prayers, should be—how we may more and more mortify the old man by daily repentance. For, the more a man dies to himself, the more Christ lives in him; the more corruptions are removed by the good Spirit of God, the more divine grace possesses the heart.

In proportion as the flesh is crucified, the spirit is quickened; as the works of darkness are put off, the armor of light from above is put on; and in the same degree as the *outward* man perisheth, the *inward* man is strengthened and renewed (2 Cor. 4:16; Col. 3:5). The decrease of the carnal life is the increase of that which is spiritual and divine. As the affections of the former, self-love, ambition, wrath, covetousness, and voluptuousness, are weakened and subdued, so are opposite affections of the spiritual life invigorated and raised. The farther a man departs from the world, from "the lust of the flesh, the lust of the eyes, and the pride of life" (1 John 2:16); the more do God, Christ, and the Holy Spirit enter into the heart and dwell there. And, on the other hand, the more nature, flesh, darkness, and the world, reign in man; the less of grace, light, the Holy Spirit, God, and Christ, is there to be found in him.

*True Christianity.* Philadelphia: Smith, English, & Co., (unk). p. 141-143.

VICTORY THROUGH SURRENDER

**WEEK FORTY SIX**     *INSIGHT and ENCOURAGEMENT*     **DAY 4**

A Word to Shepherds from 1 Thessalonians (part 1)

**The Approved Shepherd**
"but just as we have been approved by God to be entrusted with the gospel, so we speak." 2:4

*Motive:*
*Don't please men* - Not to please man, but to please God who tests our hearts. 2:4
*Don't use flattery* - For we never came with words of flattery, as you know, nor with a pretext for greed - God is witness. 2:5
*Don't seek praise* - Nor did we seek glory from people, whether from you or others, though we could have made demands as apostles of Christ. 2:6

*Model:*
*Be gentle* - But we were gentle among you, like a nursing mother taking care of her children. 2:7
*Be generous* - So, being affectionately desirous of you, we were ready to share with you not only the gospel of God but also our own selves, because you had become very dear to us. 2:8
*Work hard* - For you remember, brothers, our labor and toil: we worked night and day, that we might not be a burden to any of you, while we proclaimed to you the gospel of God. 2:9

*Method:*
*Live right* - You are witnesses, and God also, how holy and righteous and blameless was our conduct toward you believers. 2:10
*Exhort, encourage, charge* - For you know how, like a father with his children, we exhorted each one of you and encouraged you and charged you to walk in a manner worthy of God, who calls you into his own kingdom and glory. 2:12
*Be grateful* - And we also thank God constantly for this, that when you received the word of God, which you heard from us, you accepted it not as the word of men but as what it really is… 2:13

*Message:*
    …the word of God (which) is at work in you believers. 2:13

(Verses are from 1 Thessalonians 2:4-13 ESV)

| WEEK FORTY SIX | *INSIGHT and ENCOURAGEMENT* | DAY 5 |

A Word to Shepherds from 1 Thessalonians (part 2)

***The Shepherd's Joy*** – For what is our hope or joy or crown of boasting before our Lord Jesus at his coming? Is it not you? *For you are our glory and joy.* 2:19-20

***The Shepherd's Fate*** – For you, yourselves know that *we are destined for this*. For when we were with you, we kept telling you beforehand that we were to suffer affliction, just as it has come to pass, and just as you know. 3:3-4

***The Shepherd's Fear*** – For this reason, when I could bear it no longer, I sent to learn about your faith, for fear that somehow the tempter had tempted you and *our labor would be in vain*. 3:5

***The Shepherd's Goal*** – For this reason, brothers, in all our distress and affliction we have been comforted about you through your faith. For now we live, if *you are standing fast in the Lord*. 3:8

***The Shepherd's Desire*** – For what thanksgiving can we return to God for you, for all the joy that we feel for your sake before our God, as we pray most earnestly night and day that we may see you face to face and *supply what is lacking in your faith*? 3:10

***The Shepherd's Prayer*** – Now may our God and Father himself, and our Lord Jesus, direct our way to you, and *may the Lord make you increase and abound in love for one another and for all*, as we do for you, so that he may establish your hearts blameless in holiness before our God and Father, at the coming of our Lord Jesus with all his saints. 3:12-13

***The Shepherd's Attitude*** – And we urge you, brothers, admonish the idle, encourage the fainthearted, help the weak, be patient with them all. See that no one repays anyone evil for evil, but always seek to do good to one another and to everyone. 5:14-15

***The Shepherd's Principles*** – Rejoice always, pray without ceasing, give thanks in all circumstances; for this is the will of God in Christ Jesus for you. Do not quench the Spirit. Do not despise prophecies, but test everything; hold fast what is good. Abstain from every form of evil. 5:16-22

***The Shepherd's Hope*** – He who calls you is faithful; he will surely do it. 5:24

(Verses are from 1 Thessalonians 2:19-3:13; 5:14-24 ESV. Emphasis mine.)

VICTORY THROUGH SURRENDER

| WEEK FORTY SIX | Confession of a Minister | DAY 6 |

Read Malachi 2

As a minister of the Gospel and the Kingdom of God, I will take my responsibility to give glory to your name with the utmost seriousness. Fulfilling the obligation to hear and heed your voice will be my chief aim and my highest priority. Your commandments are the basis upon which your covenant promises continue to be in effect. That covenant produces life and peace for me when I am obedient. I will walk in obedience and reverence to your holy name. When I speak in your name, let me only speak the truth of your Word. I will never pervert your truth for unjust means. By your grace, I will live daily in your presence, complete and upright according to your word. My dependence on and obedience to your voice will result in many turning from the darkness of sin to the light of life in Jesus. If people seek my advice, I will share the knowledge you have shared with me. Never let me say anything that will cause someone else to stumble, especially in my role as your messenger. Never let me present a false or corrupted view of your covenant promises or incorrectly communicate in any way your just and righteous commandments. My heart's desire and my commitment is always to keep your ways and follow all the Word of the Lord totally and completely.

| WEEK FORTY SIX | *INSIGHT and ENCOURAGEMENT* | DAY 7 |

First Lessons in the School of Jesus

G. Campbell Morgan (1863-1945)

1. *Supremacy of Character* (Matt. 5: 1-12). The very first word that falls from His lips is a revelation of the will of God for man. "Blessed." "Happy." That is the Divine thought and intention for us. Sorrow, tears, pain, disappointment, all these may be and are of inestimable value in the Father's discipline; but they are means to an end made necessary by man's sin. The end, in the purpose of God, is blessedness. Happiness is that after which all men in every age seek, and the first note in the Savior's teaching reveals it as what God is seeking also. Henceforth for the disciples of Jesus themselves, and for a basis of their estimate of others, character is to be supreme.

2. *Influence the Intention* (Matt. 5:13-16). This grows out of the former and is at once the statement of a fact and declaration of an intention. The fact is that character tells upon others. If a man lives in the atmosphere of the beatitudes of Jesus, his life being of the character described, he will, apart from any effort along the line of actual work exert certain influences. This the Master intends us to understand and hence the terrific force of His figures of speech.

3. *The New Moral Code* (Matt. 5:17-48). Having thus seen the supremacy of character as the secret of happiness and source of influence, we ask what are the laws which govern the development of such character. The new code of ethics is startling. The former is done away in the sense in which the less is included in the greater. Let this section be carefully read, remembering the following points: — a. The

righteousness of the disciples is to exceed that of the Pharisees, as inner purity exceeds external whiteness. b. Gifts on the altar do not expiate wrongdoing. c. To look on sin with desire is sin. d. Retaliation is forbidden and love is to be the one law of relative life.

4. *Self-stricken* (Matt. 6). This chapter may, and undoubtedly does, contain very much teaching along other lines but the underlying principle is that of self-abnegation. Note how the injunctions run counter to every popular idea of life: — a. Alms are to be given privately. b. Prayer is preeminently a matter twixt the soul and God; certainly not to be a means of advertising self's piety. c. Men are still to fast but with glad face. d. Wealth is not to be held, save on trust. e. Self is to be smitten so that anxiety concerning necessities cannot exist.

5. *Relative Charity* (Matt. 7:1-5). The consideration of my brother's fault is to drive me to self-examination rather than to the passing of judgment on him. I am ever to count my fault a beam and his a mote.

6. *The Open Treasure House* (Matt. 7:7-14). Just as one's spirit is in danger of being over-whelmed with the sense of the impossibility of realizing such ideals, He reveals to us the wealth that lies at our disposal in the love and power of the Father, and in simplest and best understood words, He reveals our privilege in that matter.

7. *Warning* (Matt. 7:15-23). What solemn words of warning are these? Siren voices will seek to lure us. No teaching but His can produce the true character. The truth of every message is to be tested by the life of the Teacher and if failure is found there, we are to know him for "false" no matter how cleverly the sheep's clothing conceals the devouring wolf. To the learning of these first great lessons, let us set ourselves with all submission of spirit and surrender of life.

Excerpted from, *Discipleship*.  Pathos Publishers EBook, 2015.  p. 14-17 (reprint from 1897).

**Record your insights, revelations, and meditations from this week.  DATE:**

_____

_____

_____

_____

_____

**WEEK FORTH SEVEN**  *HYMNS and POEMS*  **DAY 1**

Lie Still and Let Him Mold Thee
by Ada Ruth Habershon (1861-1918)

Lie still, and let Him mould thee!
Oh, Lord I would obey;
Be Thou the skillful Potter,
And I the yielding clay.

In Thy dear hand I'm resting,
Oh hold me quiet there;
Then soften me and mould me,
And for Thy will prepare.

I need not fear to trust Thee,
Thy love and skill are such,
New lessons Thou wilt teach me,
While yielding to Thy touch.

Impress Thine image on me,
Fulfill Thy blest design,
Till others see upon me,
That beauteous face of Thine.

https://www.hymnal.net/en/hymn/h/450

Tim Tremaine

**WEEK FORTY SEVEN**     *INSIGHT and ENCOURAGEMENT*     **DAY 2**

Phantoms of Devotion

by Francis de Sales (1567-1622)

You aspire to devotion, dearest Philothea, because being a Christian, you know that it is a virtue extremely pleasing to the divine Majesty: inasmuch as small faults committed in the beginning of any affair, in the progress thereof grow infinitely greater and in the end become almost irreparable, it is necessary before all things that you should know what the virtue of devotion is; for since there is but one true devotion, and very many which are false and vain, if you know not which is the true, you may very easily be deceived, and waste your time in following some devotion which is false and superstitious.

Aurelius was wont to paint all the faces in his pictures to the air and resemblance of the women whom he loved, and each one paints devotion according to his own passion and fancy. He that is given to fasting holds himself for very devout, if he do but fast, though his heart be full of rancour: and though he dare not moisten his tongue in wine or even in water for fear of transgressing sobriety, yet he scruples not to plunge it in the blood of his neighbour, by detraction and calumny.

Another will account himself devout, for reciting a great multitude of prayers every day, although afterwards he gives his tongue full liberty to utter peevish, arrogant and injurious words among his familiars and neighbours. Another will readily draw an alms out of his purse to give it to the poor, but he cannot draw any gentleness out of his heart to forgive his enemies. Another will forgive his enemies, but will not make satisfaction to his creditors, unless forced by the law to do so. And yet all these persons are, in the common estimation, held to be devout, though they are by no means so. The servants of Saul sought for David in his house; but Michal having laid a statue in his bed, and having covered it with David's apparel, made them believe that it was David himself sick and sleeping: even so do many persons cover themselves with certain external actions belonging to holy devotion, and the world believes them to be truly devout and spiritual; whereas in reality they are but statues and phantoms of devotion.

In short, devotion is no other thing than a spiritual nimbleness and vivacity, by means of which charity works in us, or we by her, readily and heartily; and as it is the office of charity to make us observe all the commandments of God generally and universally, so it is the office of devotion to make us observe them readily and diligently. Hence it is that he who keeps not all the commandments of God, cannot be esteemed either good or devout, since to be good one must have charity, and to be devout one must have, besides charity, a great alacrity and readiness in carrying out the actions prompted by charity.

Excerpted from *Introduction to the Devout Life*. Mineola, NY: Dover Publications, Inc., (unk). p. 53-54.

VICTORY THROUGH SURRENDER

**WEEK FORTY SEVEN**  **Confession of Priorities**  **DAY 3**

From Haggai

I began to wonder why I never see success. I work hard, but I can never seem to get ahead. I always seem to be "a day late and a dollar short." I'm not suffering, I'm not starving, I'm not homeless or destitute, but I just can't seem to get ahead. The harder I try, the more behind I get. It's like I try to plant a garden, and the seeds rot in the ground before they can sprout. I try to water the garden, but the water evaporates before it hits the ground. It rains and rains before I plant, but once I do, the skies dry up, and the ground hardens like cement. So I asked you, what am I missing? What am I doing wrong? Here was your answer, "Is it right for you to live in a well-built house while my house lies in ruins?" What were you talking about? I give regularly, and the church building is in fine shape. Then it dawned on me; you weren't talking about the church building. You were talking about me. I am the temple of the Holy Spirit. I was neglecting your "house" while trying to build my own, and both suffered. I remember when I was new in the faith and had a passion for the Lord. My Christian life now can't compare with my Christian life then. By neglecting my life with you, I'm really neglecting myself. The only path to true success is to work hard on your "house" first. The blessings of God come from obedience.


**WEEK FORTY SEVEN**  *INSIGHT and ENCOURAGEMENT*  **DAY 4**

The Necessity of Prayer

by Francis de Sales (1567-1622)

Inasmuch as prayer places our understanding in the clearness of the divine light, and exposes our will to the warmth of heavenly love, there is nothing which so purges our understanding of its ignorance and our will of its depraved inclinations; it is the water of benediction, which, when our souls are watered therewith, makes the plants of our good desires revive and flourish, cleanses our souls of their imperfections, and quenches the thirst caused by the passions of our hearts.

But above all I recommend to you prayer of the mind and heart and especially that which has for its subject the life and passion of our Lord; for by beholding him often in meditation, your whole soul will be filled with him; you will learn his disposition, and you will form your actions after the model of his. He is *the light of the world,* and therefore it is in him, by him, and for him that we must be enlightened and illuminated; he is the tree of desire, in the shadow of which we must seek refreshment; he is the *living well of Jacob,* for the cleansing of all our stains. In fine, as children by listening to their mothers, and prattling with them, learn to speak their language, so we, by keeping close to the Saviour in meditation, and observing his words, his actions, and his affections, shall learn, with the help of his grace, to speak, to act, and to will like him.

We must stop there, Philothea, and believe me, we cannot go to God the Father, but by this door; for just as the glass of a mirror could not catch our reflection if the back thereof were not covered with tin or lead, so the Divinity could not well be contemplated by us in this world below if it were not united to the sacred humanity of the Saviour, whose life and death are the most appropriate, sweet, delicious and profitable subjects which we can choose for our ordinary meditations. The Saviour does not call himself for nothing, *the bread which came down from heaven,* for, as bread should be eaten with all sorts of meat, so the Saviour ought to be meditated upon, considered, and sought after in all our prayers and actions. His life and death have been arranged and distributed into divers points by many authors, in order to serve for meditation: those whom I recommend to you are St Bonaventure, Bellintani, Bruno, Capiglia, Granada, and Da Ponte.

Spend an hour in meditation every day, sometime or other before the midday meal, if possible in the early part of your morning, because your mind will be less distracted and more refreshed after the repose of the night. But do not spend more than an hour therein, unless your spiritual Father should expressly say so.

Begin all your prayers, be they mental or vocal, with the presence of God, and make no exception to this rule, and you will soon perceive how profitable it will be to you.

Excerpted from *Introduction to the Devout Life*. Mineola, NY: Dover Publications, Inc., (unk). p. 143-145.


**WEEK FORTY SEVEN**  *INSIGHT and ENCOURAGEMENT*  **DAY 5**

Energized by the Spirit
by Smith Wigglesworth (1859-1947)

So there is a necessity for every one of us to be filled with God. It is not sufficient to have just a touch or to be filled with just a desire. Only one thing will meet the needs of people, and that is for you to be immersed in the life of God. This means that God takes you and fills you with His Spirit until you live right in God. He does this so that *"whether you eat or drink, or whatever you do,* [it may be] *all to the glory of God"* (1 Corinthians 10:31). In that place you will find that all your strength and all your mind and all your soul are filled with a zeal, not only for worship, but for proclamation. This proclamation is accompanied by all the power of God, which must move satanic power and disturb the world.

The reason the world is not seeing Jesus is that Christian people are not filled with Jesus. They are satisfied with attending meetings weekly, reading the Bible occasionally, and praying sometimes. Beloved, if God lays hold of you by the Spirit, you will find that there is an end of everything and a beginning of God. Your whole body will become seasoned with a divine likeness of God. Not only will He have begun to use you, but He will have taken you in hand, so that you might be *"a vessel for honor"* (2 Timothy 2:21). Our lives are not to be for ourselves, for if we live for ourselves we will die (Romans 8:13); but if *"by the*

*Spirit* [we] *put to death the deeds of the body,* [we] *will live*" (v. 13). He who lives in the Spirit is subject to the powers of God, but he who lives for himself will die. The man who lives in the Spirit lives a life of freedom and joy and blessing and service – a life that brings blessing to others. God would have us see that we must live in the Spirit.

I do not know what your state of grace is – whether you are saved or not – but it is an awful thing for me to see people who profess to be Christians lifeless, powerless, and in a place where their lives are so parallel to unbelievers' lives that it is difficult to tell which place they are in, whether in the flesh or in the Spirit. Many people live in the place that is described to us by Paul in Romans 7:25: *"With the mind I myself serve the law of God, but with the flesh the law of sin."* That is the place where sin is in the ascendancy. But when the power of God comes to you, it is to separate you from yourself. It is destruction of yourself, annihilation. It is to move you from nature to grace, making you mighty over the powers of the enemy and making you know that you have now begun to live a life of faith in the Son of God.

Excerpted from *Smith Wigglesworth on Healing*. New Kensington, PA: Whitaker House, 1999. p. 129-131.

**WEEK FORTY SEVEN**     *HYMNS and POEMS*     **DAY 6**

### The Believer's Covenant and Confidence
by Richard Baxter (1615-1691)

My whole though broken heart, O Lord!
From henceforth shall be thine;
And here I do my vow record,
This hand, these words, are mine;
All that I have, without reserve,
I offer here to Thee:
Thy will and honor all shall serve
That thou bestow'dst on me.

I know that thou wast willing first,
And then drew my consent:
Having thus loved me at the worst,
Thou wilt not now repent.
Now I have quit all self-pretense,
Take charge of what's thine own:
My life, my health, and my defense,
Now lie on thee alone.

All that exceptions save I lose;
All that I lose I save:
The treasures of thy love I choose,
And thou art all I crave.
My God, thou hast my heart and hand;
I all to thee resign:
I'll ever to this covenant stand,
Though flesh hereat repine.

Lord, it belongs not to my care
Whether I live or die:
To love and serve thee is my share,
And this thy grace must give.
If life be long, I will be glad,
That I may long obey:
If short, yet why should I be sad,
That shall have the same pay?

| | |
|---|---|
| Christ leads me through no darker rooms | Then I shall end my sad complaints |
| Than he went through before: | And weary sinful days, |
| He that into God's kingdom comes | And join with the triumphant saints |
| Must enter by this door. | That sing Jehovah's praise. |
| Come, Lord, when grace hath made me meet | My knowledge of that life is small: |
| Thy blessed face to see: | The eye of faith is dim: |
| For if thy work on earth be sweet | But 'tis enough that Christ knows all, |
| What will thy glory be? | And I shall be with him. |

Hamilton, James. *Our Christian Classics: Reading from the Best Divines. Vol. 1.* London: James Nisbet and Co., 1859. p. 416-417.

---

**WEEK FORTY SEVEN**  *HYMNS and POEMS*  **DAY 7**

In the Name of Jesus

by Søren Kierkegaard (1813-1855)

To pray "in the name of Jesus" may perhaps be explained most simply in this way. The magistrate orders this and the other thing in the name of the King. What does that mean? In the first place it means: I myself am nothing. I have no power, nothing to say for myself – but it is in the name of the King. Thus to pray in the name of Christ means: I dare not approach God without a mediator; if my prayer is to be heard, then it will be in the name of Jesus; what gives it strength is that name.

Next, when a magistrate gives of command in the name of the King it naturally follows that what he commands must be the King's will, he cannot command his own will in the King's name. The same thing is true of praying in the name of Jesus, to pray in such a way that it is in conformity with the will of Jesus. I cannot pray in the name of Jesus to have my own will; the name of Jesus is not a signature of no importance, but the decisive factor; the fact that the name of Jesus comes at the beginning is not prayer in the name of Jesus; but it means to pray in such a manner that I dare name Jesus in it, that is to say think of Him, think His holy will together with whatever I am praying for.

Finally, when a magistrate gives an order in the name of the King it means that the King assumes the responsibility. So too with prayer in the name of Jesus, Jesus assumes the responsibility and all the consequences, He steps forward for us, steps into the place of the person praying.

Baillie, John. *A Diary of Readings*. New York: Macmillan Publishing Co., 1955. p. 21.

**Record your insights, revelations, and meditations from this week. DATE:**

Tim Tremaine

**WEEK FORTY EIGHT**  *HYMNS and POEMS*  **DAY 1**

Every Thread I wind This Day
by Sister Eva of Friedenshort (1866-1930)

Every thread I wind this day,
Every footstep on life's way,
Every clod I shall unearth,
Every task, whate'er its worth:
Only for God's glory living,
Blessing, praise and honor giving!

All the burdens of the day,
All the words which I shall say,
All the works my God may send,
All the hours in rest I spend:
Ever for His glory living,
Blessing, praise and honor giving!

Every blood-drop in the heart,
Every grief and aching smart,
Every bitter pulse of pain,
Every hour of joy again:
Only for God's glory living,
Blessing, praise and honor giving!

As I take my daily food,
Greet another on life's road,
Pluck a flower beside the way,
Stoop to lift a wisp of hay:
Ever for God's glory living,
Blessing, praise and honor giving!

All, from deeds of little worth,
To the greatest things on earth;
Mine to build some world to be,
Or to lie and gaze on Thee:
For Thy glory daily living,
Blessing, praise and honor giving!

https://www.hymnal.net/en/hymn/h/455

**WEEK FORTY EIGHT**  *INSIGHT and ENCOURAGEMENT*  **DAY 2**

Divine Union
by Hannah Whitall Smith (1832-1911)

Your joy in the Lord is to be a far deeper thing than a mere emotion. It is to be the joy of knowledge, of perception, of actual existence. It is a far gladder thing to *be* a bird, with all the actual realities of flying, than only to *feel* as if you were a bird, with no actual power of flying at all. Reality is always the vital thing. Now having guarded against this danger of an emotional experience of Divine union, let us consider how the reality is to be reached. And first I would say that it is not a new attitude to be taken by God, but only a new attitude to be taken by us. If I am really a child of God, then of necessity my heart is already the temple of God, and Christ is already within me. What is needed, therefore, is only that I shall recognize His presence and yield fully to His control.

## VICTORY THROUGH SURRENDER

It seems to me just in this way: as though Christ were living in the house, shut up in afar off closet, unknown and unnoticed by the dwellers in the house, longing to make Himself known to them, and to be one with them in all their daily lives, and share in all their interests, but unwilling to force Himself upon their notice, because nothing but a voluntary companionship could meet or satisfy the needs of His love. They come and go about all their daily affairs, with no thought of their wonderful Guest. Their plans are laid without reference to Him. His wisdom to guide and His strength to protect are all lost to them. Lonely days and weeks are spent in sadness which might have been full of the sweetness of His presence.

I make the glad announcement to thee that the Lord is in thy heart. Every moment during all that time might have been passed in the sunshine of His sweet presence, and every step have been taken under His advice. But because thou knew it not, and did not look for Him there, thy life has been lonely and full of failure. Wilt thou throw wide open every door to welcome Him in?

The steps are but three: first, we must be convinced that the scriptures teach this glorious indwelling of God; then we must surrender our whole selves to Him to be possessed by Him; and, finally, we must believe that He *has* taken possession, and *is* dwelling in us. We must begin to reckon ourselves dead, and to reckon Christ as our only life. We must maintain this attitude of soul unwaveringly. It will help us to say, "I am crucified with Christ: nevertheless I live, yet not I, but Christ liveth in me," over and over, day and night, until it becomes the habitual breathing of our souls. We must let this become, by its constant repetition, the attitude of our whole being. And as surely as we do, we shall come at last to understand something of what it means to be made one with Christ as He and the Father are one. As the Lord prayed, "that they all may be one; as thou, Father, art in me, and I in thee, that they also may be one in us." (Emphasis hers)

Adapted from *The Christian's Secret of a Happy Life*, Revell, 1952. p. 222-226.

**WEEK FORTY EIGHT** *HYMNS and POEMS* **DAY 3**

Jesus, Take This Heart of Mine
by Ernest G. Wesley (1847-1929)

Jesus, take this heart of mine;
Cleanse from sin and make it Thine.
Thou for me hast bled and died;
I to Thee my heart confide.

*Refrain:*
*Jesus, take this heart of mine,*
*Make it ever, wholly Thine;*
*May I daily watch and pray:*
*Never from Thy path to stray.*

> Jesus, take these hands of mine;
> Hold them in Thy power divine;
> Safe am I when led by Thee,
> I Thy child would ever be.
>
> Jesus, take these feet of mine;
> May they to Thy paths incline;
> May I never from Thee stray;
> Keep me faithful day by day.
>
> Jesus, take this heart of mine;
> May it with Thy glory shine;
> I would live for Thee alone;
> Make me, keep me, all Thine own.

*The Methodist Sunday School Hymnal*, New York: Methodist Book Concern, 1911, according to http://www.hymntime.com/

**WEEK FORTY EIGHT** *INSIGHT and ENCOURAGEMENT* **DAY 4**

Your Prayers Answered

by Charles C. Price (1887-1947)

Do you not know that your prayers can be answered? Do you not know that your burdens and cares can be left at His feet; that you never need bow your shoulders again with the weight of sorrow and care? I am praying, please God, that thousands who will read these lines will come to the place of abandonment of the trail of self-endeavor, realizing that it has led them into doubts and fears which destroy confidence and trust in God.

Know ye not that faith cometh by hearing, and hearing by the Word of God? In my Greek Testament it reads, "and hearing by a word of God." There is a finer ear than the one with which we listen to the music of the organ in the church service. There is another ear than the one we use when we listen to the reading of the grand old Book. It is not merely the intonation of a human voice that speaks as the Bible is read, for men hear that Book and yet do not hear the voice of God. The Bible is a book through which God speaks; yet all do not hear His voice in the lines!

Faith cometh by hearing, and hearing by a word of God. Let Jesus speak to this heart of mine and doubts will take the wings of the morning and fly away. Let Jesus breathe a little word to this poor mind of mine and heaven is brought to earth. Fear is gone like a shadow in the light of His glorious truth. Let Him say, "Bring him to me," and then cometh faith—God's faith—His faith—and my poor heart will cry, "Lord, that I may receive my sight." Let Jesus breathe on me, with His love and presence, and mountains will commence to tremble, and the fingers of the foundations will lose their grip!

That is how faith comes! Not through the channels of human concepts. Not along the paths of human understandings. Not by the abilities of minds to comprehend, or the power of the intellect to affirm. Reach with fingers such as those for the moon and you will struggle and groan in vain to possess it. But let Jesus speak, and the soul is lifted. One little word from Jesus is worth all the words in a dictionary of human language.

There is hope for the blind Bartimaeus of the Jericho Road of today, when Jesus of Nazareth is passing this way. "Hope," did I say? Yes, hope – and more than hope; for when He hears our cry of helplessness, He will not pass us by. When He speaks, hope is kindled until it becomes a fire that burns away all doubt and unbelief, and the warmth of a divine and beautiful faith brings healing to the soul.

Excerpted from *The Real Faith*. Self-published, 1941. Chapter 7. Jawbone Digital, Kindle ed.

**WEEK FORTY EIGHT**      Confession of the Blessings of Obedience      **DAY 5**

Read Deuteronomy 28

I will diligently obey the voice of the Lord my God and observe all his commandments carefully. No matter where I go, in the city or in the countryside, I will be blessed if I obey. My children and grandchildren, the work of my hands, the produce of my business will all be blessed if I obey. I will be blessed coming and blessed going out if I obey. I will face the problems, difficulties, trials, and tribulations that rise up against me and will overcome them, scattering them in every direction because I am blessed when I obey. You will command the blessing on everything you have given me to keep and everything that I find to do in the place you have given me to live. According to your promise, you have established me as part of your holy people because I keep your commandments and walk in your ways. People shall know that I am called by the name of the Lord because the Lord will grant me sufficient supply of everything I need in every area of life. I will live under an open heaven with access to all the good treasures of the Lord. I will be the head and not the tail. I will live above and not beneath because I heed the commandments of the Lord and am careful to observe them. I will not turn aside from any of the words which you command to me, to one side or the other, for to do so would be to follow after other gods and serve them.

**WEEK FORTY EIGHT**      *INSIGHT and ENCOURAGEMENT*      **DAY 6**

The Apprehension of God's Will

by Andrew Murray (1828-1917)

The great mistake here is that God's children do not really believe that it is possible to know God's will. Or if they believe this, they do not take the time and trouble to find it out. What we need is to see clearly in what way it is that the Father leads His waiting, teachable child to know that his petition is according to His will. It is through God's holy word, taken up and kept in the heart, the life, the will; and through

God's Holy Spirit, accepted in His indwelling and leading, then we shall learn to know that our petitions are according to His will. (I John 5:14-15)

In the Word the Father has revealed in general promises the great principles of His will with His people. The child has to take the promise and apply it to the special circumstances in his life. Whatever he asks within the limits of that revealed will, he can know to be according to the will of God, and he may confidently expect. In His word, God has given us the revelation of His will and plans with us, with His people, and with the world, with the most precious promises of the grace and power with which through His people He will carry out His plans and work. As faith becomes strong and bold enough to claim the fulfillment of the general promise in the special case, we may have the assurance that our prayers are heard: they are according to God's will.

This apprehension of God's will is something spiritual, and must be spiritually discerned. It is not a matter of logic that we can argue it out: God has said it; I must have it. Nor has every Christian the same gift of calling. While the general will revealed in the promise is the same for all, there is for each one a special different will according to God's purpose. And herein is the wisdom of the saints, to know this special will of God for each of us, according to the measure of grace given us, and so to ask in prayer just what God has prepared and made possible for each. It is to communicate this wisdom but the Holy Spirit dwells in us. The personal application of the general promises of the word to our special personal needs – it is for this that the leading of the Holy Spirit is given us.

It is this union of the teaching of the Word and Spirit that many do not understand, and so there is a twofold difficulty in knowing what God's will may be. Some seek the will of God in an inner feeling or conviction, and would have the Spirit lead them without the word. Others seek it in the Word, without the living leading of the Holy Spirit. The two must be united: only in the Word, only in the Spirit, can we know the will of God, and learn to pray according to it. In the heart the word and the Spirit must meet: it is only by indwelling that we can experience their teaching. Only he who yields himself entirely to the supremacy of the Word and the will of God, who can expect in special cases to discern what that word and will permit him boldly to ask. (Emphasis his.)

*With Christ in the School of Prayer.* Old Tappan, NJ: Fleming H. Revell, Co., 1953. p. 163-165

## MONTH TWELVE

*Journal entry from Latvia, June 30, 2018*

Camp is over, and we are heading home. It takes three flights to get from Latvia to Texas. Every night this week, I have pulled up something to watch on YouTube. One night, I saw a message by Pastor Cho from Korea. I watched the whole message on tabernacle prayer. It was awesome, and I immediately put the Isaiah 11 prayer into practice. I will work on the rest. But Cho also talked about the *rhema* word of Christ. I know the difference between *logos* and *rhema,* but he had a great analogy. *Logos* is rice. *Rhema* is cooked rice. The main point I heard was the emphasis on the person of the Holy Spirit. Not to take Him for granted and not to treat Him as a thing. He is the senior partner in our relationship, and He needs to call the shots.

As I was going to sleep last night, I was listening to Galatians and heard chapter 5 verse 14, where it says the whole law is fulfilled in one word: "Love your neighbor as yourself." The Holy Spirit helped me see that this was an example of cooked rice (a *rhema* word). I checked the Greek, and it does say, "one word." But the quote is from Leviticus 19:18, and it is not just one word. It must mean that Paul is talking about the quote like we use the term "getting a word from the Lord." We don't mean a single word but rather a message, understanding, interpretation, or application of Scripture. This quote is in the section of Leviticus that has long lists of rules. But the Holy Spirit has here apparently given Paul a *rhema* word, insight into the Old Testament text, to show him, and us, that this one commandment sums up all of them. Learning what the glory of God was and where to find it, Cho's tabernacle prayer, *rhema* as "cooked rice," and this insight into getting a "word" from the Lord were the highlight revelations of my week at camp.

Something else amazing just happened. I'm writing this on the plane from Riga to Helsinki, and I am reading from *The Real Faith* by Charles S. Price. "It is in Him we find our completeness…" Right in the middle of the paragraph, I nodded off, and as my head drops, I heard the Lord say, "Micah 3:8." I have never had that happen before, but it was as clear as a bell. It reads, "But as for me, I am filled with power, with the Spirit of the Lord, and with justice and might, to declare to Jacob his transgression and to Israel his sin" (Micah 3:8 ESV).

We are about four hours into the flight. I have been reading the last three chapters of the book most of that time. This is the last paragraph of the book: "If, perchance, the trials of the road become heavy; we learn to find our sufficiency not in human attainment—but in that Faith, THE FAITH *OF* THE LORD JESUS CHRIST, which worketh by love; and which will surmount every difficulty, be it physical, material, or spiritual. This sufficiency can be found only in the outworking of the Indwelling Christ, for it is in Him and through Him that all our needs are met." I can learn to live with the same faith Jesus had as I surrender to His will.

This is what the life of absolute surrender has been like for me so far—an amazing adventure of discovery and service with the Lord. Hearing specific words, getting specific instructions, seeing the glory of God on the faces of transformed people is my blessing and the desire of my heart.

**WEEK FORTY EIGHT**  *HYMNS and POEMS*  **DAY 7**

### I Will! I Will!

by Barney E. Warren (1867-1951)

*(The verses have been converted from questions to statements. Speak this out to the Lord.)*

Yes, I will count the cost today.
Yes, I will leave my sinful way.
*I will, I will.*
Yes, I will bear the cross for Him.
Yes, I will start the prize to win.
*I will, I will.*

*Refrain:*
*I'll give up sin, the prize to win,*
*And meekly bear my cross for Him,*
*I will, I will.*

Yes, I will count the cost today.
Yes, I will walk the narrow way
*I will, I will.*
Yes, I will persecutions bear,
And fight a starry crown to wear.
*I will, I will.*

Yes, I will count the cost today.
Yes, I will come without delay.
*I will, I will.*
Yes, I will give up the world this hour,
And prove His mighty saving pow'r.
*I will, I will.*

Yes, I will count the cost today.
Despite what men and demons say.
*I will, I will.*
Yes, I will stand with Christ alone,
The Rock of Truth and Corner Stone.
*I will, I will.*

Yes, I will count the cost today.
Yes, I will speak and sing and pray.
*I will, I will.*
Yes, I will read the word He's giv'n,
And do His will as 'tis is heav'n.
*I will, I will.*

Modified from https://library.timelesstruths.org/music/I_Will_I_Will/

**Record your insights, revelations, and meditations from this week.  DATE:**

Tim Tremaine

**WEEK FORTY NINE**  *HYMNS and POEMS*  **DAY 1**

My Surrender
by Gertrude E Worthington (unknown)

I have given up all to my Savior so dear,
And His praises I ever will sing;
And though all of this world should forsake me while here,
To my Savior I ever will cling.

*Refrain:*
*He leads me each day in the heavenly way,*
*So onward and upward I'll climb;*
*In the straight, narrow way, I'm determined to stay,*
*Till I leave this old dark world behind.*

I've received such great light, and its beams are so bright,
That the past of my life's way seems dim;
I will walk in this light by day and by night,
Still closer I'll cling unto Him.

Some think I've done wrong by leaving the throng,
Who abide in sectarian strife;
But I've only come back where God's people belong,
From Babel I fled for my life.

I have a good home in the fold of my Lord,
Where His sanctified children all dwell;
I am glad that I heard the truth from His word,
And now with my soul all is well.

Someday when my life and its labors are o'er,
And my sheaves at His feet I lay down,
I will meet all the saints on that beautiful shore,
And receive a bright, glittering crown.

https://library.timelesstruths.org/music/My_Surrender/ from 1949

**WEEK FORTY NINE** *INSIGHT and ENCOURAGEMENT* DAY 2

Instability of the Heart

by Bernard of Clairvaux (1090-1153)

Nothing can be more restless and unstable than my heart, which, as often as it wanders and flows forth in evil thoughts, so often offends my God. My heart is vain, roving, wavering: while it is led by its own choice and lacks the Divine guidance, it has no steadfastness; but, more variable than all things, it is in countless ways distracted. And while it seeks rest in diverse objects, it yet finds none, but continues unhappy, laboring, without true repose. It disagrees with itself, recoils from its own purposes, changes its volitions and designs, builds up the new, destroys the old, rebuilds what it destroyed.

As a millstone is turned rapidly, and rejects nothing, but grinds whatever comes, and if nothing is offered, then consumes itself, so is my heart ever in ceaseless motion, and, whether I sleep or watch, still dreams or ruminates. And as sand would damage, and pitch defile, and straw obstruct the millstone, so angry thoughts disturb, impure thoughts stain, vain thoughts fatigue my heart.

Thus while it cares not for future joy nor seeks Divine aid, it is far remote from the love of the heavenly, engrossed by what is earthly and perishing. Thus while it shuns the former and is entangled in the latter, variety absorbs, curiosity persuades, cupidity attracts, sensuality pollutes, envy torments, anger perturbs, sadness dejects it, and so it is miserably plunged in vices, because it has forsaken that only God and Lord, who would suffice for its healing and welfare. Such are its falls and its miseries when unsustained by Divine grace. And when it examines itself and considers its course, it finds nought but fruitless cogitation, which has fashioned many things out of nothing; deceits of imagination and delusions of the evil one.

God commands me to give my heart to Him; and because I have been disobedient and resisted His will, I am become also a rebel and a foe to myself. I cannot have rest in myself until I am in willing submission and adherence to Him, and I must be an unwilling slave to self, if His service is refused.

If I am not united to God, I am divided and distracted within myself. With Him I cannot be united save by love, nor be submissive to Him except by humility, nor be truly humble, except through His word of truth. It is needful, therefore, that I thoroughly search into my heart, and learn more fully how vile, how frail, and how unsteadfast I am. And when I ascertain my utmost miseries, it is of utmost necessity that I return and cleave to Him, by whom I exist, and without whom I am nothing and can do nothing.

Shepperd, John (1785-1879). *Chosen Words from Christian Writers*. London: Hodder & Stoughton, 1869. p. 252-253.

**WEEK FORTY NINE**     *HYMNS and POEMS*     **DAY 3**

The Thought of God
by Frederick William Faber (1814-1863)

The thought of God, the thought of Thee,
Who liest in my heart,
And yet beyond imagined space
Outstretched and present art.

The thought of Thee, above, below,
Around me and within,
Is more to me than health and wealth,
Or love of kith and kin.

The thought of God is like the tree
Beneath whose shade I lie,
And watch the fleets of snowy clouds
Sail o'er the silent sky.

'Tis like that soft invading light,
Which in all darkness shines,
The thread that through life's sombre web
In golden pattern twines.

It is a thought which ever makes
Life's sweetest smiles from tears,
And is a daybreak to our hopes,
A sunset to our fears.

One while it bids the tears to flow,
Then wipes them from the eyes,
Most often fills our souls with joy,
And always sanctifies.

Within a thought so great, our souls
Little and modest grow,
And, by its vastness awed, we learn
The art of walking slow.

The wildflower on the messy ground
Scarce bends its pliant form,
When overhead the autumnal wood
Is thundering like a storm.

So is it with our humbled souls
Down in the thought of God,
Scarce conscious in their sober peace
Of the wild storms abroad.

To think of Thee is almost prayer,
And is outspoken praise;
And pain can even passive thoughts
To actual worship raise.

O Lord! I live always in pain,
My life's sad undersong,
Pain in itself not hard to bear,
But hard to bear so long.

Little sometimes weighs more than much,
When it has no relief;
A joyless life is worse to bear
Than one of active grief.

And yet, O Lord! a suffering life
One grand ascent may dare;
Penance, not self-imposed, can make
The whole of life a prayer.

All murmurs lie inside Thy Will
Which are to Thee addressed;
To suffer for Thee is our work,
To think of Thee our rest.

Tozer, A. W. *The Christian Book of Mystical Verse: A Collection of Poems, Hymns, and Prayers for Devotional Reading.* Chicago: Moody Publishers, 2016. p. 36-38.

| **WEEK FORTY NINE** | **Confession about Immorality** | **DAY 4** |

Various scriptures

How easy it is to be trapped by immorality. The flattering words of an immoral person are as smooth as butter and as sweet as honey but as deadly as any poison. There is no truth in their words. Their only purpose is to seduce me by deception to steal my potential, rob me of health and wealth, and destroy any usefulness I may have to the Kingdom of God. What a blessing from God love and physical intimacy is. What a curse when those God-given desires are met in God-forbidden ways. You see my every step and know my every thought. To even contemplate what it might be like to pursue the enticement of a wicked person shows an extreme lack of understanding. I do so at my own peril. What foolishness to think I could play with fire and not get burned. To even daydream about lust-filled fantasies would set me on a path to destruction. Your righteous instructions are clear. There is no gray area. The warning signs are plain and evident to all. There can be no compromise of principle, no rationalization, no excuses for such a blatant failure of obedience. I cannot avoid every temptation, but I do not have to entertain it. I must not give it another thought except to expose and reject it immediately. I will not give it a second look. Stronger, more talented, more intelligent people than I have lost it all by not recognizing the warning signs and heeding the cautions of others regarding their affections. By your grace and in your strength, I will stay the course of wisdom and discretion.


| **WEEK FORTY NINE** | *INSIGHT and ENCOURAGEMENT* | **DAY 5** |

"What Would Jesus Do?"

by Charles M. Sheldon (1857-1946)

"What I am going to propose now is something which ought not to appear unusual or at all impossible of execution. Yet I am aware that it will be so regarded by a large number, perhaps, of the members of this church. But in order that we may have a thorough understanding of what we are considering, I will put my proposition very plainly, perhaps bluntly. I want volunteers from the First Church who will pledge themselves, earnestly and honestly for an entire year, not to do anything without first asking the question, 'What would Jesus do?' And after asking that question, each one will follow Jesus as exactly as he knows how, no matter what the result may be. I will of course include myself in this company of volunteers, and shall take for granted that my church here will not be surprised at my future conduct, as based upon this standard of action, and will not oppose whatever is done if they think Christ would do it. Have I made my meaning clear? At the close of the service I want all those members who were willing to join such a company to remain and we will talk over the details of the plan. Our motto will be, 'What would Jesus do?' Our aim will be to act just as He would if He was in our places, regardless of immediate results. In other words, we propose to follow Jesus' steps as closely and as literally as we believe He taught His disciples to do. And those who volunteer to do this will pledge themselves for an entire year, beginning with today, so to act."

Henry Maxwell paused again and looked out over his people. It is not easy to describe the sensation that such a simple proposition apparently made. Men glanced at one another in astonishment. It was not like Henry Maxwell to define Christian discipleship in this way. There was evident confusion of thought over his proposition. It was understood well enough, but there was, apparently, a great difference of opinion as to the application of Jesus' teaching and example.

He calmly closed the service with a brief prayer. The organist began his postlude immediately after the benediction and the people began to go out. There was a great deal of conversation. Animated groups stood all over the church discussing the minister's proposition. It was evidently provoking great discussion. After several minutes he asked all who expected to remain to pass into the lecture room which joined the large room on the side. He himself detained at the front of the church talking with several persons there, and when he finally turned around, the church was empty. He walked over to the lecture room entrance and went in. He was almost startled to see the people who were there. He had not made up his mind about any of his members, but he had hardly expected that so many were ready to enter into such a testing of their Christian discipleship as now awaited him.

*In His Steps.* Nashville: Broadman Press, 1935. p. 15-16. (From the 1896 story by Sheldon.)

**WEEK FORTY NINE**  *INSIGHT and ENCOURAGEMENT*  **DAY 6**

The Nearness of God

by Andrew Murray (1828-1917)

It has been said that the holiness of God is the union of God's infinite distance from sinful man with God's infinite nearness in His redeeming grace. Faith must seek to realize both the distance and the nearness.

In Christ God has come near, so very near to man, and now the command comes: If you want to come still nearer, you must make the move. The promised nearness of Christ Jesus expressed in the promise, "Lo, I am with you alway," can only be experienced as we move near to Him.

That means, at the beginning of each day to yield ourselves for His holy presence to rest upon us. It means a voluntary, intentional, and wholehearted turning away from the world, to wait for God to reveal Himself. It is impossible to expect the abiding presence of Christ with us through the day, unless there be a definite

# VICTORY THROUGH SURRENDER

daily exercise of strong desire and childlike trust in His word: "Draw nigh to God, and He will draw nigh to you."

Further, it means the simple, childlike offering of ourselves and our lives in everything to do His will and to please Him. His promise is sure: "If a man love Me he will keep My words, and My Father will love him, and we will make our abode in him."

Then comes the quiet assurance of faith, even if there is not much feeling or sense of His presence, that God is with us, and that as we go out to do His will He strengthens us in the inner man for the work we do for Him. Child of God, let these words come to you with a new meaning each morning: "Draw nigh to God, and he will draw nigh to you." Wait patiently, and He will speak in divine power: "Lo, I am with you alway."

*Growing in Christ*. Westchester, IL: Good News Publishers, 1979. p. 34-35.

**WEEK FORTY NINE**  *HYMNS and POEMS*  **DAY 7**

Since I Am Sanctified

by Barney E. Warren (1867-1951)

The Comforter abides within,
Since I am sanctified;
He cleanseth all my heart from sin,
Since I am sanctified.
The blood by faith now reaches me,
In soul and body I am free,
And now I've constant victory,
Since I am sanctified.

The Comforter is all I need,
Since I am sanctified;
I've nothing but His grace to plead,
Since I am sanctified.
He guides me in the truth and right,
He helps me conquer in the fight,
His service is my heart's delight,
Since I am sanctified.

The Comforter is life and peace,
Since I am sanctified;
His grace and glory do increase,
Since I am sanctified.
My heart with rapture overflows,
My life on earth much sweeter grows,
And in me dwells no hind'ring foes,
Since I am sanctified.

The Comforter is life complete,
Since I am sanctified;
In His rich favor I'm replete,
Since I am sanctified.
I'm never lonely, tired with care,
For He, a present help, is there,
And all my burdens He doth bear,
Since I am sanctified.

https://library.timelesstruths.org/music/Since_I_Am_Sanctified/

**Record your insights, revelations, and meditations from this week. DATE:**

VICTORY THROUGH SURRENDER

WEEK FIFTY  *HYMNS and POEMS*  DAY 1

Resignation

by Jeanne Marie De La Motte-Guyon (1648-1717)

A little bird I am,
Shut from the fields of air;
And in my cage I sit and sing
To Him who placed me there;
Well pleased a prisoner to be,
Because, my God, it pleases Thee.

Naught have I else to do;
I sing the whole day long;
And He whom most I love to please
Doth listen to my song;
He caught and bound my wandering wing,
But still He bends to hear me sing.

Thou hast an ear to hear,
A heart to love and bless;
And though my notes were e'er so rude,
Thou wouldst not hear the less;
Because Thou knowest, as they fall,
That love, sweet love, inspires them all.

My cage confines me round;
Abroad I cannot fly;
But though my wing is closely bound,
My heart's at liberty.
My prison walls cannot control
The flight, the freedom, of the soul.

O, it is good to soar
These bolts and bars above,
To Him whose purpose I adore,
Whose providence I love;
And in Thy mighty will to find
The joy, the freedom, of the mind.

Tozer, A. W. *The Christian Book of Mystical Verse: A Collection of Poems, Hymns, and Prayers for Devotional Reading.* Chicago: Moody Publishers, 2016. p. 131.


WEEK FIFTY  *INSIGHT and ENCOURAGEMENT*  DAY 2

The Law of Exchange

by S. D. Gordon (1859-1936)

Every man needs power. Every earnest man covets power. Every willing man has the Master's promise of power. But every man does not possess the promised power. And many, it is to be feared, never will. Many a man's life today is utterly lacking in power. Some of us will look back at the close of life with a sense of keen disappointment and of bitter defeat. And the reason is not far to seek, nor hard to see through. If we do not have power it is because we are not willing to pay the price.

Everything costs. There is a law of exchange that rules every sphere of life. It is this, "to get, you must give." It rules the business world. If I want a house or a hat I must give the sum agreed upon. It rules the intellectual world. If the young man wants a disciplined mind he must give time, and close application, and some real, hard work. It holds true in the spirit realm. If you and I wish to have business transactions in this upper world of spirit-life we must be governed by the same law. To have power in our lives over sin and selfishness, and passion, and appetite; over tongue, and temper, and self-seeking ambition; to have power in prayer, and in winning others over from sin to Jesus Christ, one must first lay down the required price.

What is the price of power? Turn to Jesus' talk with Peter and the others in the latter part of the 16$^{th}$ chapter of Matthew's gospel. Jesus has been telling them of the awful cross-experiences which He clearly saw ahead. Peter probably fearful that whatever came to his Master might possibly come to himself also, and shrinking back in horror from that, has the hardihood to rebuke Jesus. The Master, recognizing the suggestion is coming from a far subtler individual than Peter, who is using ignorant Peter's selfishness to repeat the suggestion of the wilderness, again bids *him* be gone. Then in a few simple words of far-reaching significance, He states first the standard of power, and then the price to be paid by one who would reach that standard. Listen to Him: "If any man would come after Me, let him deny himself and take up his cross and follow Me."

Let us look a little into these familiar words. "*If* any man *would come after Me*" – that is the standard set before us. Not to be regarded as a pillar in the church, a leader in religious circles, the good Bible student, a generous giver, an earnest speaker, an energetic worker, a spiritually minded person, but, what may be coupled with any or all of these admirable things, *to tread in the footprints of Jesus*.

*Quiet Talks on Power*. New York: Fleming H. Revell Co, 1903. p. 87-88.

**WEEK FIFTY**     **Confession of Forgetfulness**     **DAY 3**

Read Psalm 78

Lord, you have done so many marvelous things for me. Even the little things you do are mind-blowing. And I know there are things you do that I don't realize or don't recognize and don't acknowledge. Even from my youth, you have done amazing and wonderful things for me. But how many times have I forgotten that? How many times have I looked at what you have done and questioned why you didn't do more or complained about the provision you have graciously given? How often have I been confronted with a situation and tried to figure out how to fix it without even consulting you? I didn't believe in you. I didn't remember your Word. I didn't trust in your salvation. I cannot imagine how frustrating, how aggravating that must be to you. Instead of being a testimony to the next generations of your tender mercies and gracious provisions, they have seen me get fearful and depressed and angry at circumstances I didn't understand and could not control. All I had to do was trust you. All I had to do was acknowledge you. All I had to do was remember you are the God who saves. You know that my life is but a breath of air compared to eternity. You are the all-powerful, all-loving God. Nothing is impossible for you. In my weakest hour, in every hour, help me not to forget again, but to always look to you and remember.

**WEEK FIFTY**  *HYMNS and POEMS*  **DAY 4**

The Disciple to His Lord
by John S. B. Monsell (1811-1875)

Teach me to do the thing that pleaseth Thee;
Thou art my God, in Thee I live and move;
Oh, let Thy loving Spirit lead me forth
Into the land of righteousness and love.

Thy love the law and impulse of my soul,
Thy righteousness its fitness and its plea,
Thy loving Spirit mercy's sweet control
To make me liker, draw me nearer Thee.

My highest hope to be where, Lord, Thou art,
To lose myself in Thee my richest gain,
To do Thy will the habit of my heart,
To grieve the Spirit my severest pain.

Thy smile my sunshine, all my peace from thence,
From self alone what could that peace destroy?
Thy joy my sorrow at the least offense,
My sorrow that I am not more Thy joy.

Tozer, A. W. *The Christian Book of Mystical Verse: A Collection of Poems, Hymns, and Prayers for Devotional Reading.* Chicago: Moody Publishers, 2016. p. 161

**WEEK FIFTY**  *INSIGHT and ENCOURAGEMENT*  **DAY 5**

The Revelation of Jesus
by Andrew Murray (1828-1917)

The great work of the Holy Spirit is to reveal Christ to the believer in the glory of His heavenly life and in His power at work in our hearts. As a preparation for this, His first work is to convict us of the sin of unbelief. The salvation God has prepared for us is complete in Jesus Christ. His life of humility and obedience has been prepared for us and can be received and lived through simple faith alone.

The great secret of the true Christian lies in the daily, unceasing faith in what Jesus will work in us each moment of our life. When this faith is not exercised and sought after, the Christian life becomes feeble. Nothing grieves the Holy Spirit as much as the unbelief which prevents Jesus from showing His power to deliver men from the power of sin and the world.

We need to see the simplicity and the glory of the gospel we profess. In Jesus Christ all that His life, death, and resurrection accomplished is stored up for us. The fullness of life that is in Jesus is reproduced in us, enabling us to grow into the likeness of His humility, love, and obedience.

This is not accomplished by any power in ourselves. The Holy Spirit is given and lives in us to communicate and maintain the life of Christ in the soul. Feel the urgency of the command, "Grieve not the Holy Spirit of God." What an unspeakable blessing will come if we yield to Him!

We are in search of the New Testament standard of a life of devotion. Suppose we could ask Paul about his personal experience. He would answer, "I am sure that the child of God, living fully in the power of the Holy Spirit can please God. There is no reason to grieve the Spirit every day."

The different standard of our modern Christianity is simply the result of ignorance and unbelief in the supernatural working of the Spirit in the heart. Paul lived his life of devotion in the fullness and the joy of the Holy Spirit. Is our standard limited because such an experience is seldom taught and lived? Is the reason for this that our knowledge is too intellectual and that the Holy Spirit is not honored as the only Teacher of spiritual truth?

Let us return to the prayer in Ephesians 1:15-23. Let it teach us to receive the Spirit of wisdom as the only Teacher that can enable us to experience the heavenly life God has prepared for us.

Excerpted from *Living to Please God*. Pittsburgh, PA: Whitaker House, 1984. p. 68-70.

**WEEK FIFTY**        **Confession of Emotional Dependence**        **DAY 6**

Read Psalm 130

Out of the depths of depression, I cry out to you, oh Lord my God. Hear my voice and be attentive to my cries for help and pleas for mercy. Lord, if you kept a record of sins, who could stand in your presence? No one, least of all me. But with you, there is forgiveness. I am in awe of that and amazed. Because of that, I will serve you in godly fear and reverence. I wait for you, Lord. My heart, soul, and body will wait, and I place my hope on every word you have spoken, on every promise you have made. My mind, will, and emotions will wait for you like the watchman waits for the morning and longs for the sunrise. I will put all my hope in you, Lord. Your lovingkindness is steadfast. Your faithful love and mercy are never failing. With you, there is redemption in abundance. You yourself have redeemed me from all my iniquities and saved me from all my sins. On you, oh Lord, I call and upon you, my God, I will wait.

**WEEK FIFTY**        *HYMNS and POEMS*        **DAY 7**

Come Savior, Jesus, From Above
by Antoinette Bourignon (1616-1680)

Come, Savior, Jesus, from above!
Assist me with Thy heavenly grace;
Empty my heart of earthly love,
And for Thyself prepare the place.

O let Thy sacred presence fill,
And set my longing spirit free!
Which pants to have no other will,
But day and night to feast on Thee.

While in this region here below,
No other good will I pursue:
I'll bid this world of noise and show,
With all its glittering snares, adieu!

That path with humble speed I'll seek,
In which my Savior's footsteps shine,
Nor will I hear, nor will I speak,
Of any other love but Thine.

Henceforth may no profane delight
Divide this consecrated soul;
Possess it, Thou who hast the right,
As Lord and Master of the whole.

Published in *Hymns and Sacred Poems*, by Charles & John Wesley, 1730 according to http://www.hymntime.com/

**Record your insights, revelations, and meditations from this week. DATE:**

_____

_____

_____

_____

_____

_____

_____

Tim Tremaine

**WEEK FIFTY ONE**          *HYMNS and POEMS*          **DAY 1**

I Am Trusting Thee

by Frances Ridley Havergal (1836-1879)

I am trusting Thee, Lord, Jesus,
Trusting only Thee;
Trusting Thee for full salvation,
Great and free.

I am trusting Thee for pardon;
At Thy feet I bow;
For Thy grace and tender mercy,
Trusting now.

I am trusting Thee for cleansing
In the crimson flood;
Trusting Thee to make me holy
By Thy blood.

I am trusting Thee to guide me;
Thou alone shalt lead;
Every day and hour supplying
All my need.

I am trusting Thee for power,
Thine can never fail;
Words which Thou Thyself shalt give me
Must prevail.

I am trusting Thee, Lord Jesus;
Never let me fall;
I am trusting Thee forever,
And for all.

Lyrics first published in *Loyal Responses* in 1878 according to http://www.hymntime.com/.

**WEEK FIFTY ONE**  *INSIGHT and ENCOURAGEMENT*  **DAY 2**

Christian Standing and Privilege

by J. Sidlow Baxter (1903-1999)

All the New Testament epistles are written to Christian recipients, and they all alike assume that the new Christian's standing has fundamentally changed all the relationships of those who are "in Christ Jesus." The standpoint is, not that we are fervently *seeking* forgiveness but that we are *already* forgiven in a way which puts us on a new footing – "even as God for Christ's sake hath forgiven you" (Eph. 4:32). We're not just *seeking* peace with God, but "being justified by faith we *have* peace with God" (Rom. 5:1). We are *already* "delivered out of the power of darkness, and translated into the kingdom of God's dear Son" (Col. 1:13). We are *already* the restored, regenerated "children of God" (1 John 3:2). We are *already* "sealed with the Holy Spirit" as the "earnest of our inheritance" (Eph. 1:13-14).

All the many such New Testament references add up to a magnificent certitude of ASSURANCE – an assurance of eternal salvation in Christ, and of unlimited welcome *as sons of God* at the throne of "the Majesty on high." Therefore we no longer limp there in prodigal's rags, or uncertainly beg as abject aliens. We draw near with filial confidence, gratefully to appropriate what has already been guaranteed. To do so is not presumption; it is God-honoring faith with a blood-sealed warrant. The whole Hebrews epistle is written to show us that it is doubt, not faith, which is God-dishonoring. We are two "come BOLDLY to the Throne."

Such, I insist, is the true attitude of the born-again in Christ; and it alone is the approach which prepares Christian hearts to receive, through consecration and faith, the promised blessing of inwrought holiness. Yet although that attitude undoubtedly concurs with the New Testament epistles, you would scarcely think so, according to much of the "miserable-sinner" emphasis which is supposed to glorify God to more by dwelling with mournful constrictedness on our ugly sinfulness and destitute wretchedness.

But is that the true language of the cleansed and regenerated Christian heart? "Our *guilt*" – but has not all our guilt been borne and removed by the great Sin-bearer? Must we keep speaking of it as though it hangs over our heads? Is *that* honoring to God? It has been truly said, "The Christian belongs to what he is to *become*; not to what he has left behind." The same New Testament which humbles us to the dust as sinners, also calls us "*saints*." It says that we already *are* saints, positionally, in Christ, and that we are to *become* saints of His in our *character*. (Emphasis his.)

Excerpted from *A New Call to Holiness*. Zondervan: Grand Rapids, 1973. p. 36-39.

Tim Tremaine

**WEEK FIFTY ONE**  Confession of a Worshipper  **DAY 3**

Read Psalm 8

Lord, your name is so great and powerful! People everywhere see your splendor. Your glorious majesty streams from the heavens, filling the earth with the fame of your name! You have built a stronghold by the songs of babies. Strength rises up with the chorus of singing children. This kind of praise has the power to shut Satan's mouth. Childlike worship will silence the madness of those who oppose you. Look at the splendor of your skies, your creative genius glowing in the heavens. When I gaze at your moon and your stars, mounted like jewels in their settings, I know you are the fascinating artist who fashioned it all! But when I look up and see such wonder and workmanship above, I have to ask you this question: Compared to all this cosmic glory, why would you bother with puny, mortal man or be infatuated with Adam's sons? Yet what honor you have given to men, created only a little lower than Elohim, crowned like kings and queens with glory and magnificence. You have delegated to them mastery over all you have made, making everything subservient to their authority, placing earth itself under the feet of your image-bearers. All the created order and every living thing of the earth, sky, and sea— the wildest beasts and all the sea creatures— everything is in submission to Adam's sons. All the created order and every living thing of the earth, sky, and sea— the wildest beasts and all the sea creatures— everything is in submission to Adam's sons. Lord, your name is so great and powerful. People everywhere see your majesty! What glory streams from the heavens, filling the earth with the fame of your name!

From *The Passion Translation*® Copyright © 2017 by Passion & Fire Ministries, Inc.


**WEEK FIFTY ONE**  *HYMNS and POEMS*  **DAY 4**

Since Jesus Gave His Life for Me

by Mildred E. Howard (unknown)

Since Jesus gave His life for me,
Should I not give Him mine?
I'm consecrated, Lord, to Thee,
I shall be wholly Thine.

*Refrain:*
*My life, O Lord, I give to Thee,*
*My talents, time, and all;*
*I'll serve Thee, Lord, Thine own to be,*
*I'll hear Thy faintest call.*

I care not where my Lord directs,
His purpose I'll fulfill;
I know He everyone protects
Who does His holy will.

Though He may call across the sea,
With Jesus I will go;
And tell the lost of love so free,
Till all His pow'r may know.

My home and friends are dear to me,
　Yet He is dearer still;
In my affections first He'll be,
　And first His righteous will.

My all, O Lord, to Thee I'll give,
　Accept it as Thine own;
For Thee alone I'll ever live,
　My heart shall be Thy throne.

https://library.timelesstruths.org/music/Consecration/ from 1907.

**WEEK FIFTY ONE**　　　　*INSIGHT and ENCOURAGEMENT*　　　　**DAY 5**

Is Christianity Hard or Easy?

by C. S. Lewis (1898-1963)

The ordinary idea which we all have before we become Christians is this. We take as starting point our ordinary self with its various desires and interests. We then admit that something else – call it "morality" or "decent behavior," or "the good of society" – has claims on this self: claims which interfere with its own desires. What we mean by "being good" is giving in to those claims. Some of the things the ordinary self wanted to do turn out to be what we call "wrong": well, we must give them up. Other things, which the self did not want to do, turn out to be what we call "right": well, we shall have to do that. But we are hoping all the time that when all the demands have been met, the poor natural self will still have some chance, and some time, to get on with its own life and do what it likes. In fact, we are very like an honest man paying his taxes. He pays them all right, but he does hope that there will be enough left over for him to live on. Because we are still taking our natural self as the starting point.

As long as we are thinking that way, one or other of two results is likely to follow. Either we give up trying to be good, or else we become very unhappy indeed. For, make no mistake: if you are really going to try to meet all the demands made on the natural self, it will not have enough left over to live on. The more you obey your conscience, the more your conscience will demand of you. And your natural self, which is thus being starved and hampered and worried at every turn, will get angrier and angrier. In the end, you will either give up trying to be good, or else become one of those people who, as they say, "lives for others" but always in a discontented, grumbling way.

The Christian way is different: harder, and easier. Christ says "Give me All. I don't want so much of your time and so much of your money and so much of your work: I want you. I have not come to torment your natural self, but to kill it. No half measures are any good. I don't want to cut off a branch here and a branch there, I want to have the whole tree down. I don't want to drill the tooth, or crown it, or stop it, but have it out. Hand over the whole natural self, all the desires which you think innocent as well as the ones you think wicked – the whole outfit. I will give you a new self instead. In fact, I will give you Myself: My own will shall become yours."

Both harder and easier than what we are all trying to do. You have noticed, I expect, that Christ Himself sometimes describes the Christian way as very hard, sometimes as very easy. He says, "Take up your

Cross" – in other words, it is like going to be beaten to death in a concentration camp. Next minute he says, "My yoke is easy and my burden is light." He means both. And one can just see why both are true. The terrible thing, the almost impossible thing, is to hand over your whole self – all your wishes and precautions – to Christ. But it is far easier than what we are all trying to do instead. For what we are trying to do is to remain what we call "ourselves," to keep personal happiness as our great aim in life, and yet at the same time be "good." And that is exactly what Christ warned us you could not do. As He said, a thistle cannot produce figs.

Excerpted from *Mere Christianity*. Westwood, NJ: Barbour and Co., Inc. 1952. p. 165-167.

**WEEK FIFTY ONE** *HYMNS and POEMS* **DAY 6**

Take My Heart, O Father!

by Charles Wesley (1707-1788)

Take my heart, O Father! take it;
Make and keep it all Thine own;
Let Thy Spirit melt and break it—
This proud heart of sin and stone.

Father, make me pure and lowly,
Fond of peace and far from strife;
Turning from the paths unholy
Of this vain and sinful life.

Ever let Thy grace surround me,
Strengthen me with power divine,
Till Thy cords of love have bound me;
Make me to be wholly Thine.

May the blood of Jesus heal me
And my sins be all forgiv'n;
Holy Spirit, take and seal me,
Guide me in the path of Heav'n.

http://www.hymntime.com/tch/htm/t/a/k/e/takemhof.htm

# WEEK FIFTY ONE *INSIGHT and ENCOURAGEMENT* DAY 7

### The Church as the Counterculture
by Ed Silvoso (1945-present)

Jesus' recruitment of marketplace people who were not members of the religious establishment was intentional. The same can be said about how the Holy Spirit led the early church to operate in the marketplace. The Great Commission begins with the city, Jerusalem, and it will be fulfilled when the last city on earth is reached. To accomplish this, the city's most vital component, the marketplace, has to be transformed just as it happened in Ephesus and the other cities mentioned in Acts.

Because the marketplace embodies the societal systems that define and give life to a metropolis, Jesus recruited people from the marketplace to be the backbone of His redemptive movement. His objective was to create a new social vehicle – the Church, a movement that freely expanded, rather than a monument to be gazed at. This movement was meant to be the counterculture, rather than a subculture. People in a subculture are satisfied with surviving under the dominant culture, whereas those in a counterculture have as their irretrievable objective to debunk and replace it. According to the dictionary a counterculture is "a culture with values and mores that run counter to those of established society." [book footnote: *Merriam-Webster's Collegiate Dictionary*, 10th ed., s.v. "counterculture."]

This is why New Testament teaching is intentionally focused on curing social ills and repairing broken relationships as a means to transform society's institutions: marriage, family, work and government. This is true because Jesus' mission was not only to save individuals but also to bring people groups and nations to himself (see Rev. 21:24-27). If He had come only to save people, believers would be transferred to heaven right after their conversions. Instead, they are left in the world and entrusted with the commission to disciple the nations.

Jesus always spoke of his disciples taking the Kingdom of God to the people. He also compared his Kingdom to leaven, light, salt and seeds. Each of these elements must come in contact with the physical world to fulfill its destiny: to infiltrate, shine, preserve or sprout. Jesus' design was for the Church to be the counterculture, not another subculture merely satisfied with survival.

This is where the marketplace comes into a sharper focus. Since business is what makes the marketplace go, we need to understand that the God of ministry is also the God of business.

[Why include an excerpt from a book on ministering to the marketplace in a devotional tool about absolute surrender? The purpose of surrendering your life has amazing and wonderful benefits for you as an individual, but it must be viewed in the wider context of God's will for the world. We do not go through this process just for our own benefit, but so that we can be fit and positioned to function in the Church, and in the world, as God desires.]

*Anointed for Business.* Ventura, CA: Regal Books, 2002. Pp. 50-51.

**Record your insights, revelations, and meditations from this week.  DATE:**

VICTORY THROUGH SURRENDER

**WEEK FIFTY TWO**     *HYMNS and POEMS*     **DAY 1**

A Hymn

by J. Sidlow Baxter (1903-1999)

With all my longing heart
Now may I be
Completely set apart,
Dear Lord, for Thee.

And may there now begin
The cure divine;
Work miracles within
This heart of mine.

Enchained by subtle fear,
My bondage see;
Break in upon me here,
And set me free.

All dark allure to sin
In me replace
By holy light within,
From Thy dear face.

At last, true holiness
May I now find
In having Thee possess
And fill my mind.

Let risk seem what it will,
My *all* I give
Lord, all my being fill,
For Thee to live.

Within each stanza of this hymn, Baxter reveals a pearl of wisdom regarding the surrendered life. Look at each stanza and record below what you hear to be the theme or lesson within.

Stanza One  _____

Stanza Two  _____

Stanza Three  _____

Stanza Four  _____

Stanza Five  _____

Stanza Six  _____

*A New Call to Holiness*, Zondervan, Grand Rapids, 1973. p. 183.

**WEEK FIFTY TWO**      *INSIGHT and ENCOURAGEMENT*      **DAY 2**

Disciplined Habits

by E. Stanley Jones (1884-1973)

Conversion is a gift and an achievement. It is the act of a moment and the work of a lifetime. You cannot attain salvation by disciplines – it is the gift of God. But you cannot retain it without disciplines. If you try to attain salvation by disciplines, you will be trying to discipline an unsurrendered self. You will be sitting on a lid. The result will be tenseness instead of trust. "You will wrestle instead of nestle." While salvation cannot be obtained by discipline around an unsurrendered self, nevertheless when the self is surrendered to Christ and a new center formed, then you can discipline your life around that new center – Christ. Discipline is the fruit of conversion – not the root.

This passage gives the double-sidedness of conversion: "As therefore you received Christ Jesus the Lord, so live in him, rooted and built up in him and established in the faith" (Col. 2:6-7, RSV). Note, "received" – receptivity; "so live" – activity. It appears again, "rooted" – receptivity; "built up in him" – activity.

The "rooted" means we take from God as the roots take from the soil; the "built up" means we build up as one builds a house, a character and life by disciplined effort. So we take and try; we obtain and attain. We trust as if the whole thing depended on God and work as if the whole thing depended on us. The alternate beats of the Christian heart are receptivity and response – receptivity from God and response in work from us.

The best man that ever lived on our planet illustrated this receptivity and response rhythm. No one was so utterly dependent on God and no one was more personally disciplined in his habits.

He did three things by habit: (1) "He stood up to read as was his custom" – he read the word of God by habit. (2) "He went out into the mountain to pray as was his custom" – he prayed by habit. (3) "He taught them again as was his custom" – he passed on to others by habit what he had and what he had found.

The simple habits were the foundation habits of his life. They are as up to date as tomorrow morning. No converted person can live without those habits at work mightily in his life.

Develop the habit of reading the Word of God daily, preferable in the morning. Pray in private by habit. Pass on to others what you have found. Cultivate the new life by daily disciplines. Pray for those who have wronged you. Give up habits that cannot be Christianized. Constantly enlarge the area of your conversion, taking in new areas of your life every day.

Excerpted from Foster, Richard J. and Smith, James Bryan. *Devotional Classics*. New York: Harper One, 2005. p. 281-285.

## VICTORY THROUGH SURRENDER

**WEEK FIFTY TWO**  Confession about My Life  **DAY 3**

John Baillie prayer

HERE I am, O God, humbly yours, lifting up my heart to you, before whom all created things are as dust and mist. You are hidden behind the curtain of our limited sight and hearing, incomprehensible in your greatness, mysterious in your almighty power; yet here am I, speaking to you with the familiarity of a child to a parent, a friend to a friend. If I could not speak to you like this, then I would indeed be without hope in the world. I have little power to do or control anything; it is not by my will that I am here or will one day pass away. Of all that will come to me today, very little will have been what I have chosen for myself. It is you, O hidden One, who has given me my heritage, and you determined the place of my birth. It is you who have given me the power to do one kind of work and have withheld the skill to do another. It is you who hold in your hand the threads of this day's life and you alone who know what lies before me to do or to suffer. But because you are my Father, I am not afraid. Because it is your Spirit that stirs within my heart's most secret room, I know that all is well. What I desire for myself I cannot achieve, but whatever you desire in me, you can help me to achieve. The good that I want to do, I fail to do, but you can give me the power to do good. Dear Father, take this day's life into your keeping. Guide all my thoughts and feelings. Direct all my energies. Instruct my mind. Sustain my will. Take my hands and give me the skill to serve you. Take my feet and make them quick to do whatever you ask. Take my eyes and keep them fixed on your everlasting beauty. Take my mouth and give me the words to tell others of your love. Make this day a day of obedience, a day of spiritual joy and peace. Make this day's work a little part of the work of the kingdom of my Lord Jesus, in whose name these prayers are said. Amen.

*A Diary of Private Prayer.* New York: Scribner, 1949. p. 38-39.

**WEEK FIFTY TWO**  *INSIGHT and ENCOURAGEMENT*  **DAY 4**

The Method of Advancement

by G. Campbell Morgan (1863-1945)

The truth taught must become incarnate in the disciples. As we insisted at the outset, discipleship is not a condition for amassing information. Every doctrine has its issue in some clearly defined duty, every theory taught reveals a practical application and responsibility. To the soul in right relationship with the Teacher, He reveals some new aspect of truth and straightway there occurs some circumstance in which that doctrine may be tested by duty; and as we are most real in ordinary circumstances – it is in the simple and commonplace experiences that these testing places are mostly to be found. This is a great comfort. He knows the capacity and weakness and strength of everyone in His school and His examinations do not consist in a common testing for a common standard, and so are not competitive.

Now, advancement is dependent always on our obedience in these hours of testing, in our manifesting in actual practice the power of the truth we have heard in theory. No lesson is considered learned in the school of Jesus, which is only committed to memory. That lesson only is learned which is incarnate in the life and becomes beautiful in its realization and declaration in that way; and until this is so there can be no progress. You cannot leave first principles and go on unto perfection, save as these first things have become principles and not merely theories.

Here we touch the secret of much of the failure in Christian living today. The powerlessness in service, the unattractiveness in life, what do they mean? Has the system of Jesus failed in these lives? Have the great lessons He came to teach humanity broken down in their application to human life? Take any single example – it may be that of your own experience. When you first became a disciple, your days were days of delight and joy, the words and will of the Master thrilled and comforted you and you walked in His ways with a joy and gladness that filled the days with song. (But now,) Your Christianity has become a restriction through which you would like to break, an encumbrance of which you would fain be rid.

These are confessions you never make, but they tell the true inner story of your life. No other lesson has been given, nor can be. Every other depended upon that. That was not final. It was preparatory, and until that is learned by obedience there can be no advancement, and so for weeks, perchance months, aye, even years, you have been a disciple making no progress and there is no wonder that you are weary of it all.

The Teacher's love is marked in your case by His fidelity to Himself and His own lessons. Time after time, in meetings, in conversations, in loneliness, He brings you back to that old point and reiterates with a persistence and a patience passing all human understanding: "If any man willeth to do His will, he shall know of the teaching." [Are you willing to be willing?]

Excerpted from, *Discipleship*. Pathos Publishers EBook, 2015. p. 19-20 (reprint from 1897).

**WEEK FIFTY TWO**  *HYMNS and POEMS*  **DAY 5**

*A*nother Step Is Made With God

by A. H. Francke (1663-1727).

Another step is made with God
Towards mine eternal station
To thee through all this pilgrim road
I've made my hearts oblation;
O source! From who my life depends,
And every heavenly grace descends
Into my longing bosom.

I'm counting minutes, days and years,
Which seem too slowly moving,
Till that long wished for time appears,
To embrace thee, Lord, so loving:
Till all what mortal is in me
Be wholly shallowed up in thee,
And I become immortal.

## VICTORY THROUGH SURRENDER

'Tis from thy flaming love I find,
My soul is thus delighted,
That all the power of heart and mind
Are so with thee united;
That thou in me, and I in thee,
And yet I cannot cease to be,
Forever drawing nearer.

And since the oil of gladness is
Poured in my soul and spirit,
And I rejoice in present bliss
With what I shall inherit.
The light of life shines forth in me,
And keeps my lamp thus trimmed for thee,
To welcome my beloved.

Though to my wisdom he refined,
The proper time and measure,
Yet thou art always well inclined,
To hear me call with pleasure:
And see me thus improve they grace,
With carefulness to run my race,
To meet thee my redeemer.

I am content with nought of all
Can breed a separation
'Twixt me and thee, when I can call
My bridegroom and salvation;
And that thou, dearest prince of life!
Wilt make me thine espoused wife,
And coheir of thy kingdom.

Lord! I adore thy lasting grace
For this new date and station,
That thou hast brought me to these days
And nearer to salvation:
Thus stepping forward by degrees,
Still reaching at that blessed place
Jerusalem above me.

And should my hands be tired at length,
My feeble knees grow sinking,
Then Lord afford new grace and strength,
To keep my faith from shrinking,
That through thy powerful aid, O God!
My feet may run the heavenly road
Without an intermission.

My soul march boldly on in faith,
Be not dismayed or frighted,
Nor trifles turn thee from thy path,
With what the world's delighted:
But should thy race too slowly move,
Then stretch the wings of fervent love,
And soar aloft like eagles.

Jesu! My soul has taken flight
From earth to heaven already:
Thou hast, O source of love and light
Exhausted soul and body,
Farewell ye fleeting hours of time,
Mine element is more sublime,
Since I'm in Jesu living.

John Kunze. *A Hymn and Prayer Book*. New York: Hurtin & Commardinger, 1795. p. 189-192.

**WEEK FIFTY TWO**          *INSIGHT and ENCOURAGEMENT*          **DAY 6**

Practical Results in Daily Life
by Hannah Whitall Smith (1832-1911)

The life hid with Christ in God is a hidden life, as to its source, but it must not be hidden as to its practical results. People must see that we walk as Christ walked, if we say that we are abiding in Him. We must prove that we "possess" that which we "profess." We must, in short, the real followers of Christ, and not theoretical ones only. And this means a great deal. It means that we must really and absolutely turn our backs on everything that is contrary to the perfect will of God. It means that we are to be a "peculiar people," not only in the eyes of God, but in the eyes of the world around us; and that, wherever we go, it will be known from our habits, our tempers, our conversation and our pursuits, that we are followers of the Lord Jesus Christ, and are not of the world, even as He was not of the world. We must no longer look upon our money as our own, but as belonging to the Lord, to be used in His service. We must not feel at liberty to use our energies exclusively in the pursuit of worldly means, but must recognize, that, if we seek first the kingdom of God and His righteousness, all needful things shall be added unto us. We shall find ourselves forbidden to seek the highest places, or to strain after worldly advantages. We shall not be permitted to make self, as heretofore, the center of all our thoughts and all our aims. Our days will have to be spent, not in serving ourselves, but in serving the Lord; and we shall find ourselves called upon to bear one another's burdens, and so will fulfill the law of Christ. And all our daily homely duties will be more perfectly performed than ever, because whatever we do will be done, "not with eye-service, as men-pleasers, but as the servants of Christ, doing the will of God from the heart."

Into all this we shall undoubtedly be led by the Spirit of God if we give ourselves up to His guidance. But unless we have the right standard of Christian life set before us, we may be hindered by our ignorance from recognizing His voice; and it is for this reason I desire to be very plain and definite in my statements.

I have noticed that wherever there has been a faithful following of the Lord in a consecrated soul, several things have, sooner or later, inevitably followed.

Meekness and quietness of spirit become in time the characteristics of the daily life. A submissive acceptance of the will of God, as it comes in the hourly events of each day, is manifested; pliability in the hands of God to do or to suffer all the good pleasure of His will; sweetness under provocation; calmness in the midst of turmoil and bustle; a yielding to the wishes of others, and an insensibility to slights and affronts; absence of worry or anxiety; deliverance from care and fear, – all these, and many other similar graces, are invariably found to be the natural outward development of that inward life which is hid with Christ in God. Then as to the habits of life; we always see such Christians sooner or later laying aside thoughts of self, and becoming full of consideration for others; they dress and live in simple, healthful ways; they renounce self-indulgent habits, and surrender all purely fleshly gratifications. Some helpful work for others is taken up, and useless occupations are dropped out of the life. God's glory and the welfare of His creatures become the absorbing delight of the soul. The voice is dedicated to Him, to be used in singing His praises. The purse is placed at His disposal. The pen is dedicated to write for Him, the lips to speak for Him, the hands and the feet to do His bidding. Year after year such Christians are seen to grow more unworldly, more serene, more heavenly-minded, more transformed, more like Christ, until even their faces express the beautiful inward life, and everyone can see that they live with Jesus.

Adapted from *The Christian's Secret of a Happy Life*. Grand Rapids: Revell, 1952. p. 200-202.

**WEEK FIFTY TWO**  *HYMNS and POEMS*  **DAY 7**

Take My Life, and Let It Be
>by Frances Ridley Havergal (1836-1879)

Take my life, and let it be
Consecrated, Lord, to Thee;
Take my moments and my days,
Let them flow in ceaseless praise.

Take my hands and let them move
At the impulse of Thy love;
Take my feet, and let them be
Swift and beautiful for Thee.

Take my voice and let me sing
Always, only, for my King;
Take my lips and let them be
Filled with messages from Thee.

Take my silver and my gold,
Not a mite would I withhold;
Take my intellect, and use
Every power as Thou shall choose.

Take my will, and make it Thine,
It shall be no longer mine;
Take my heart, it is Thine own,
It shall be Thy royal throne.

Take my love; my Lord, I pour
At Thy feet its treasure-store.
Take myself, and I will be
Ever, only, all for Thee.

https://www.hymnal.net/en/hymn/h/1359

**Record your insights, revelations, and meditations from this week.  DATE:**

**DAY 365**                         **Confession about My Life with God**

Read Ephesians 2

Father God, you made me alive, who was dead in trespasses and sins, in which I once walked according to the course of this world, according to the prince of the power of the air, the spirit who now works in the sons of disobedience, among whom also I once conducted myself in the lusts of my flesh, fulfilling the desires of my flesh and my mind, and was by nature a child of wrath, just as the others.

But God, you are so rich in mercy, because of your great love with which you loved me, even when I was dead in trespasses, you made me alive together with Christ (by grace I have been saved), and raised me up together, and made me sit together in the heavenly places in Christ Jesus, that in the ages to come you might show the exceeding riches of your grace in your kindness toward me in Christ Jesus. For by grace I have been saved and that not of myself; it is your gift, O God, not based on works, lest I should boast. For I am your workmanship, created in Christ Jesus for good works, which you prepared beforehand that I should walk in them.

For I was an alien from the commonwealth of Israel and a stranger from the covenants of promise, having no hope and without God in the world. But now, in Christ Jesus, although once I was far off, now I have been brought near by the blood of Christ. For through Christ, I have access by the Holy Spirit to you, my Father.

Amen.

# EPILOGUE

Congratulations on reaching the end of your first year of walking with the Lord in absolute surrender. As you reflect on the past year, what have you learned about this way of living? Hopefully, you can look back over your journaling and see how the Holy Spirit lead you and taught you about this life with His insight and revelation. For me, this life is more peaceful and not as frenetic as living out of my own mind and resources. It is costly, in the sense of what the Lord asks us to part with, but it is so much more satisfying. This life is filled with more blessings and more opportunities. There are still challenges, but the ability to meet those challenges is inherent in the deeper relationship with Him. I have experienced a greater desire to be generous and an enhanced ability to be so through more resources and less waste. There is more waiting but less pressure. I have seen more revelation, more insights, more answers to prayer, and greater boldness in witnessing. Placing yourself entirely at the disposal of the Lord requires radical obedience that only the surrendered life can supply. I leave you with one last poem that has encouraged me these last forty years of ministry.

*Don't Quit*
by
John Greenleaf Whittier

When things go wrong as they sometimes will,
When the road you're trudging seems all uphill,
When the funds are low and the debts are high
And you want to smile, but you have to sigh,
When care is pressing you down a bit,
Rest if you must, but don't you quit.

Life is strange with its twists and turns
As every one of us sometimes learns
And many a failure comes about
When he might have won had he stuck it out;
Don't give up though the pace seems slow—
You may succeed with another blow.

Success is failure turned inside out—
The silver tint of the clouds of doubt,
And you never can tell just how close you are,
It may be near when it seems so far;
So stick to the fight when you're hardest hit—
It's when things seem worst that you must not quit.

## VICTORY THROUGH SURRENDER

This is my prayer of benediction and blessing over you from Hebrews 13 and Ephesians.

*Now may the God of peace who brought again from the dead our Lord Jesus,*
*the great shepherd of the sheep,*
*by the blood of the eternal covenant,*
*equip you with everything good that you may do his will,*
*working in us that which is pleasing in his sight,*
*through Jesus Christ, to whom be glory forever and ever.*

*I, therefore, the prisoner of the Lord,*
*beseech you to walk worthy of the calling*
*with which you were called.*
*Amen.*

Together, we are **prisoners of grace**.

Tim Tremaine

# INDEX OF AUTHORS

INSIGHT and ENCOURAGEMENT (62)

Richard Allestree (1621-1681)
Johann Arndt (1555-1621)
J. Sidlow Baxter (1903-1999)
Manley Beasley (1932-1990)
Bernard of Clairvaux (1090-1153)
Henry Blackaby (1935-present)
Paul Billheimer (1897-1984)
Dietrich Bonhoeffer (1906-1945)
Jeremy Boynton (1824-1883)
Adam Clarke (1762-1832)
Oswald Chambers (1874-1917)
Francis Chan (1967-present)
Larry Crabb, Jr. (1944-present)
Charles L. Culpepper, Sr. (1895-1986)
Francis de Sales (1567-1622)
Jonathan Edwards (1703-1758)
François Fénelon (1651-1715)
Raymond P. Findlater (1954-present)
Augustus Hermann Francke (1663-1727)
Ronnie Floyd (1955-present)
E. Stanley Jones (1884-1973)
Thomas à Kempis (1380-1471)
Ken Kessler (unknown – present)
Søren Kierkegaard (1813-1855)
Daniel Kolenda (1981-present)
A. J. Gordon (1836-1895)
S. D. Gordon (1859-1936)
Gregory of Nyssa (331-396)
John of the Cross (1542-1591)
Frank Laubach (1884-1970)
William Law (1686-1761)
Brother Lawrence (c. 1614-1691)
C. S. Lewis (1898-1963)
Walter Marshall (1628-1680)
Alexander MacLaren (1826-1910)
David McIntyre (1859-1938)
Benjamin Fay Mills (1857-1916)

G. Campbell Morgan (1863-1945)
George Müller (1805-1898)
Andrew Murray (1828-1917)
Watchman Nee (1903-1972)
John Henry, Cardinal Newman (1801-1890)
John Newton (1725-1807)
J. Edwin Orr (1912-1987)
Phoebe Palmer (1807-1874)
Isaac Pennington (1617-1680)
Fuchsia Pickett (1918-2004)
Charles S. Price (1887-1947)
Adrian Rogers (1931-2005)
J. C. Ryle (1816-1900)
J. Oswald Sanders (1917-1992)
Charles M. Sheldon (1857-1946)
Ed Silvoso (1945-present)
Hannah Whitall Smith (1832-1911)
Gary Scott Smith (unknown-present)
James Smith (1802-1862)
Johannes Tauler (1300-1361)
Jeremy Taylor (1613-1667)
Major W. Ian Thomas (1914-2007)
A. W. Tozer (1897-1963)
Alexandre Vinet (1797-1847)
George D. Watson (1845-1923)
B. F. Westcott (1825-1901)
John Wesley (1703-1791)
Smith Wigglesworth (1859-1947)

HYMNS and POEMS (70)

Joseph Addison (1672-1719)
Cecil Francis Alexander (1818-1895)
St. Francis of Assisi (c. 1182-1226)
Richard Baxter (1615-1691)
Francis Augustus Blackmer (1855-1930)
Anne Bradstreet (1612-1672)
Nicolaus Brady (1659-1726)
Martin Behm (1557-1622)

John Ernest Bode (1816-1874)
Antoinette Bourignon (1616-1680)
Mary Brown (1856-1919)
John Burton, Jr. (1803-1877)
Josiah Carley (1996-present)
Catherine Booth-Clibborn (1858-1955)
Thomas O. Chisholm (1793-1847)
Josiah Conder (1789-1855)
William Cowper (1731-1800)
Sister Eva of Friedenshort (1866-1930)
Emily May Grimes Crawford (1864-1927)
Frederick William Faber (1814-1863)
B. M. Franklin (1882-1965)
William H. Foulkes (1877-1961)
Christian F. Gellert (1715-1769)
Thomas Hornblower Gill (1819-1906)
Paul Gerhardt (1607-1676)
Ann Griffiths (1776-1805)
Homer W. Grimes (published 1934)
Jeanne Marie De La Motte-Guyon (1648-1717)
Ada Ruth Habershon (1861-1918)
Frances Ridley Havergal (1836-1879)
Marianne Hearn (1834–1909)
George Herbert (1593-1633)
Grace W. Hinsdale (1833-1902)
Oliver Holden (1765-1844)
Mildred E. Howard (unknown)
Mary Dagworthy James (1810-1883)
Calvin W. Laufer (1874-1938)
Witness Lee (1905-1997)
Karl Friedrich Lockner (1634-1697)

Henry F. Lyte (1793-1847)
George Matheson (1842-1906)
John S. B. Monsell (1811-1875)
Lelia Naylor Morris (1862-1929)
Charles W. Naylor (1874-1950)
Watchman Nee (1903-1972)
John Henry Newman (1801-1890)
John Newton (1725-1807)
Anna Olander (unknown)
J. Edwin Orr (1912-1987)
Mary Bowley Peters (1813-1856)
Jean Sophia Pigott (1845-1882)
Christina Rossetti (1830-1894)
Nikolaus Selnecker (1532-1592)
Sharla Sensenig (unknown)
A. B. Simpson (1843-1919)
Walter Sheely (1725-1786)
Alfred C. Snead (1884-1961)
Nahum Tate (1652-1715)
Georgiana M. Taylor (1857-1914)
Anna Laetitia Waring (1820-1910)
Barney E. Warren (1867-1951)
Isaac Watts (1674-1748)
Charles Wesley (1707-1788)
Ernest G. Wesley (1847-1929)
John Greenleaf Whittier (1807-1892)
Daniel W. Whittle (1840-1901)
Gertrude E Worthington (unknown)
Katharina A. von Schlegel (1697-1768)
Nicolaus Ludwig Von Zinzendorf (1700-1760)

## INDEX OF WEEKLY THEMES OR FEATURED AUTHORS

1. Salvation – Major W. Ian Thomas
2. Obedience
3. New Beginnings
4. The Two-Step Process
5. Death to Self
6. Sacrifice
7. Sanctification
8. Conditions of Discipleship – Oswald Chambers
9. Holiness
10. Heart Circumcision
11. Consecration
12. Five Keys to the Christian Life
13. Longsuffering
14. Refining
15. Watchman Nee
16. Christ-likeness
17. Faith – A. H. Franke
18. Faith
19. Surrender
20. Submission
21. Prayer – Paul Billheimer
22. Selflessness
23. Faith – Cahrles Price
24. Sanctification
25. Holy Spirit
26. Being Filled with the Holy Spirit
27. Holy Spirit
28. Devotion
29. Abiding in Christ
30. Frank Laubach
31. Discipleship
32. Peace
33. Holiness
34. Discipleship – Dietrich Bonhoeffer
35. Victory
36. Ed Silvoso
37. Blessing
38. Testimony
39. Patience – Andrew Murray
40. Kingdom of God – Ed Silvoso
41. The Presence of God
42. Daniel Kolenda
43. Obedience – Andrew Murray
44. J. Edwin Orr
45. Revival
46. Shepherds
47. Discipline
48. Prayer
49. What Would Jesus Do?
50. Revelation
51. The Church
52. Set Apart

# BIBLIOGRAPHY

Allestree, Richard. *The Whole Duty of Man.* London: Society for Promoting Christian Knowledge, 1841.

Arndt, Johann. *True Christianity.* Philadelphia: Smith, English, & Co., (unk).

Baillie, John. *A Diary of Readings.* New York: Macmillan Publishing Co., 1955.

Baxter, J. Sidlow. *A New Call to Holiness.* Grand Rapids: Zondervan, 1973.

Beasley, Manley. *Adventures in Faith.* Kindle Edition, 2013. (Originally a self-published workbook.)

Billheimer, Paul. *Adventure in Adversity.* Wheaton: Tyndale House, 1984.
*Destined for The Cross.* Wheaton: Tyndale House Publishers, Inc. 1982.

Blackaby, Henry. *Holiness.* Nashville: Thomas Nelson, 2003.

Boch, Fred. *Hymns for the Family of God.* Nashville: Paragon Associates, Inc. 1976.

Bonhoeffer, Dietrich. *The Cost of Discipleship.* New York: Simon & Schuster, 2018.

Boynton, Jeremy. *Sanctification Practical.* New York: Foster & Palmer, 1867.

Brother Lawrence. *The Practice of the Presence of God.* Grand Rapids: Revell, 1958 (eBook).

Chambers, Oswald. *If Thou Wilt Be Perfect.* Fort Washington, PA: Christian Literature Crusade, 1941.
*My Utmost For His Highest.* Westwood, NJ.: Barbour and Company, 1963.

Clarke, Adam. *Sanctification.* Kansas City: The Publishing House of the Pentecostal Church of the Nazarene, 1907.

Crabb, Jr., Dr. Larry. *Finding God.* New York: Walker and Company, 1994.

Culpepper, Sr., Charles L. *The Shantung Revival.* https://www.gospeltruth.net/shantung.htm. 1968. (Based on the book of the same name by Mary K. Crawford, 1933.)

de Sales, Francis. *Introduction to the Devout Life.* Mineola, NY: Dover Publications, (unk).

Eitel, Lorraine, ed. *The Treasury of Christian Poetry*. Old Tappan, NJ: Revell, 1982.

Fénelon, François. *Christian Perfection*. New York and London: Harper & Brothers, 1947.

Findlater, Raymond P. *Victory Through Surrender*. Maitland, FL: Xulon Press, 2013.

Francke, Augustus Hermann. *Memoirs of A. H. Francke*. Philadelphia: American Sunday School Union, 1831.
*The Prayer of Faith Answered, or An Encouragement to Live by Faith, In the Promises and Faithfulness of God*. Plymouth Dock: Printed by J. Heydon. 1705.

Foster, Richard J. and Smith, James Bryan. *Devotional Classics*. New York: Harper One, 2005.

Gordon, A. J. *The Ministry of the Spirit*. Philadelphia: American Baptist Publication Society, 1894.

Gordon, S. D. *Quiet Talks on Power*. New York: Fleming H Revell Co, 1903.

Hayford, Jack, ed. *The Spirit-Filled Bible*. Nashville: Thomas Nelson, 2018.

John of the Cross. *Dark Night of the Soul*. Start Publishing eBook edition: 2012.

Jones, E. Stanley. *Victory Through Surrender*. New York: Abingdon Press, 1966.

Jorgensen, Johannes. *Saint Francis of Assisi: A Biography*. New York: Longmans, Green, and Co., 1912.

Kolenda, Daniel. *Slaying Dragons*. Lake Mary FL: Charsima House, 2019.

Law, William. *A Serious Call To A Devout and Holy Life* (1729). New York: Scriptura Press, 2015.

Lewis, C. S. *Mere Christianity*. Westwood, NJ: Barbour and Co., Inc. 1952.

MacLaren, Alexander. *Expositions of Holy Scripture. Vol. 13*. Grace-eBooks.com., (unk).
*The Secret of Power*. London: Macmillan and Co., 1882.

Marshall, Walter. *Sanctification; or The Highway of Holiness*. London: James Nisbet & Co., 1884.

McIntyre, David. *The Hidden Life of Prayer*. Originally 1891. https://www.scribd.com/document/176950429/The-Hidden-Life-of-Prayer

Mills, Benjamin Fay. *Victory Through Surrender; a Message Concerning Consecrated Living*. Chicago: Fleming H. Revell Company, 1892.

Morgan, G. Campbell. *Discipleship*. Pathos Publishers EBook, 2015.

Müller, George. *The Autobiography of George Müller*. Dallas: Gideon House Books, 2017.

Murray, Andrew. *Abide in Christ*. Readaclassic.com, 2010.
*Absolute Surrender and other addresses*. Chicago: Moody Press, (unk).
*Divine Healing*. Fort Washington, PA: Christian Literature Crusade, 1971.
*Holy in Christ*. Minneapolis: Bethan Fellowship, [original 1887].
*How to Work for God*. Pittsburgh, PA: Whitaker House, 1983.
*Growing in Christ*. Westchester, IL: Good News Publishers, 1979.
*Living the New Life*. Springdale, PA: Whitaker House, 1982.
*Living to Please God*. Pittsburgh, PA: Whitaker House, 1984.
*The Believer's Secret of Holiness*. Minneapolis: Bethany House, 1984.
*The Holiest of All*. Old Tappan, NJ: Fleming H. Revell Co, 1978.
*The School of Obedience*. Chicago: Moody Press, no date.
*Waiting on God*. Chicago: Moody Press. (reprint from 1905).
*With Christ in the School of Prayer*. Old Tappan, NJ: Revell, 1953.

Nee, Watchman. *Love Not the World*. Philadelphia: Christian Literature Crusade, 1973.

Orr, J. Edwin. *Full Surrender*. London: Marshall, Morgan & Scott, 1951.

Palmer, Phoebe. *Present to My Christian Friend on Entire Devotion to God*. London: William Nichols, 1857.

Price, Charles S. *The Meaning of Faith*. Pasedena, CA: Charles S. Price Pub. Co., 1936.
*The Real Faith*. Self-published, 1941. Jawbone Digital, Kindle ed.

Pughe, George R. G. trans. *The Hymns of Ann Griffiths*. Blackburn: Geo. H. Durham, Exchange Works, 1900.

Rogers, Adrian. The Incredible Power of Kingdom Authority. Nashville: Lifeway Press, 2002.

Ryle, J. C. *Holiness*. Dublin, CA: FirstLove Publication, 2017.

Sanders, J. Oswald.    *Cultivation of Christian Character*. Chicago: Moody Publishers, 2017.
*Spiritual Discipleship: principles of following Christ for every believer*. Chicago: Moody Publishers, 1994.

Sheldon, Charles M.    *In His Steps*. Nashville: Broadman Press, 1935.

Shepperd, John.    *Chosen Words from Christian Writers*. London: Hodder & Stoughton, 1869.

Silvoso, Dr. Ed.    *Anointed for Business*. Ventura, CA: Regal Books, 2002.
*Ekklesia*. Bloomington, MN: Chosen Books, 2018.
*Strongholds*. Bloomington, MN: Chosen Books, 2018.
*That None Should Perish*. Ventura, CA: Regals Books, 1994.
*Transformation*. Ventura, CA: Regal Books, 2007.

Smith, Hannah Whitall.    *The Christian's Secret of a Happy Life*. Grand Rapids: Revell, 1952.

Smith, James.    *Handfuls on Purpose II*. London: Pickering & Inglis, 1923.

Thomas, W. Ian.    *How to Work for God*. Pittsburgh, PA: Whitaker House, 1983.
*The Mystery of Godliness*. Carnforth, Great Britain: Capernwray Press, 1981.
*The Indwelling Life of Christ*. Colorado Springs: Multnomah Publishers, 2006.

Tozer, A. W.    *The Crucified Life: How to Live Out a Deeper Christian Experience*. Minneapolis: Bethany House, 2017.
*The Christian Book of Mystical Verse: A Collection of Poems, Hymns, and Prayers for Devotional Reading*. Chicago: Moody Publishers, 2016.

Watson, Charles D.    *Soul Food, Being Chapters on the Interior Life*. Cincinnati, OH: M. W. Knapp, 1896.
*The Secret of Spiritual Power*. Boston: The McDonald & Gill Co., 1894.

Wesley, John.    *Sermons on Several Occasions, Vol. 1*. Digireads.com Publications, 2012.
*Christian Perfection*. Franklin, TN: Seedbed Publishing, 2014.

Westcott, B. F.    *Social Aspects of Christianity*. London: Macmillan and Co., 1900.

Wigglesworth, Smith.    *Smith Wigglesworth on Healing*. New Kensington, PA: Whitaker House, 1999.

*Victory Through Surrender:*
*Confessions of a Prisoner of Grace*
*Volume One*

is available on
www.amazon.com

or contact
The Tremaine Co. LLC
at
www.tntremaine.com

www.ingramcontent.com/pod-product-compliance
Lightning Source LLC
Chambersburg PA
CBHW081356070526
44583CB00020B/2569

*9781648304040*